ULTIMATE COMICS™

X-MEN™

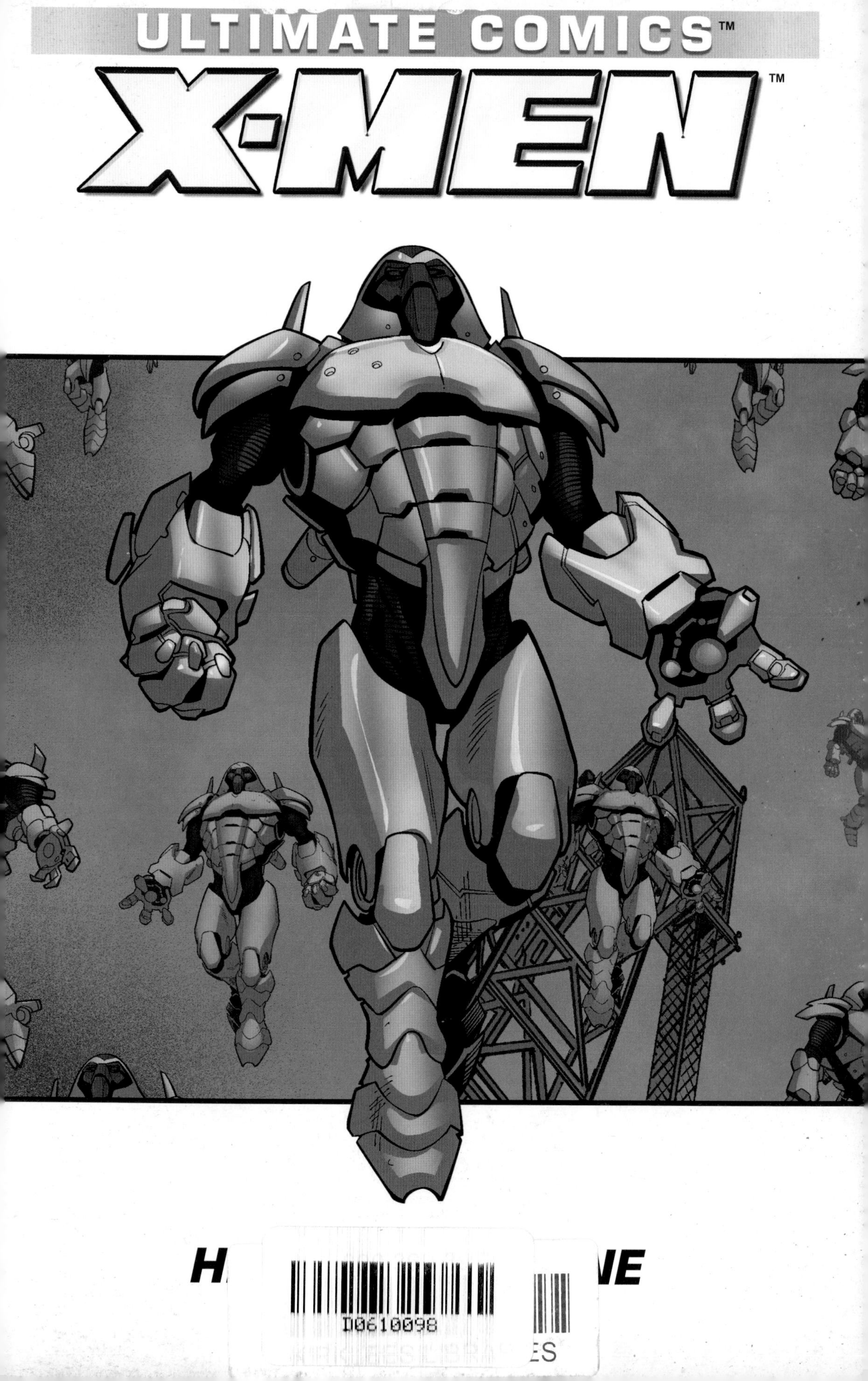

H… …NE

ULTIMATE COMICS™

X-MEN™

HIS WILL BE DONE

NICK SPENCER
WRITER

CARLO BARBERI & PACO MEDINA
PENCILLERS

WALDEN WONG & JUAN VLASCO
INKERS

VC'S JOE SABINO
LETTERER

MARTE GRACIA
COLOURIST

KAARE ANDREWS
COVER ARTIST

JON MOISAN
ASSISTANT EDITOR

SANA AMANAT
ASSOCIATE EDITOR

MARK PANICCIA
EDITOR

AXEL ALONSO
EDITOR IN CHIEF

JOE QUESADA
CHIEF CREATIVE OFFICER

ULTIMATE COMICS X-MEN VOLUME 2: HIS WILL BE DONE Contains material originally published in magazine form as ULTIMATE COMICS X-MEN #7-12. First printing 2012. Published by Panini Publishing, a division of Panini UK Limited. All rights reserved. Mike Riddell, Managing Director. Alan O'Keefe, Managing Editor. Mark Irvine, Production Manager. Marco M. Lupoi, Publishing Director Europe. Ed Hammond, Reprint Editor. Charlotte Reilly, Designer. Office of publication: Brockbourne House, 77 Mount Ephraim, Tunbridge Wells, Kent TN4 8BS. Licensed by Marvel Characters B.V. www.marvel.com. All rights reserved. No similarity between any of the names, characters, persons and/or institutions in this edition with those of any living or dead person or institution is intended, and any such similarity which may exist is purely coincidental. This publication may not be sold, except by authorised dealers, and is sold subject to the condition that it shall not be sold or distributed with any part of its cover or markings removed, nor in a mutilated condition. Printed in Italy. ISBN: 978-1-84653-516-1

Do you have any comments or queries about this graphic novel? Email us at graphicnovels@panini.co.uk

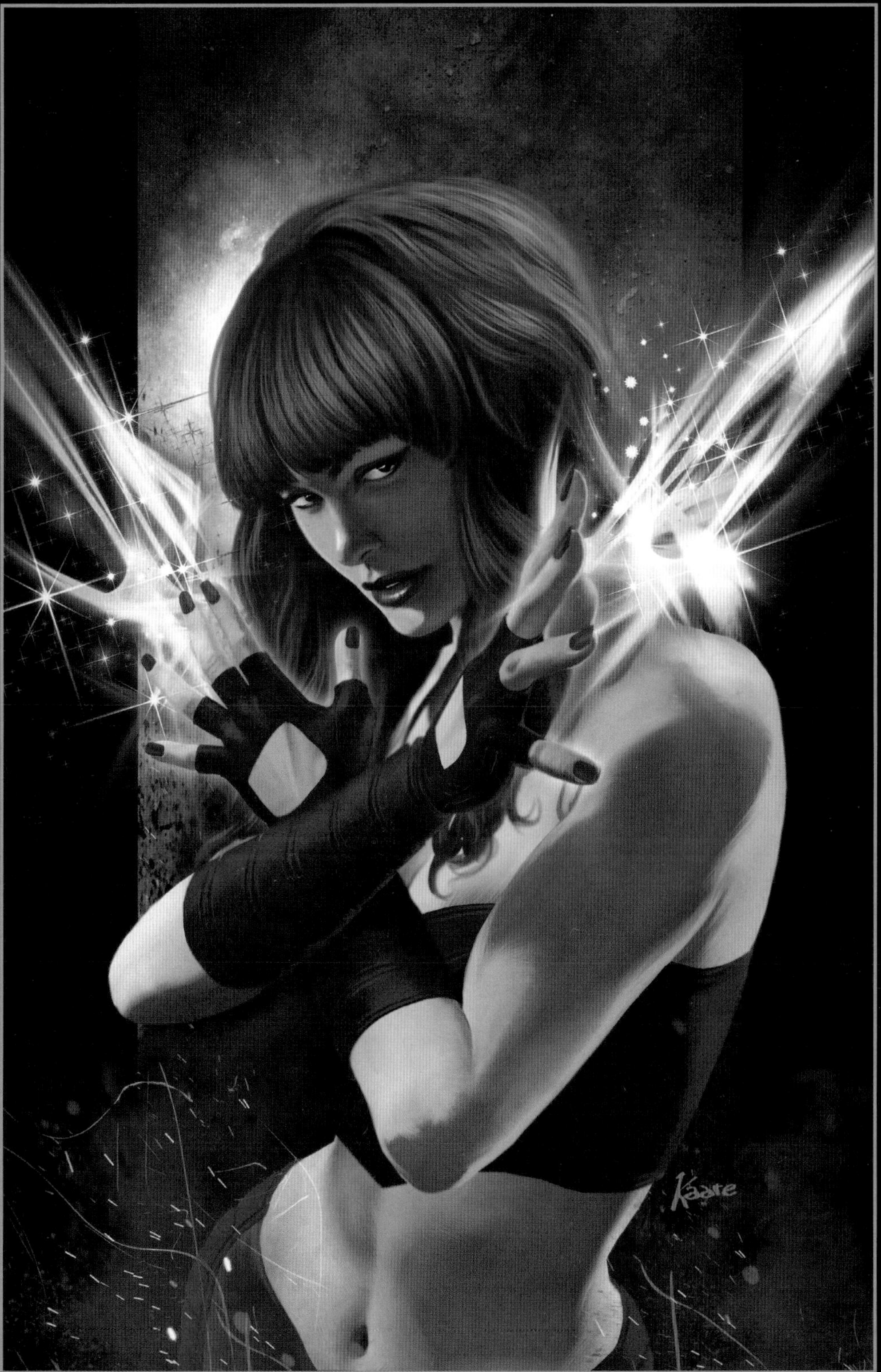

ISSUE 07 COVER

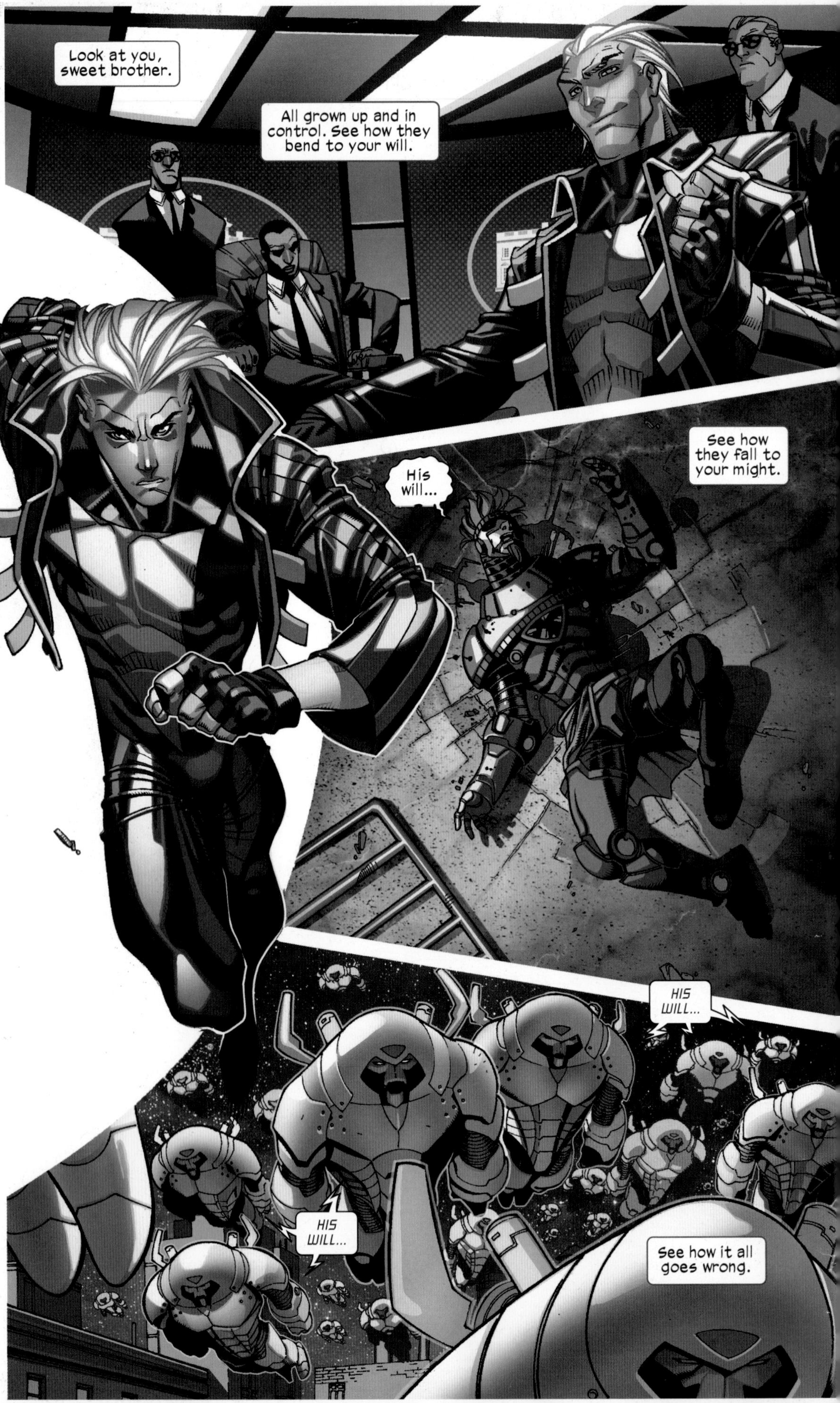

Look at you, sweet brother.
All grown up and in control. See how they bend to your will.
His will...
See how they fall to your might.
HIS WILL...
HIS WILL...
See how it all goes wrong.

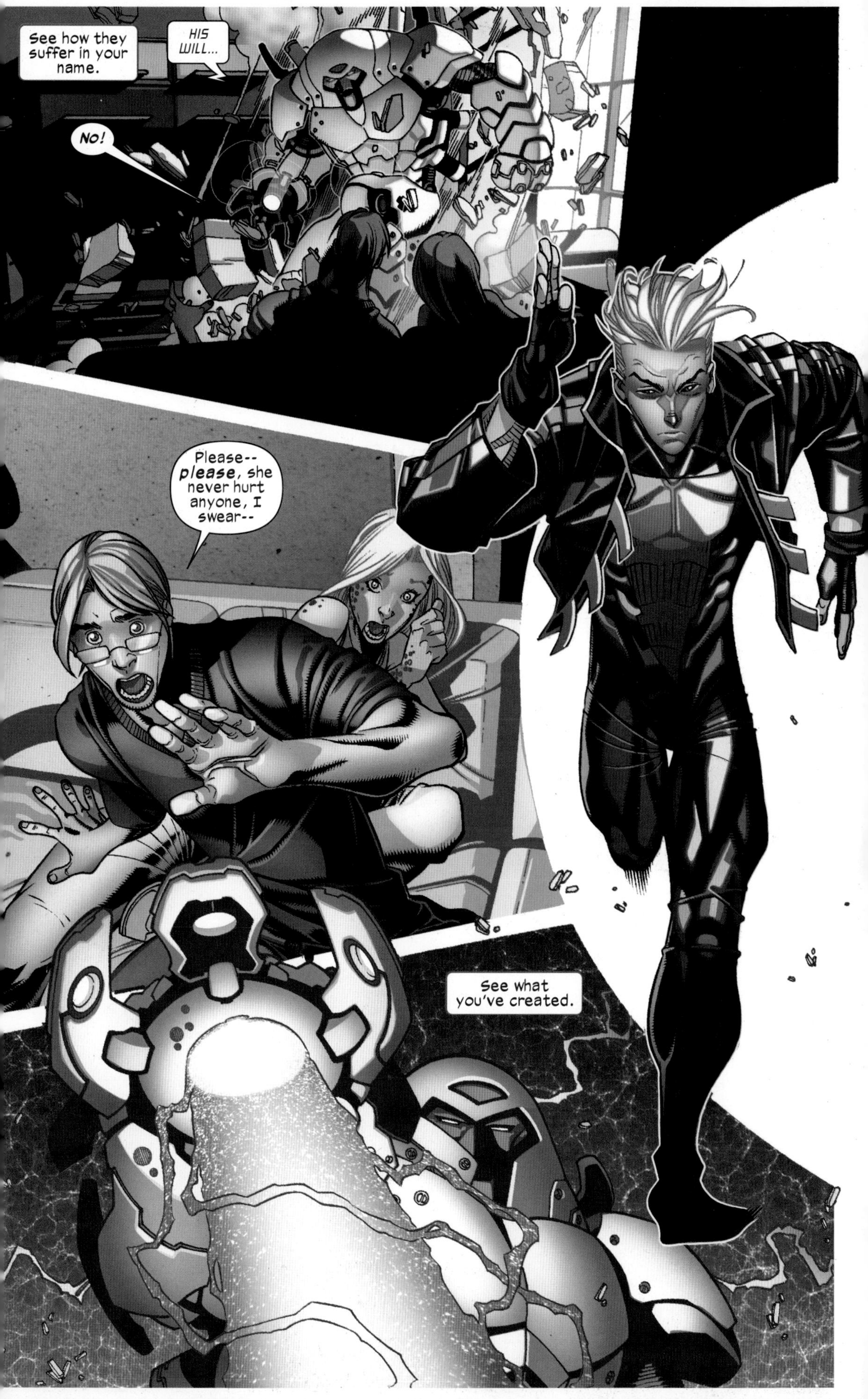
See how they suffer in your name.
HIS WILL...
NO!
Please-- please, she never hurt anyone, I swear--
See what you've created.

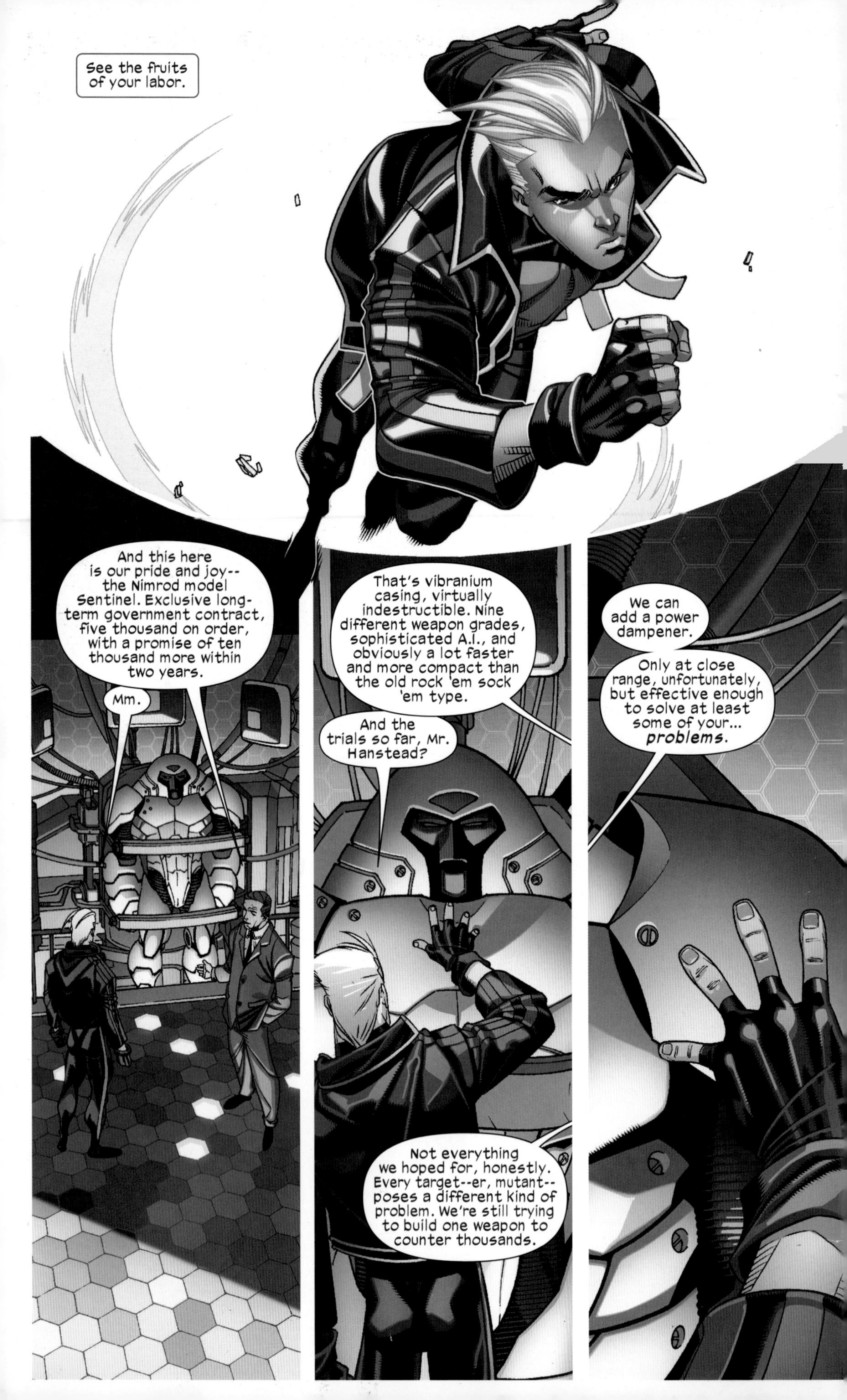
See the fruits of your labor.
And this here is our pride and joy-- the Nimrod model Sentinel. Exclusive long-term government contract, five thousand on order, with a promise of ten thousand more within two years.
Mm.
That's vibranium casing, virtually indestructible. Nine different weapon grades, sophisticated A.I., and obviously a lot faster and more compact than the old rock 'em sock 'em type.
And the trials so far, Mr. Hanstead?
Not everything we hoped for, honestly. Every target--er, mutant--poses a different kind of problem. We're still trying to build one weapon to counter thousands.
We can add a power dampener.
Only at close range, unfortunately, but effective enough to solve at least some of your... *problems*.

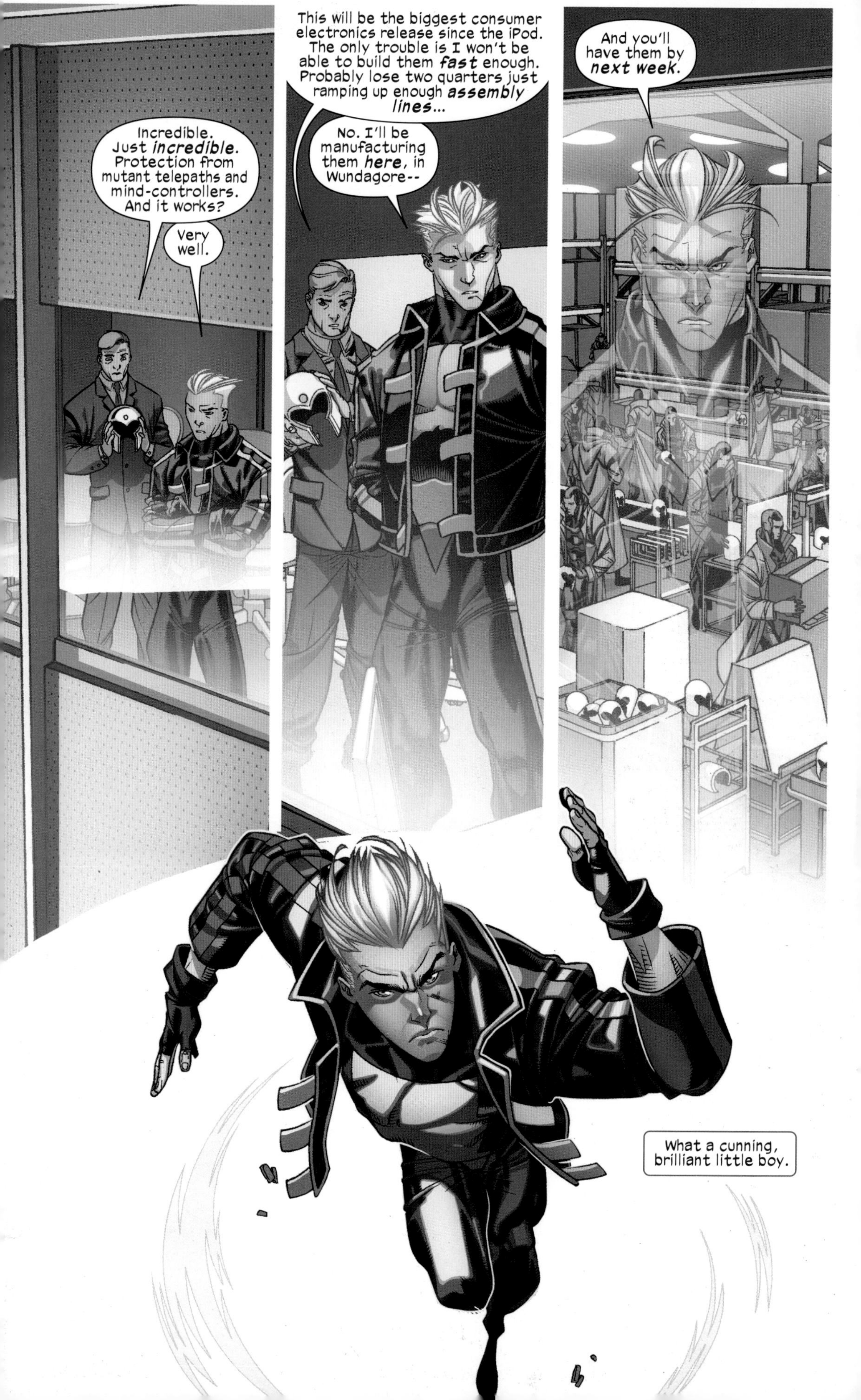
Incredible.
Just *incredible*.
Protection from
mutant telepaths and
mind-controllers.
And it works?
Very
well.
This will be the biggest consumer
electronics release since the iPod.
The only trouble is I won't be
able to build them *fast* enough.
Probably lose two quarters just
ramping up enough *assembly*
lines...
No. I'll be
manufacturing
them *here*, in
Wundagore--
And you'll
have them by
next week.
What a cunning,
brilliant little boy.

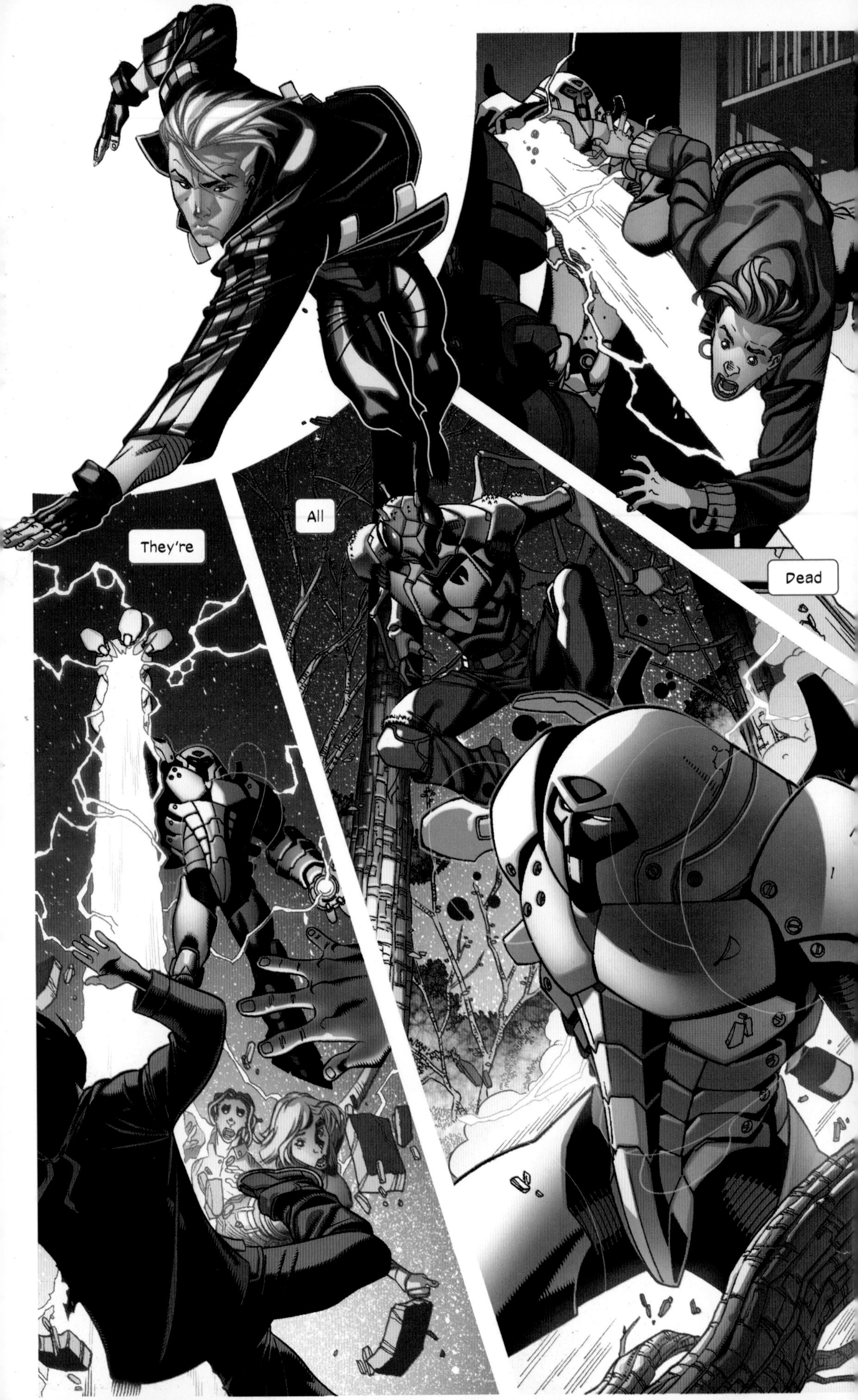
They're
All
Dead

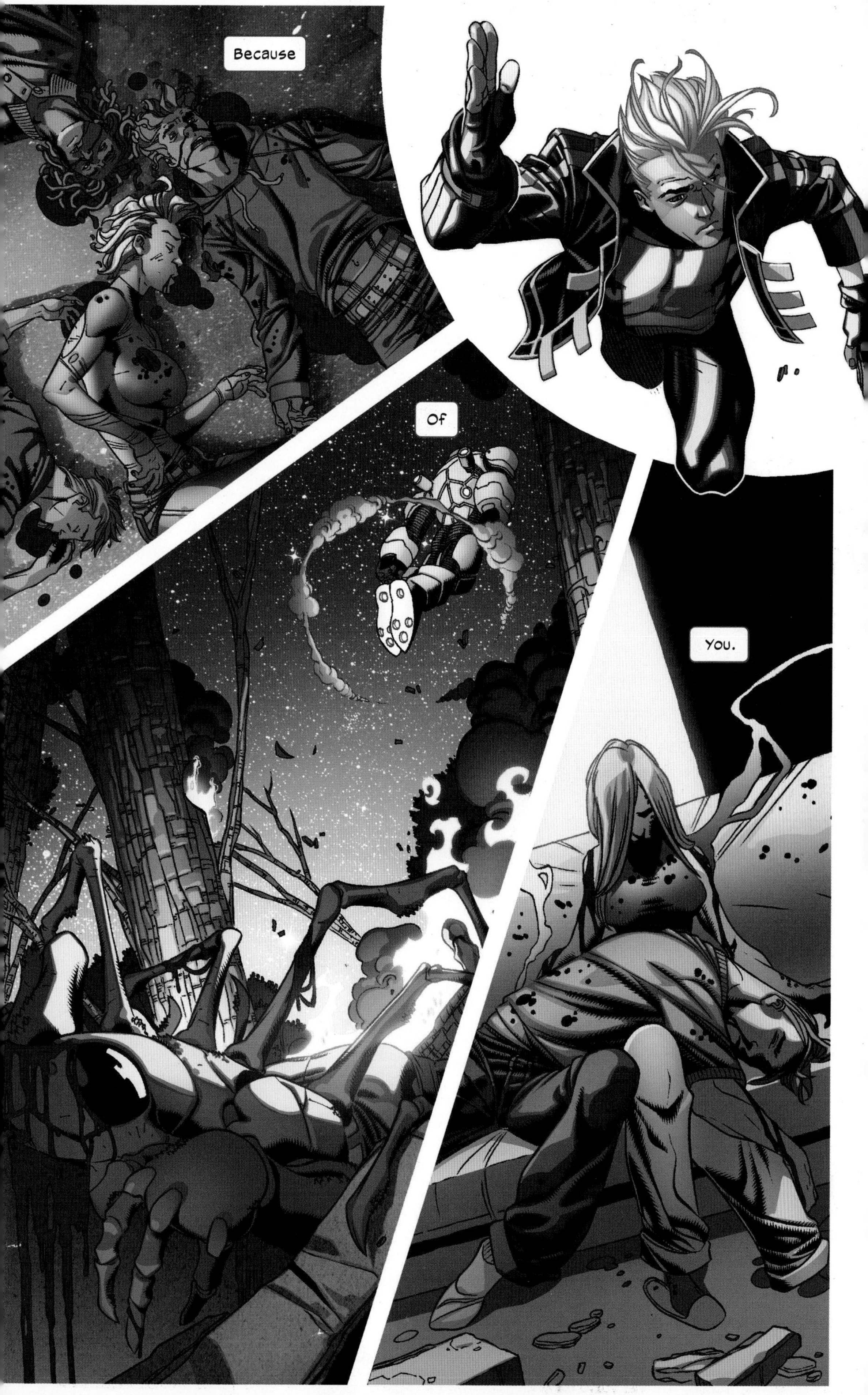
Because
Of
You.

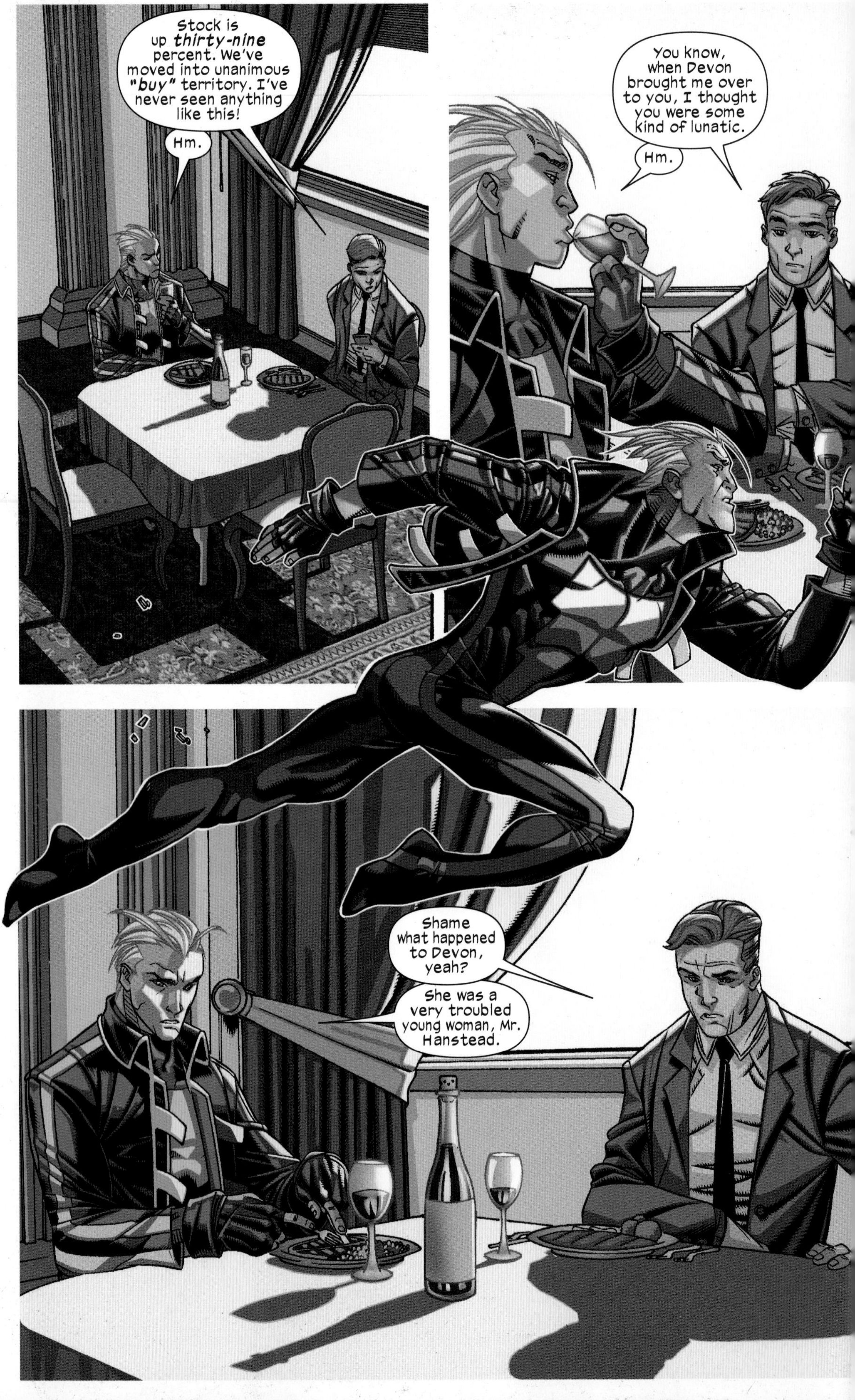

Stock is up *thirty-nine* percent. We've moved into unanimous *"buy"* territory. I've never seen anything like this!
Hm.
You know, when Devon brought me over to you, I thought you were some kind of lunatic.
Hm.
Shame what happened to Devon, yeah?
She was a very troubled young woman, Mr. Hanstead.

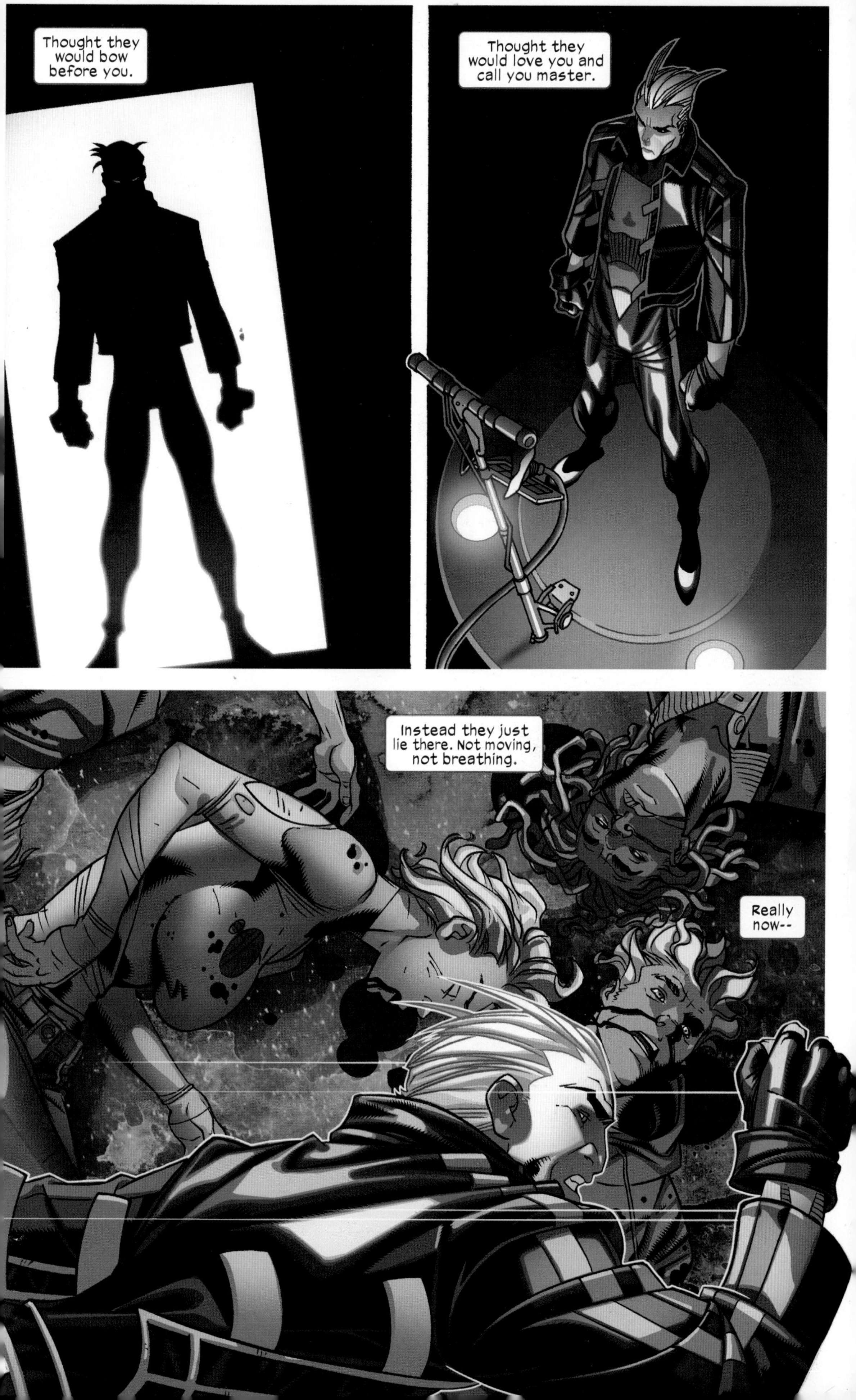
Thought they would bow before you.
Thought they would love you and call you master.
Instead they just lie there. Not moving, not breathing.
Really now--

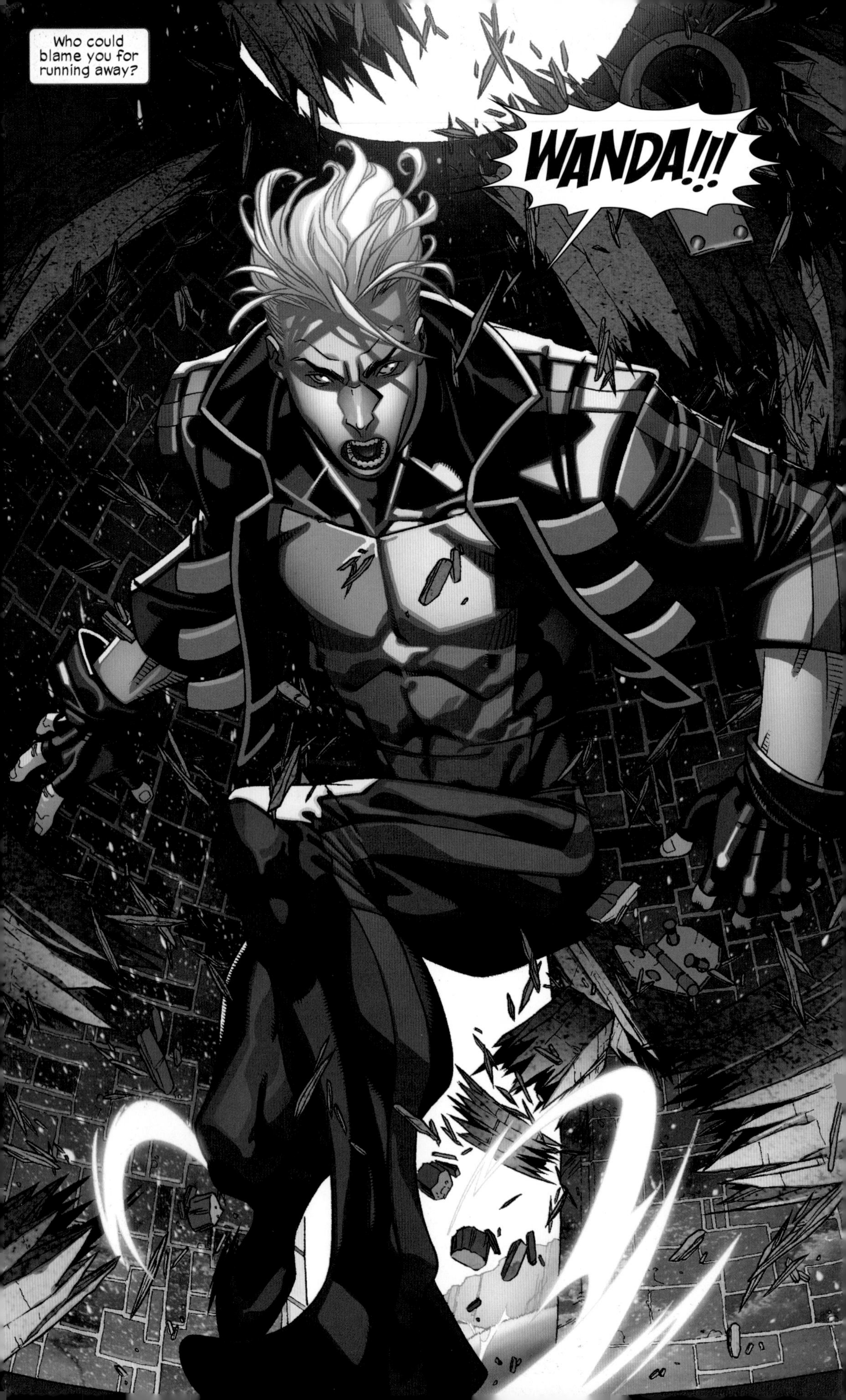
Who could blame you for running away?
WANDA!!!

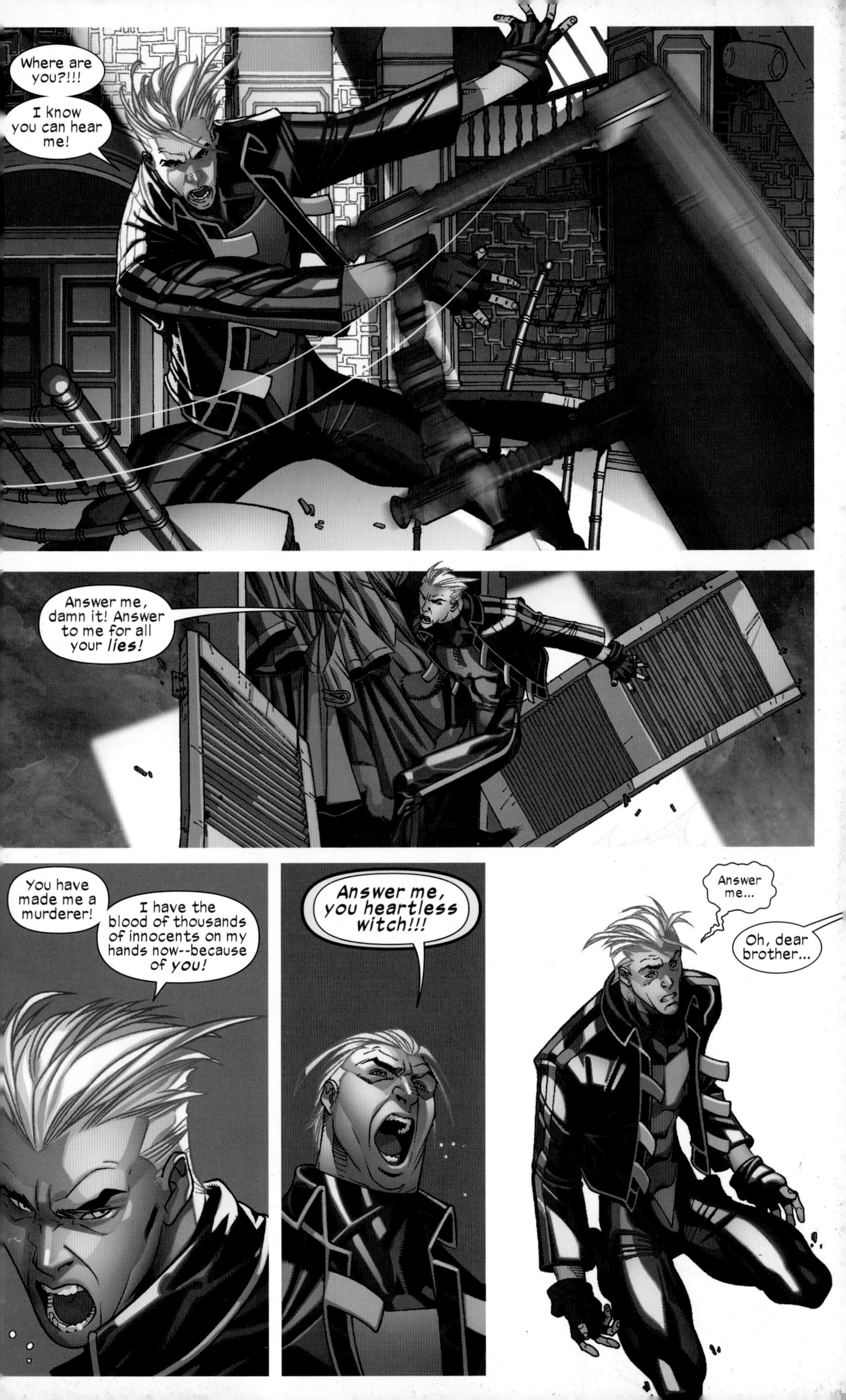
Where are you?!!!
I know you can hear me!
Answer me, damn it! Answer to me for all your lies!
You have made me a murderer!
I have the blood of thousands of innocents on my hands now--because of you!
Answer me, you heartless witch!!!
Answer me...
Oh, dear brother...

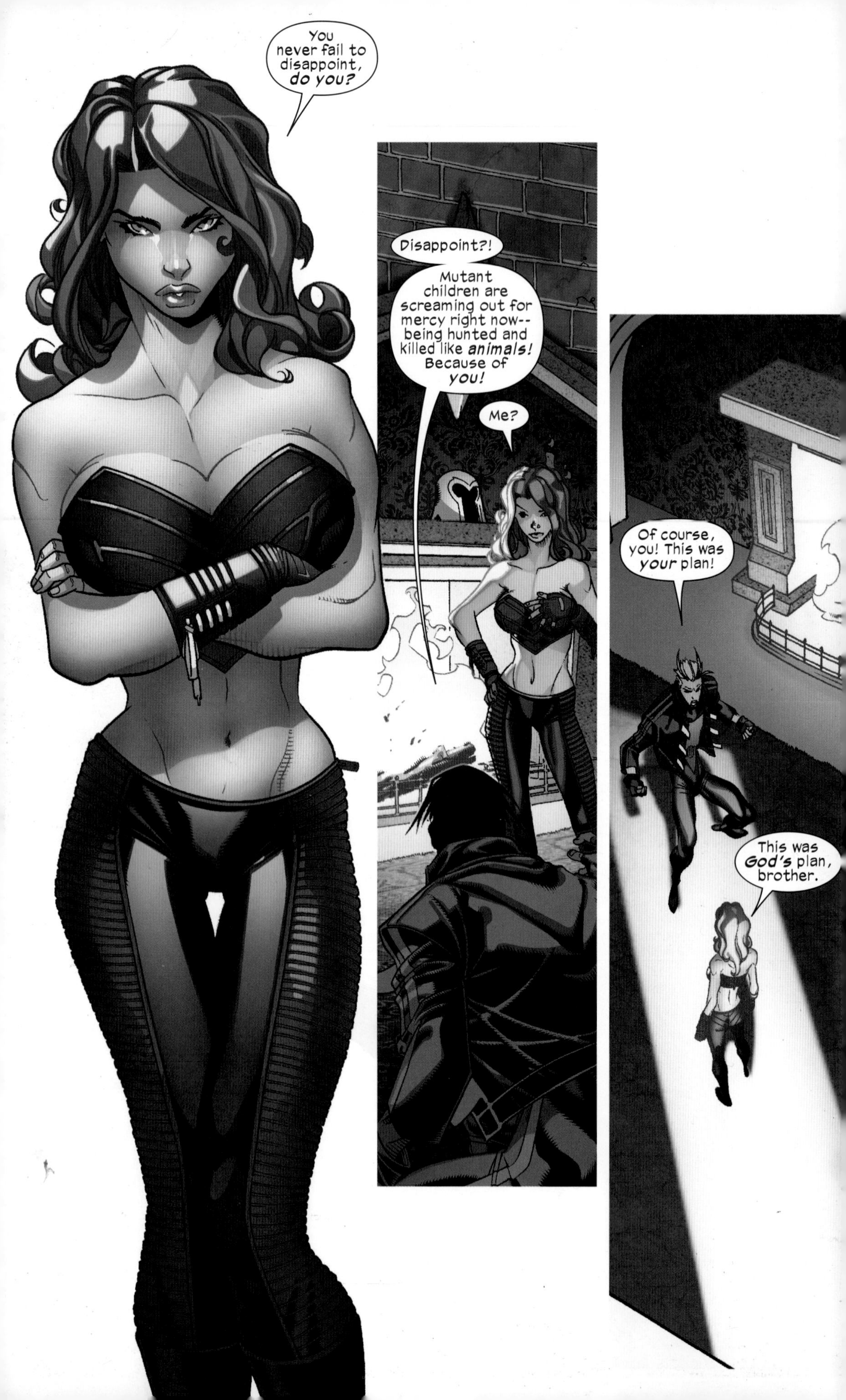
You never fail to disappoint, *do you?*
Disappoint?!
Mutant children are screaming out for mercy right now-- being hunted and killed like *animals!* Because of *you!*
Me?
Of course, you! This was *your* plan!
This was *God's* plan, brother.

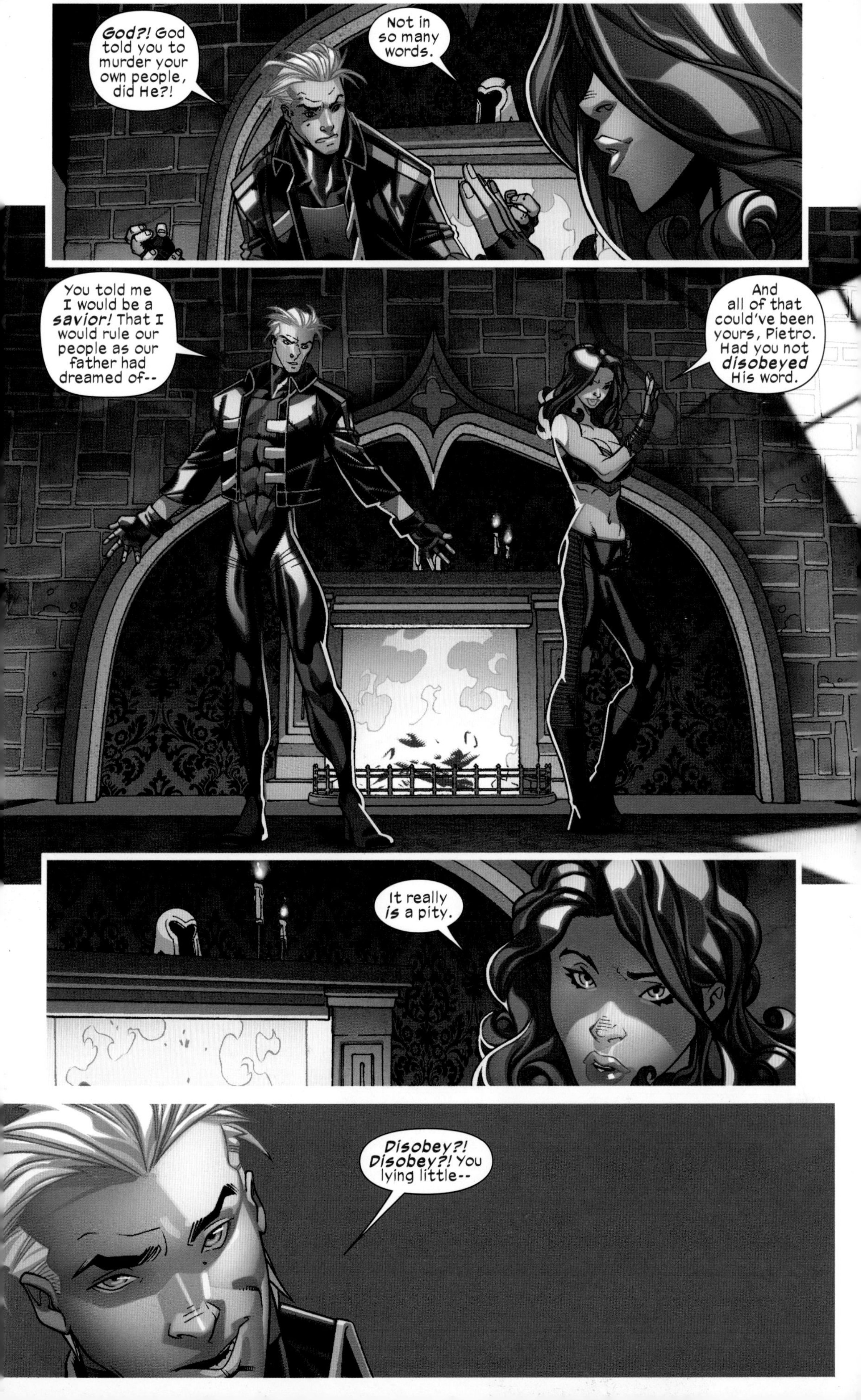
God?! God told you to murder your own people, did He?!
Not in so many words.
You told me I would be a savior! That I would rule our people as our father had dreamed of--
And all of that could've been yours, Pietro. Had you not disobeyed His word.
It really is a pity.
Disobey?! Disobey?! You lying little--

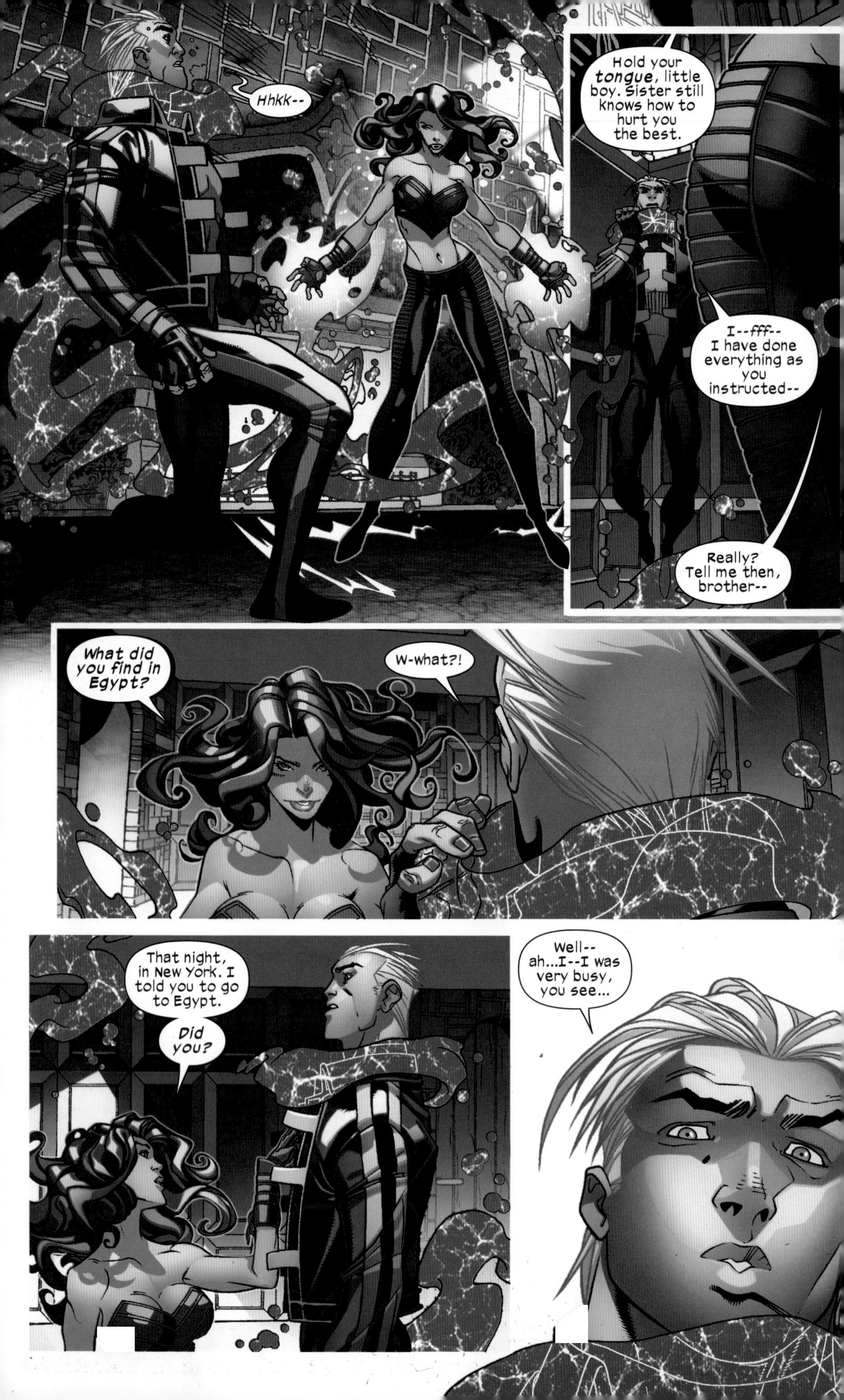
Hhkk--
Hold your *tongue*, little boy. Sister still knows how to hurt you the best.
I--*fff*-- I have done everything as you instructed--
Really? Tell me then, brother--
What did you find in Egypt?
W-what?!
That night, in New York. I told you to go to Egypt.
Did you?
Well-- ah...I--I was very busy, you see...

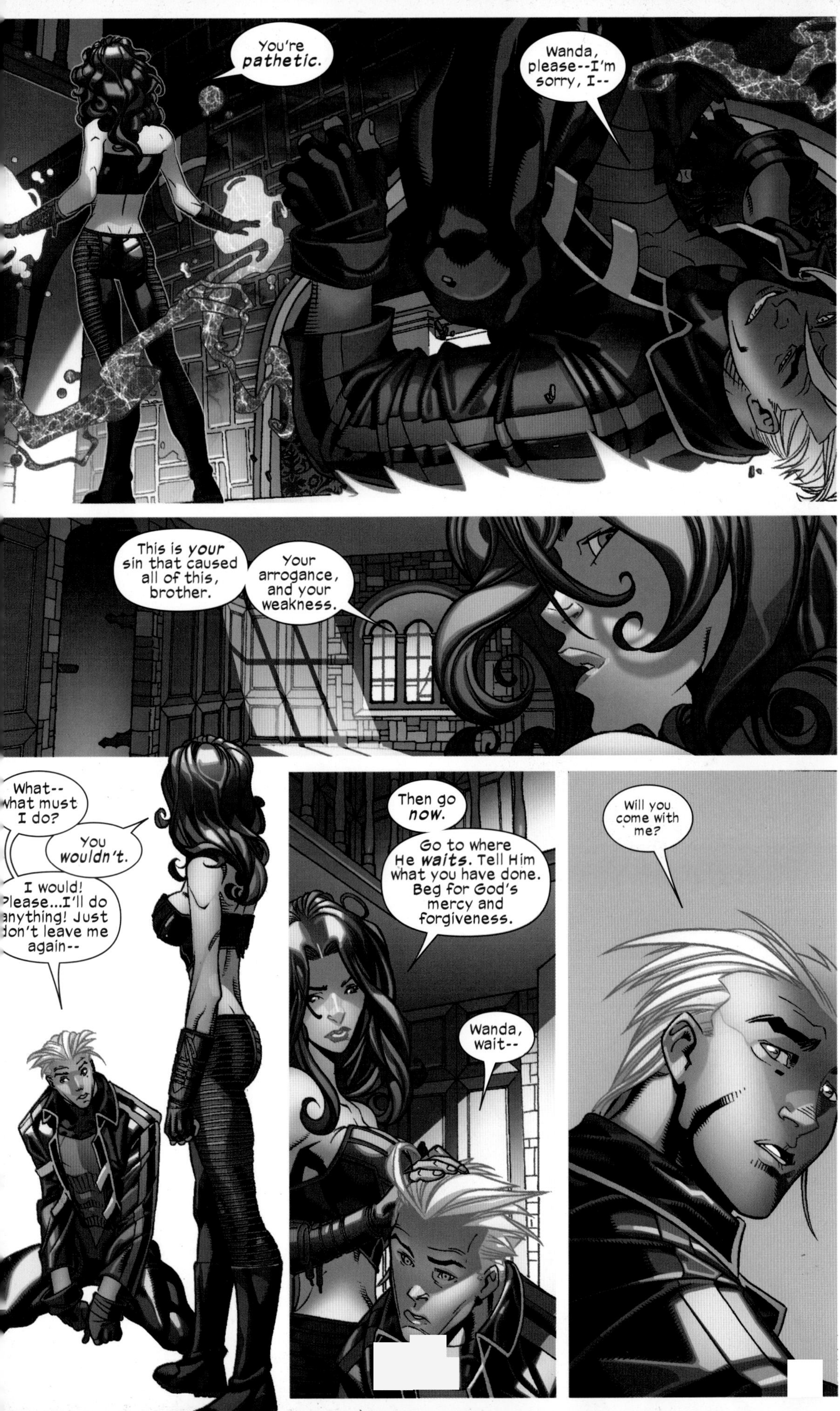

You're pathetic.
Wanda, please--I'm sorry, I--
This is your sin that caused all of this, brother.
Your arrogance, and your weakness.
What--what must I do?
You wouldn't.
I would! Please...I'll do anything! Just don't leave me again--
Then go now.
Go to where He waits. Tell Him what you have done. Beg for God's mercy and forgiveness.
Wanda, wait--
Will you come with me?

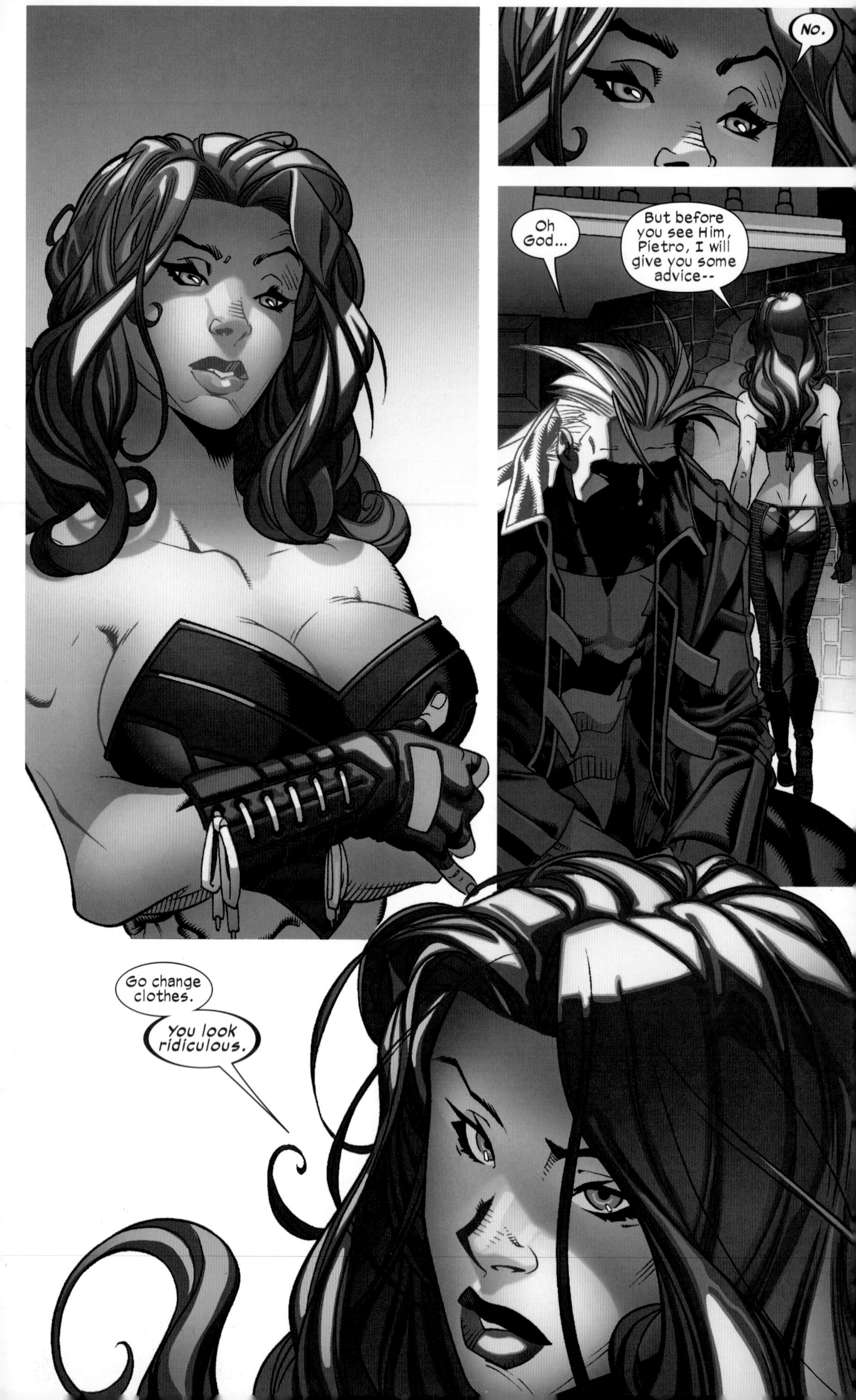
NO.
Oh God...
But before you see Him, Pietro, I will give you some advice--
Go change clothes.
You look ridiculous.

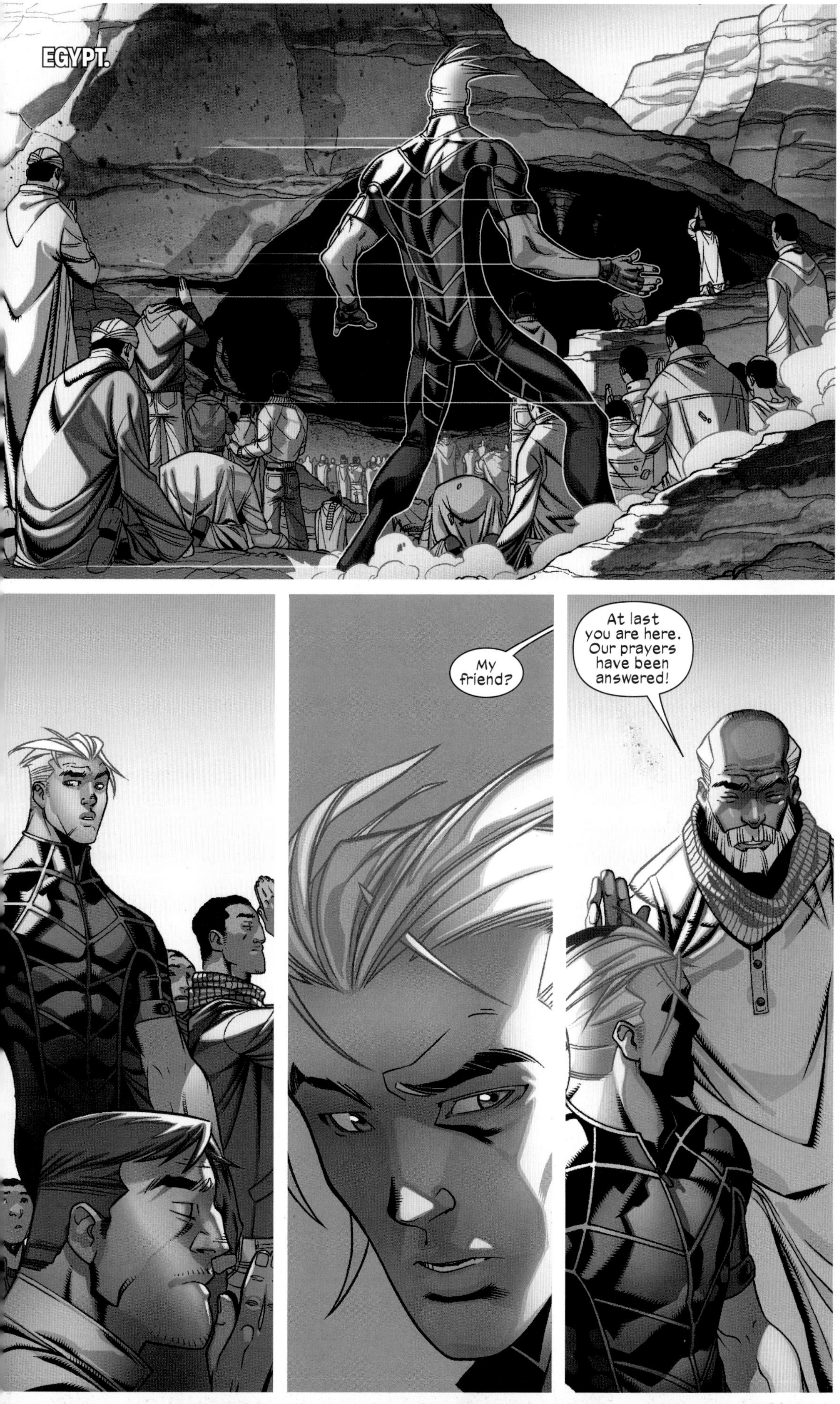
EGYPT.
My friend?
At last you are here. Our prayers have been answered!

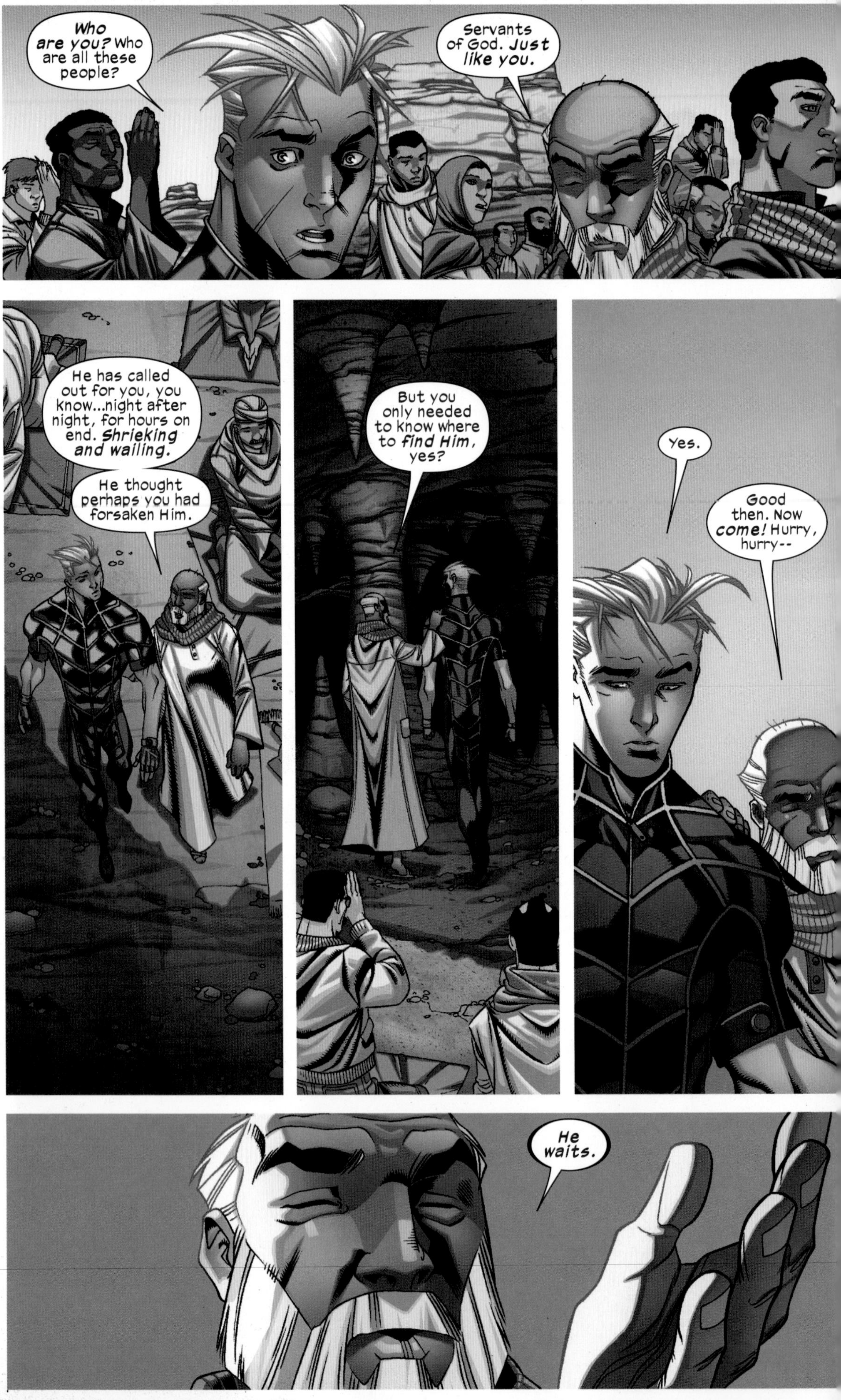
Who are you? Who are all these people?
Servants of God. Just like you.
He has called out for you, you know...night after night, for hours on end. Shrieking and wailing.
He thought perhaps you had forsaken Him.
But you only needed to know where to find Him, yes?
Yes.
Good then. Now come! Hurry, hurry--
He waits.

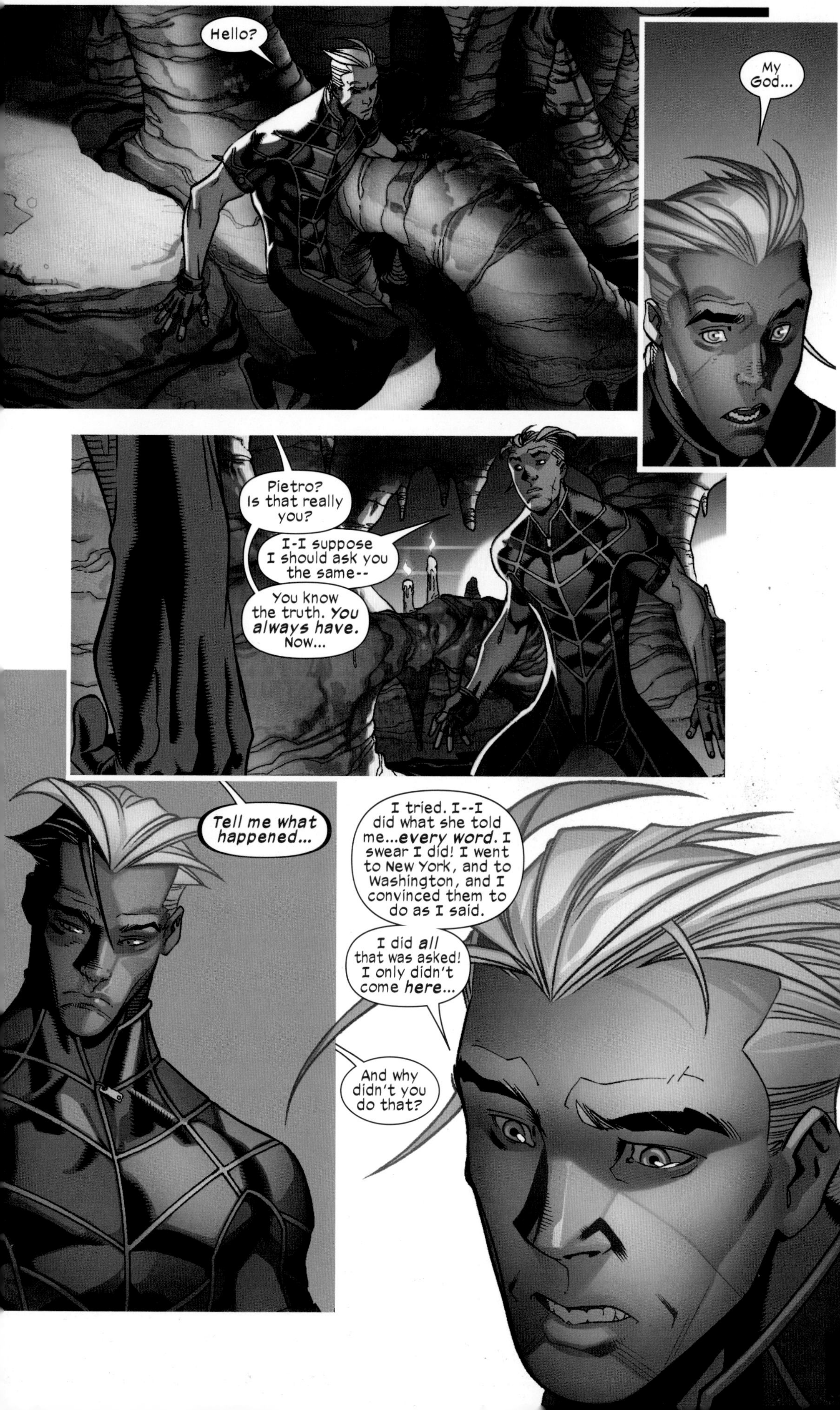
Hello?
My God...
Pietro? Is that really you?
I-I suppose I should ask you the same--
You know the truth. *You always have.* Now...
Tell me what happened...
I tried. I--I did what she told me...*every word.* I swear I did! I went to New York, and to Washington, and I convinced them to do as I said.
I did *all* that was asked! I only didn't come *here*...
And why didn't you do that?

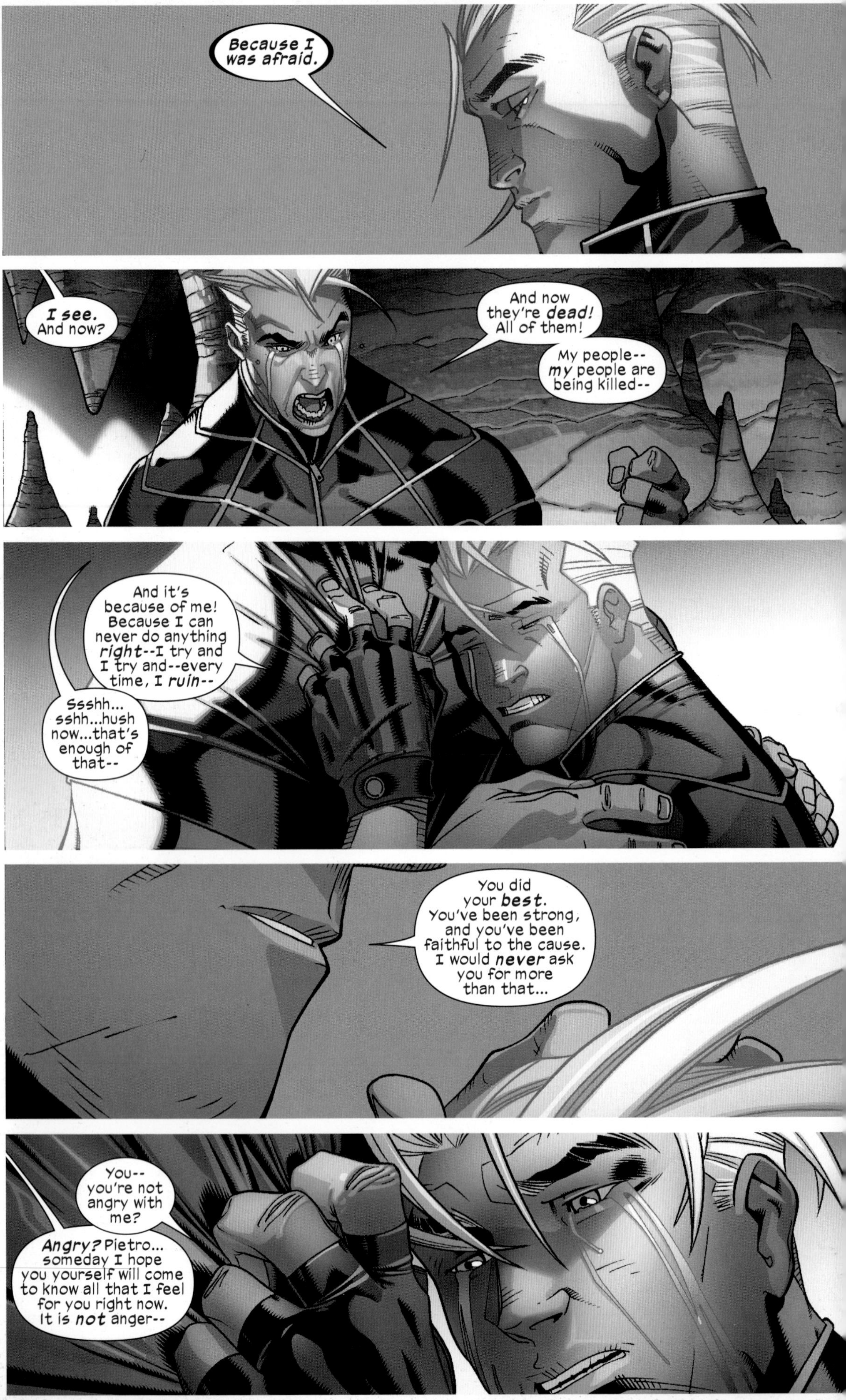
Because I was afraid.
I see. And now?
And now they're dead! All of them!
My people-- my people are being killed--
And it's because of me! Because I can never do anything right--I try and I try and--every time, I ruin--
Ssshh... sshh...hush now...that's enough of that--
You did your best. You've been strong, and you've been faithful to the cause. I would never ask you for more than that...
You-- you're not angry with me?
Angry? Pietro... someday I hope you yourself will come to know all that I feel for you right now. It is not anger--

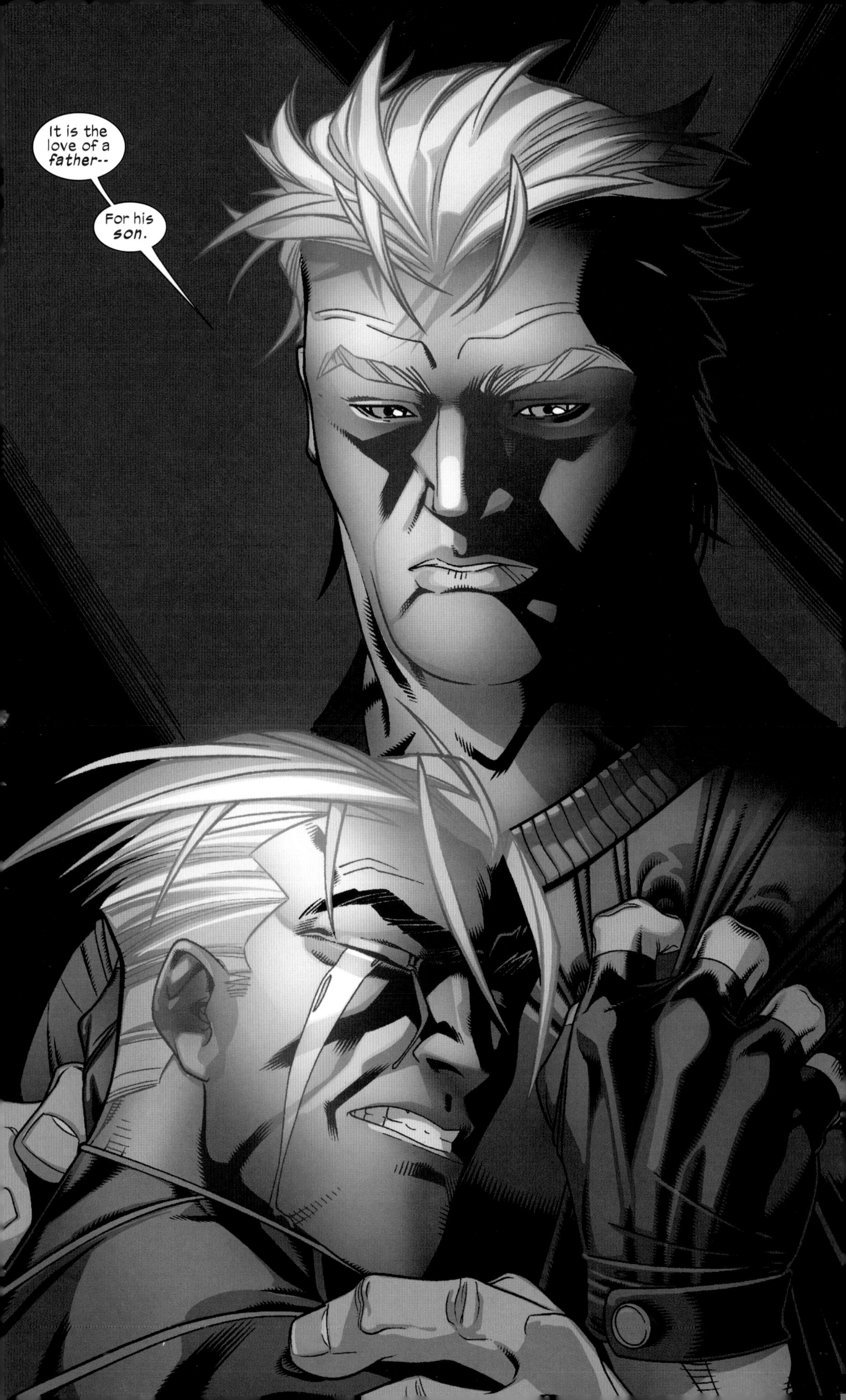
It is the love of a *father*--
For his *son*.

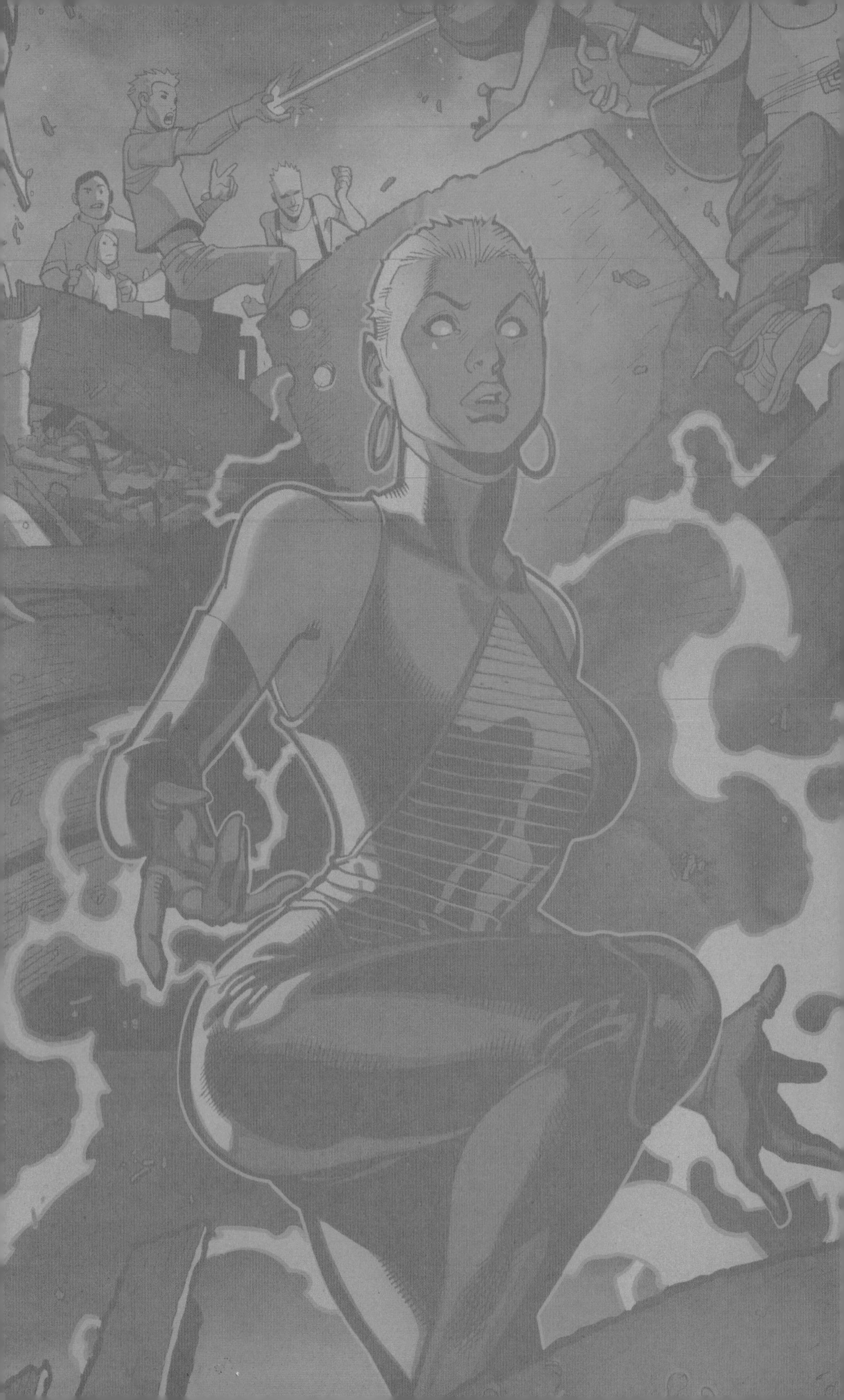

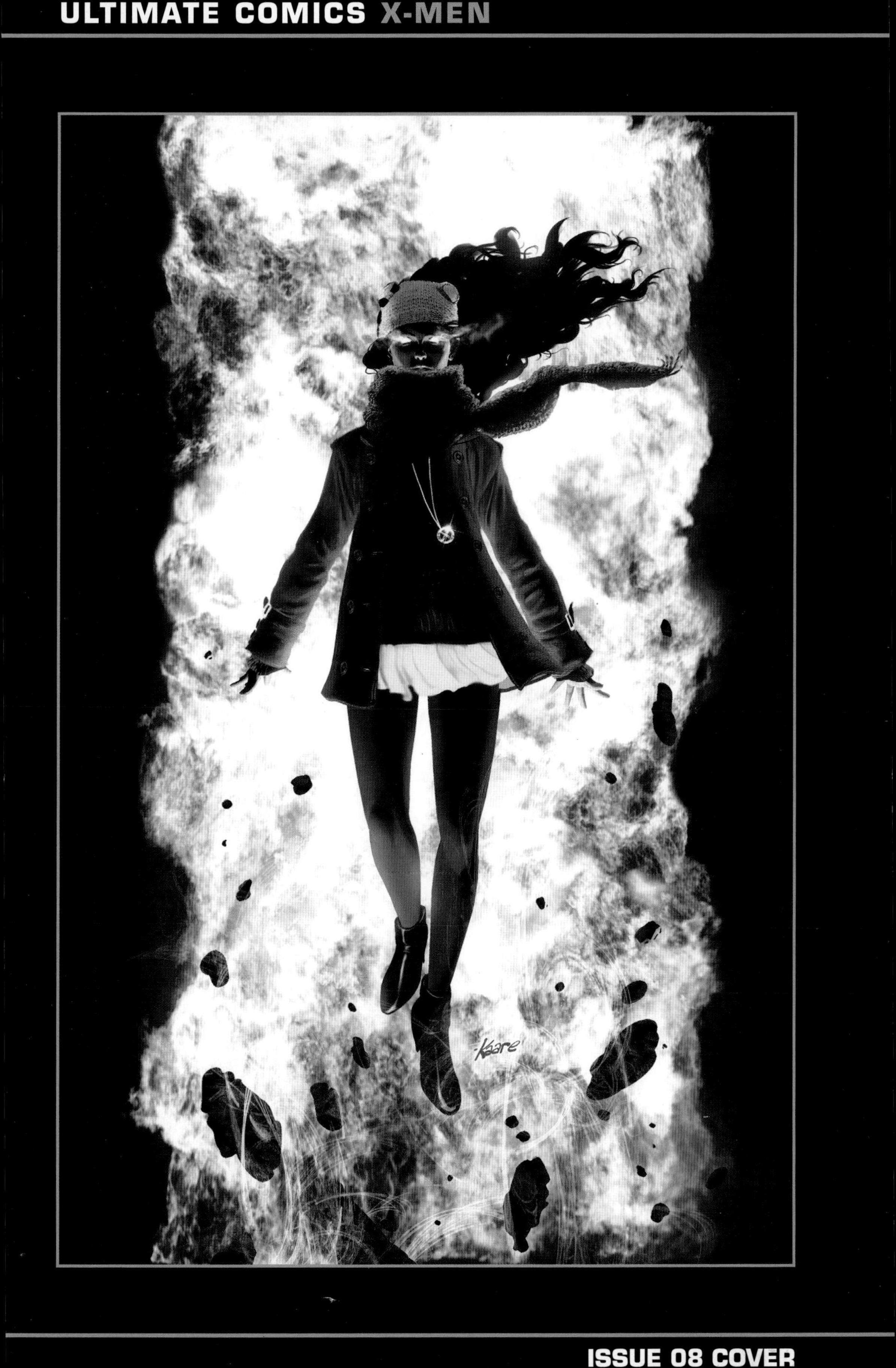
Kaare

ISSUE 08 COVER

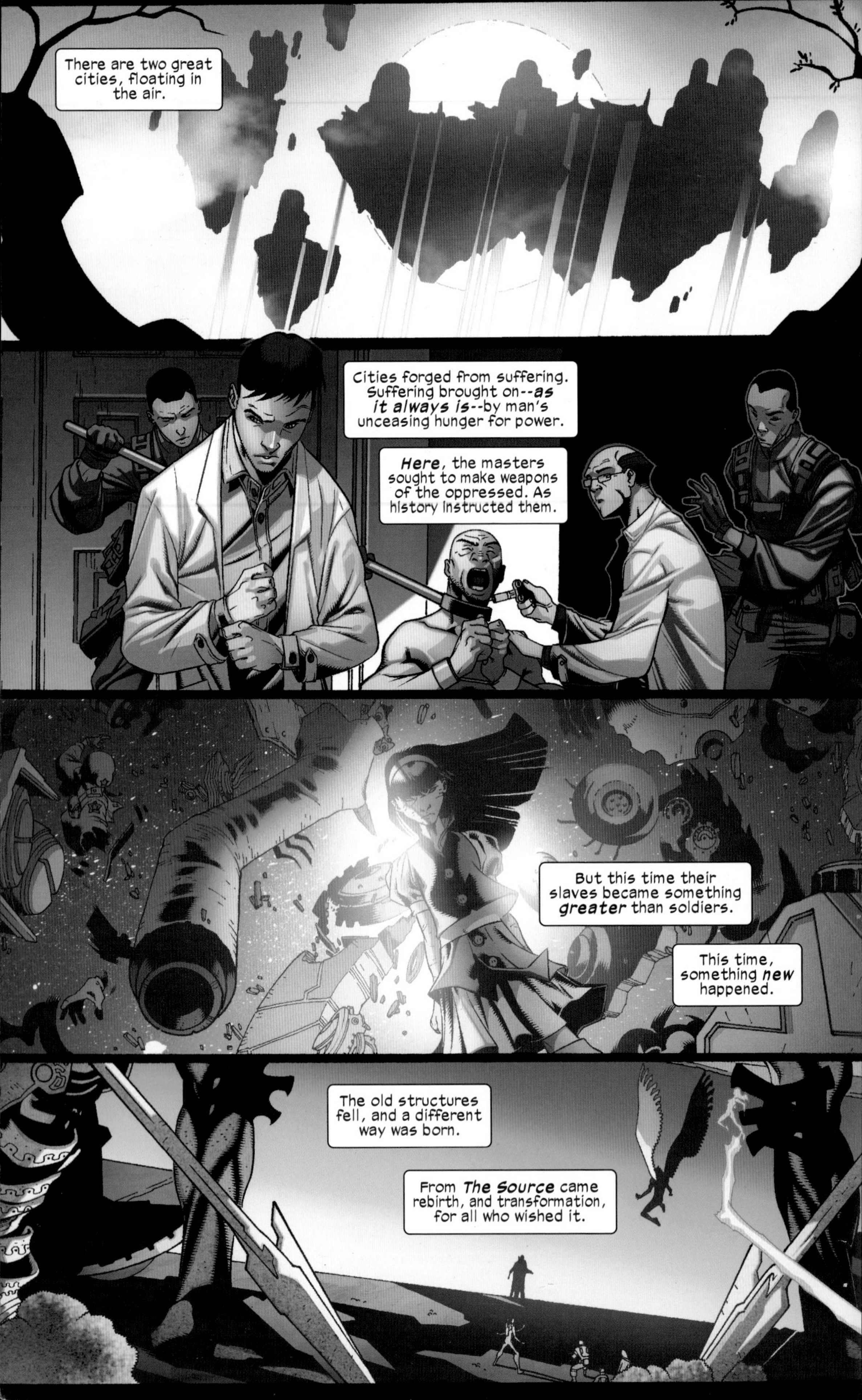
There are two great cities, floating in the air.
Cities forged from suffering. Suffering brought on--*as it always is*--by man's unceasing hunger for power.
Here, the masters sought to make weapons of the oppressed. As history instructed them.
But this time their slaves became something *greater* than soldiers.
This time, something *new* happened.
The old structures fell, and a different way was born.
From *The Source* came rebirth, and transformation, for all who wished it.

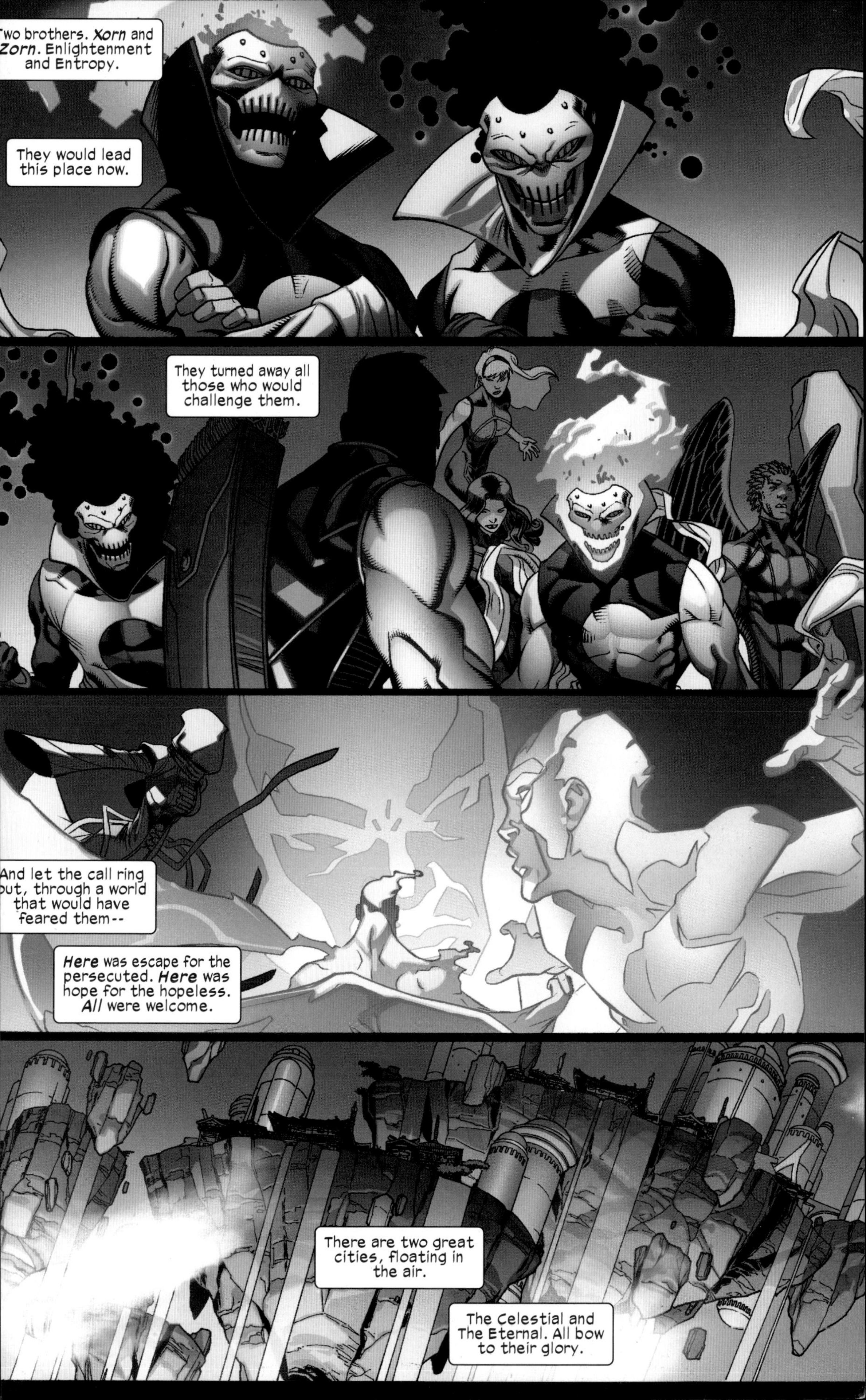
Two brothers. Xorn and Zorn. Enlightenment and Entropy.
They would lead this place now.
They turned away all those who would challenge them.
And let the call ring out, through a world that would have feared them--
Here was escape for the persecuted. Here was hope for the hopeless. All were welcome.
There are two great cities, floating in the air.
The Celestial and The Eternal. All bow to their glory.

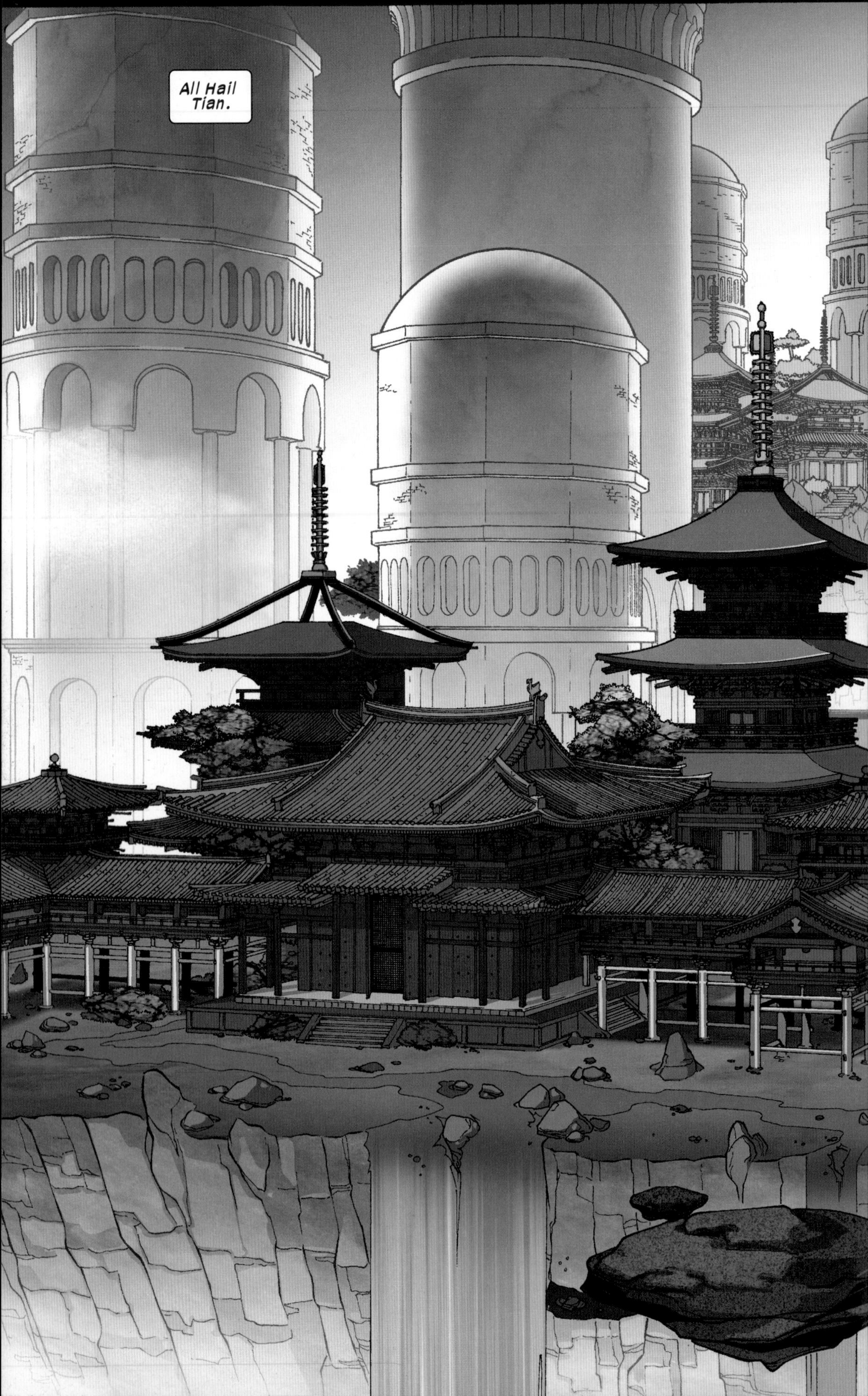
All Hail Tian.

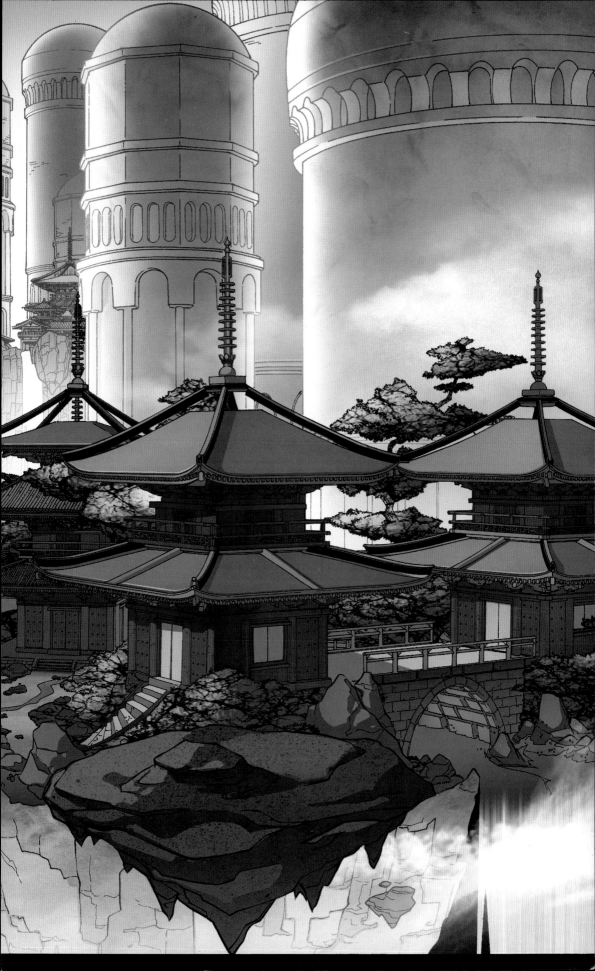

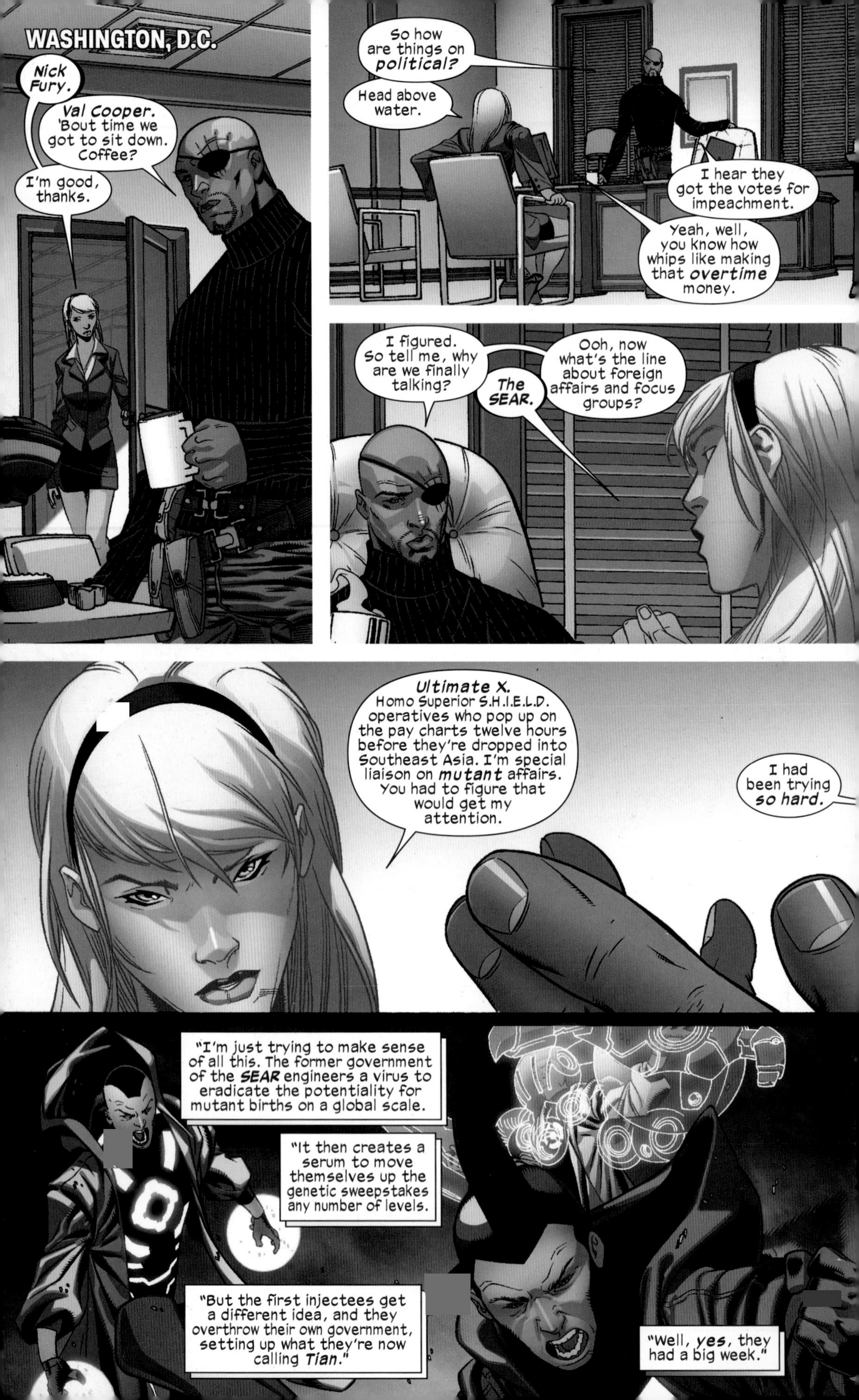
WASHINGTON, D.C.
Nick Fury.
Val Cooper. 'Bout time we got to sit down. Coffee?
I'm good, thanks.
So how are things on political?
Head above water.
I hear they got the votes for impeachment.
Yeah, well, you know how whips like making that overtime money.
I figured. So tell me, why are we finally talking?
Ooh, now what's the line about foreign affairs and focus groups?
The SEAR.
Ultimate X. Homo Superior S.H.I.E.L.D. operatives who pop up on the pay charts twelve hours before they're dropped into Southeast Asia. I'm special liaison on mutant affairs. You had to figure that would get my attention.
I had been trying so hard.
"I'm just trying to make sense of all this. The former government of the SEAR engineers a virus to eradicate the potentiality for mutant births on a global scale.
"It then creates a serum to move themselves up the genetic sweepstakes any number of levels.
"But the first injectees get a different idea, and they overthrow their own government, setting up what they're now calling Tian."
"Well, yes, they had a big week."

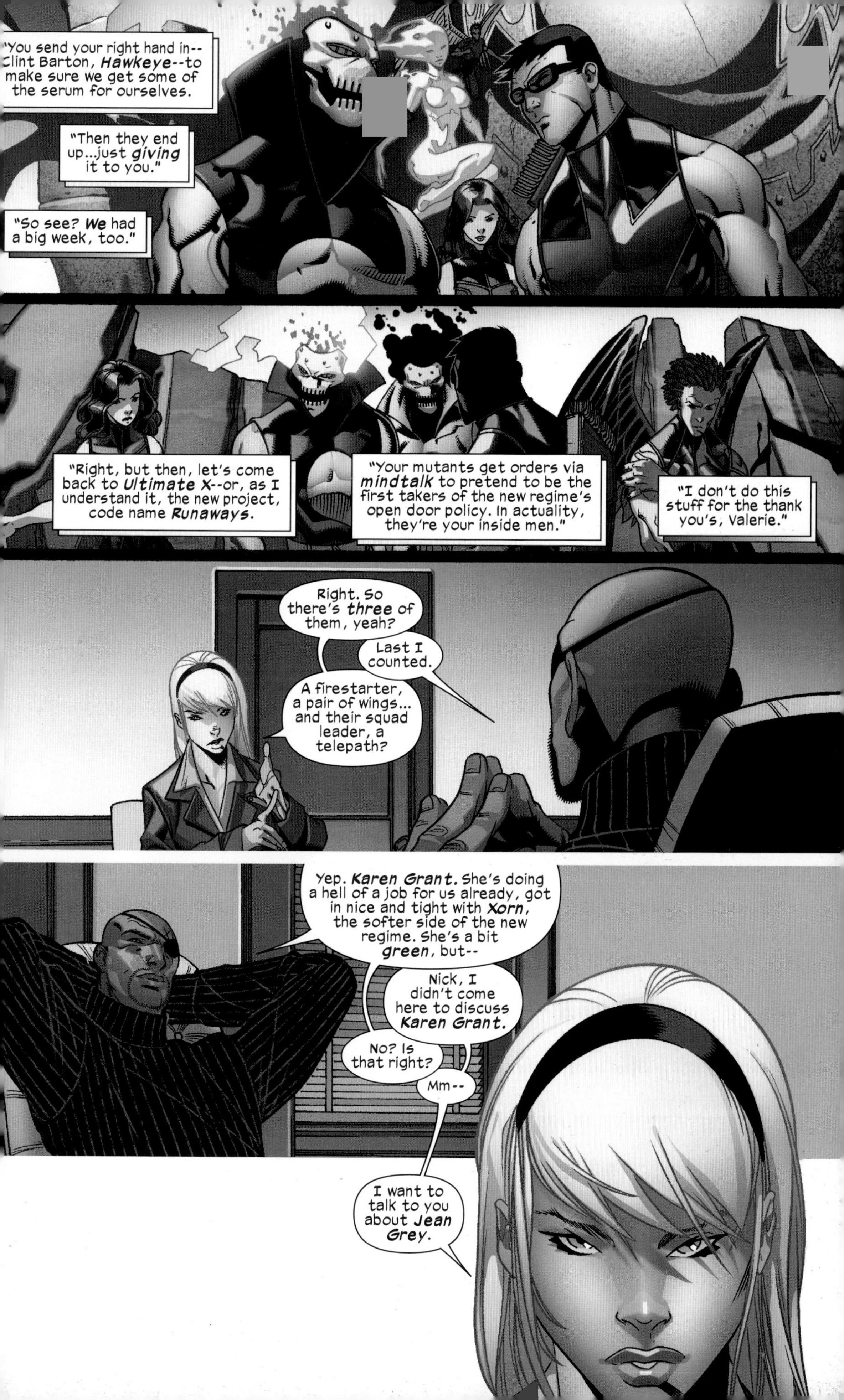
"You send your right hand in--Clint Barton, Hawkeye--to make sure we get some of the serum for ourselves.
"Then they end up...just giving it to you."
"So see? We had a big week, too."
"Right, but then, let's come back to Ultimate X--or, as I understand it, the new project, code name Runaways.
"Your mutants get orders via mindtalk to pretend to be the first takers of the new regime's open door policy. In actuality, they're your inside men."
"I don't do this stuff for the thank you's, Valerie."
Right. So there's three of them, yeah?
Last I counted.
A firestarter, a pair of wings... and their squad leader, a telepath?
Yep. Karen Grant. She's doing a hell of a job for us already, got in nice and tight with Xorn, the softer side of the new regime. She's a bit green, but--
Nick, I didn't come here to discuss Karen Grant.
No? Is that right?
Mm--
I want to talk to you about Jean Grey.

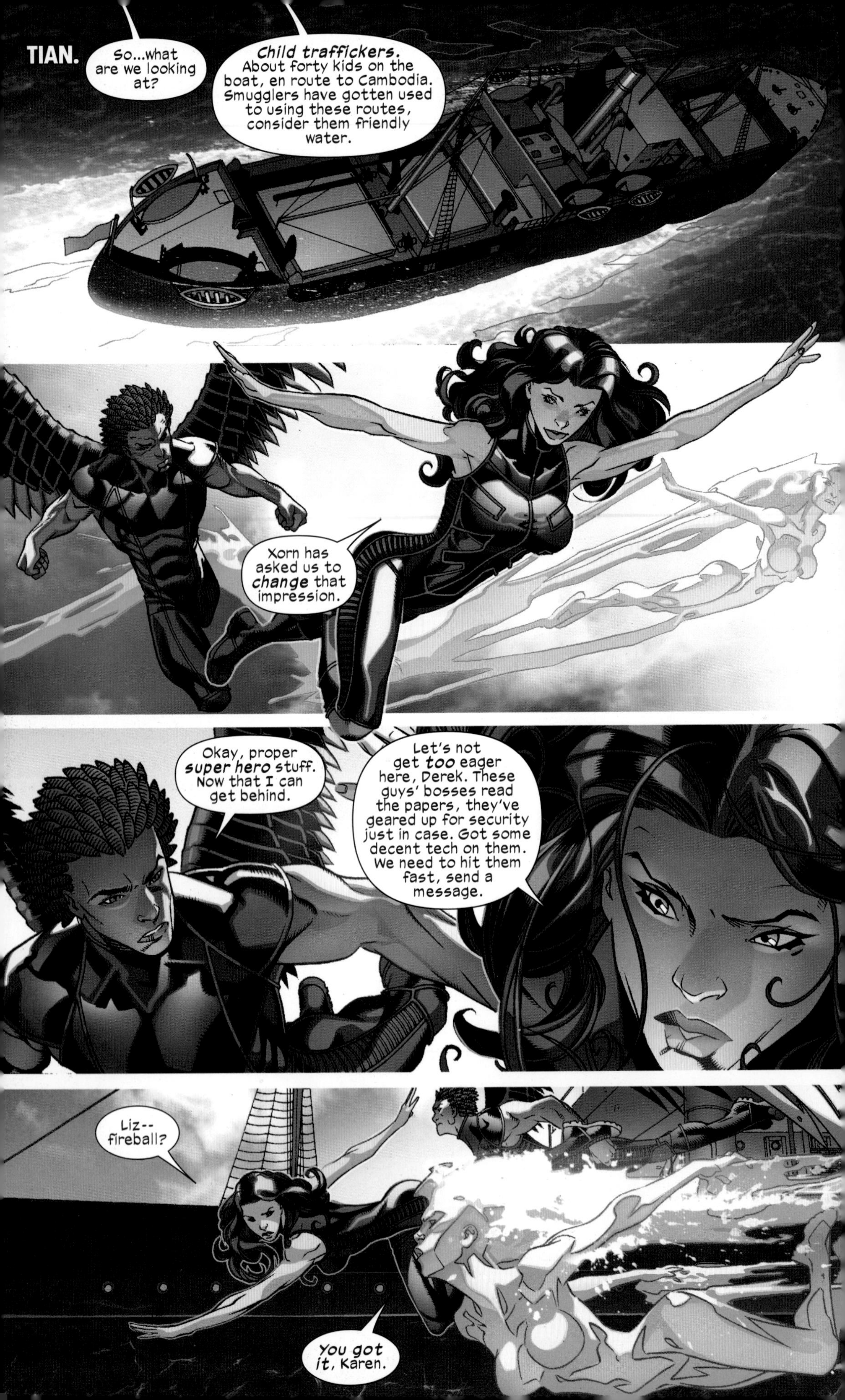
TIAN.
So...what are we looking at?
Child traffickers. About forty kids on the boat, en route to Cambodia. Smugglers have gotten used to using these routes, consider them friendly water.
Xorn has asked us to change that impression.
Okay, proper super hero stuff. Now that I can get behind.
Let's not get too eager here, Derek. These guys' bosses read the papers, they've geared up for security just in case. Got some decent tech on them. We need to hit them fast, send a message.
Liz--fireball?
You got it, Karen.

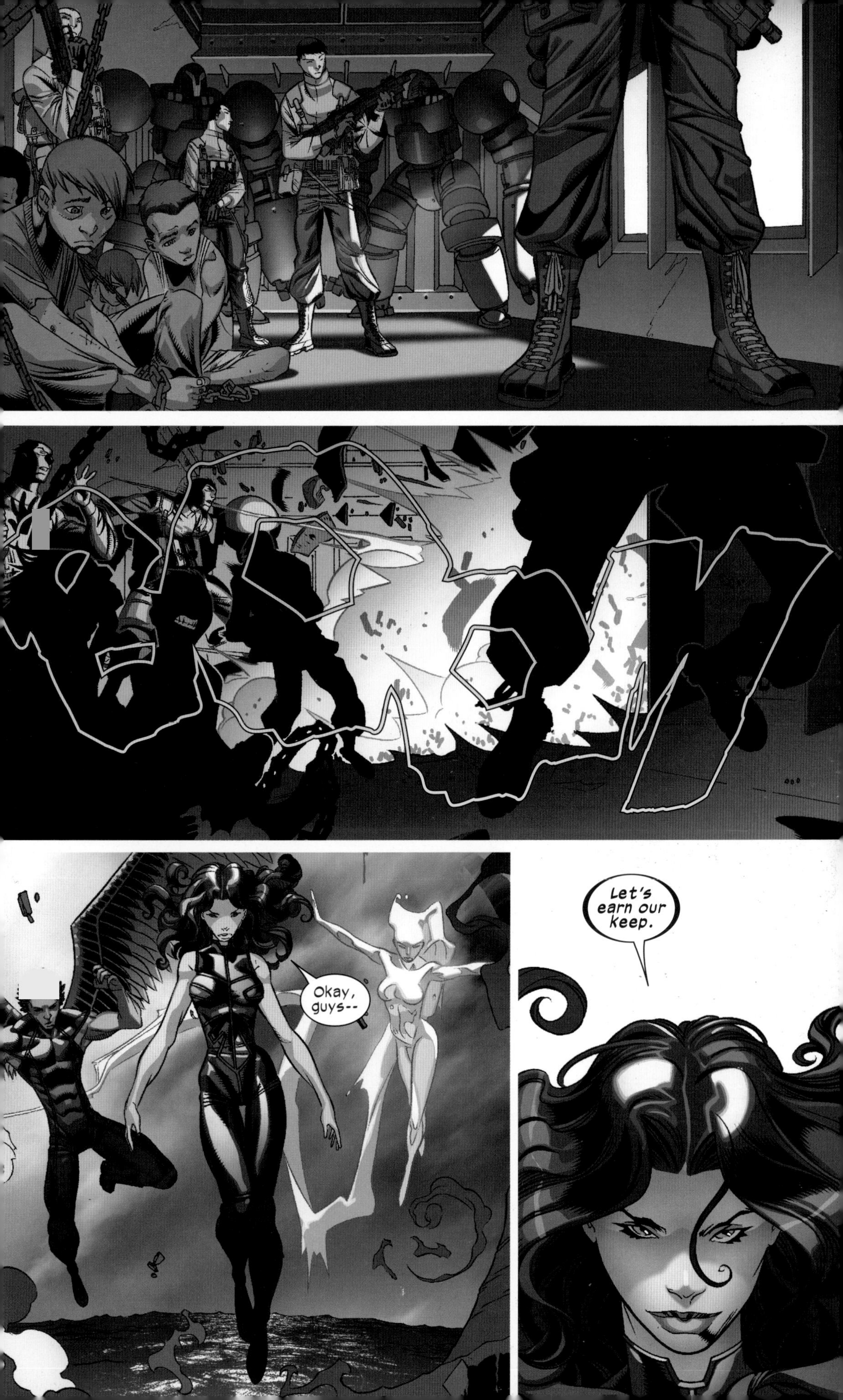
Okay, guys--
Let's earn our keep.

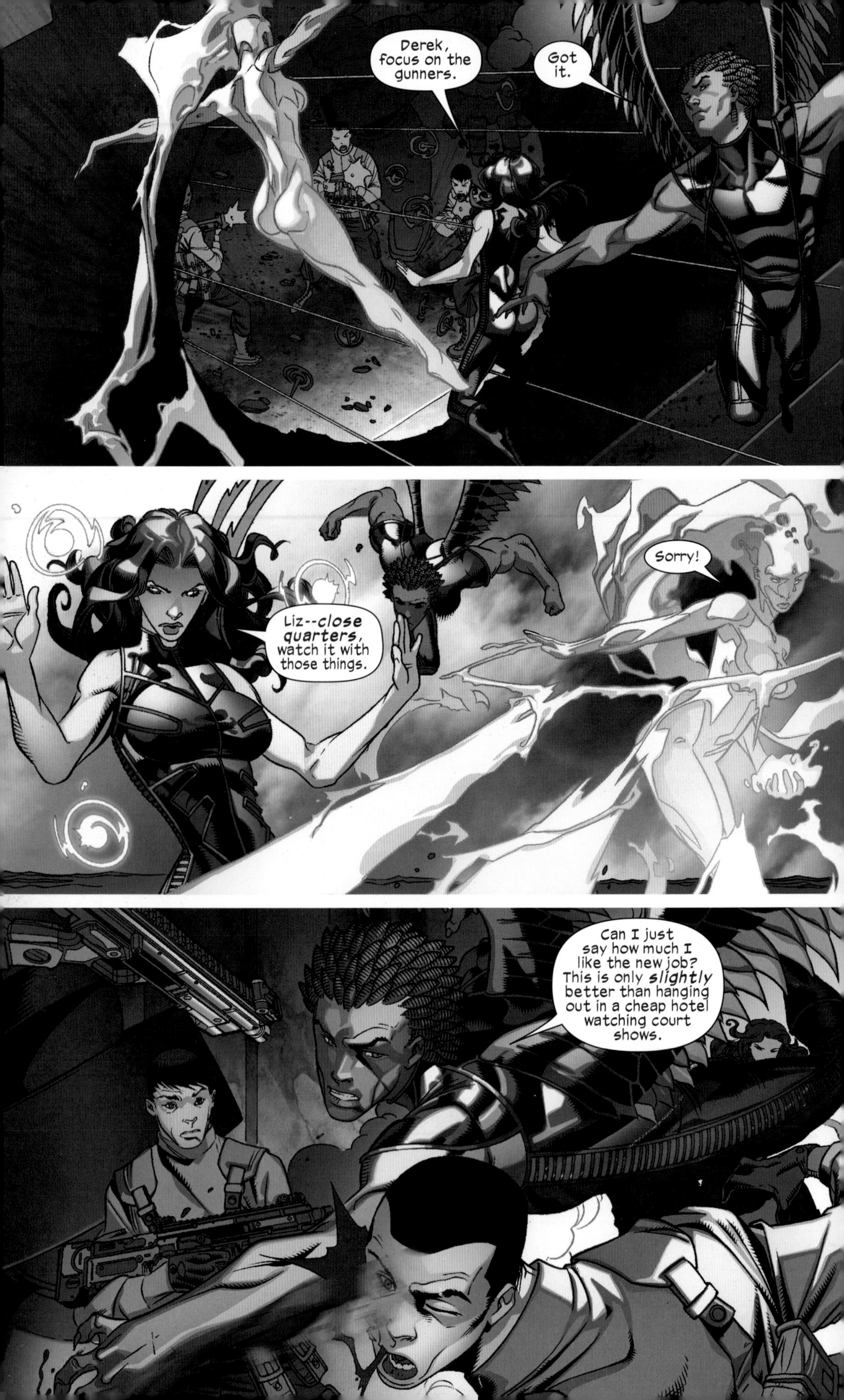
Derek, focus on the gunners.
Got it.
Liz--*close quarters*, watch it with those things.
Sorry!
Can I just say how much I like the new job? This is only *slightly* better than hanging out in a cheap hotel watching court shows.

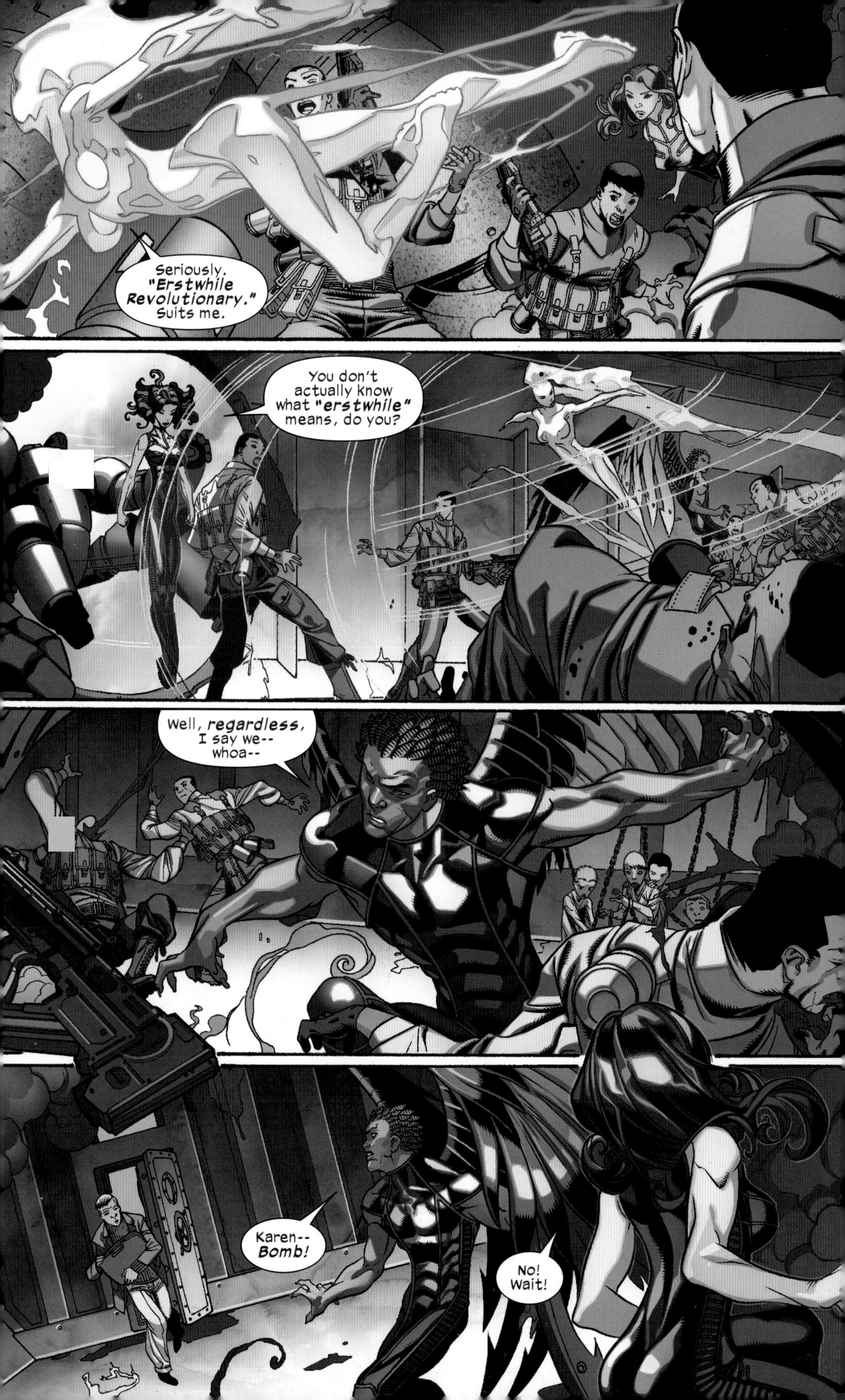
Seriously. "Erstwhile Revolutionary." Suits me.
You don't actually know what "erstwhile" means, do you?
Well, regardless, I say we-- whoa--
Karen-- Bomb!
No! Wait!

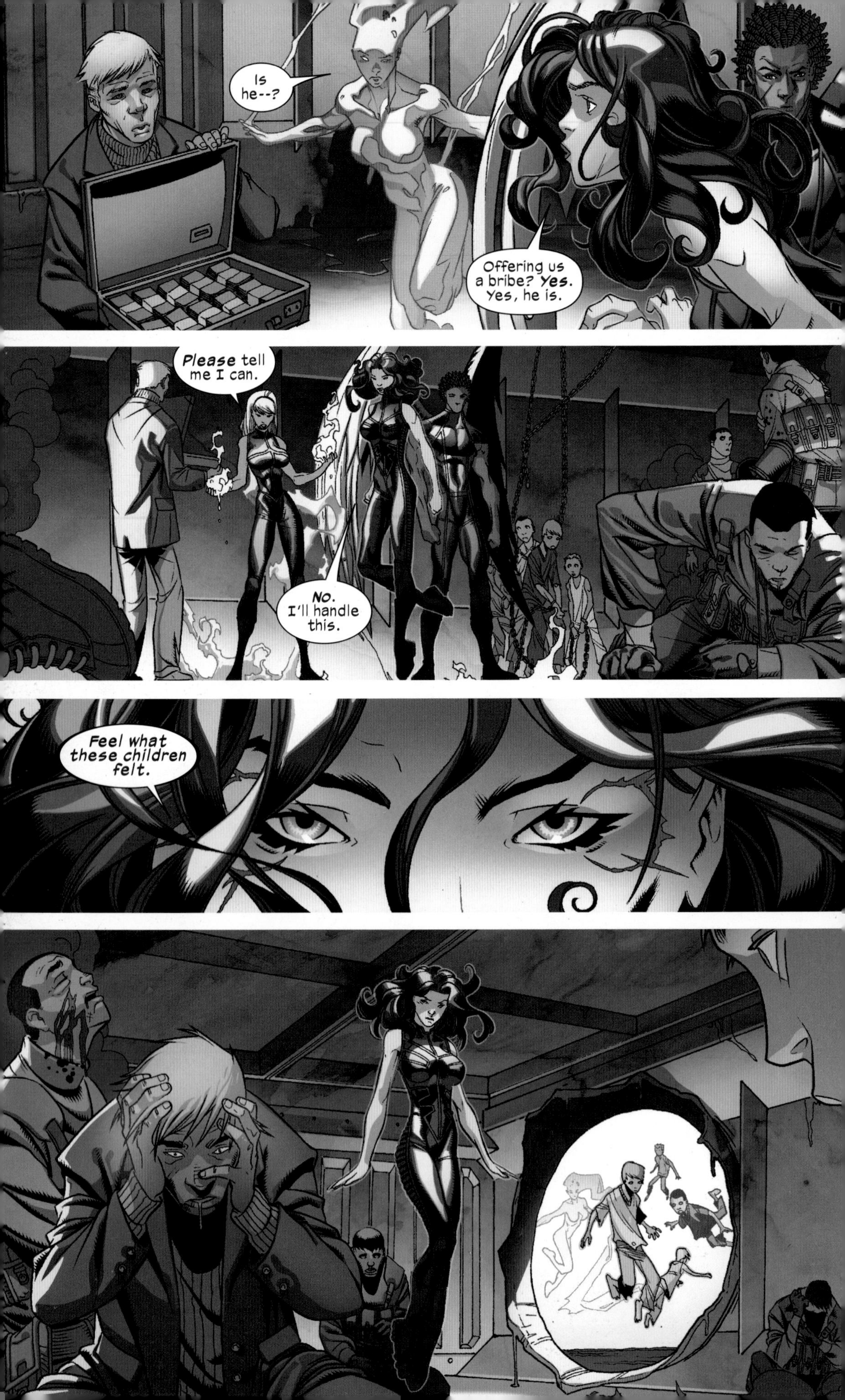
Is he--?
Offering us a bribe? *Yes*. Yes, he is.
Please tell me I can.
No. I'll handle this.
Feel what these children felt.

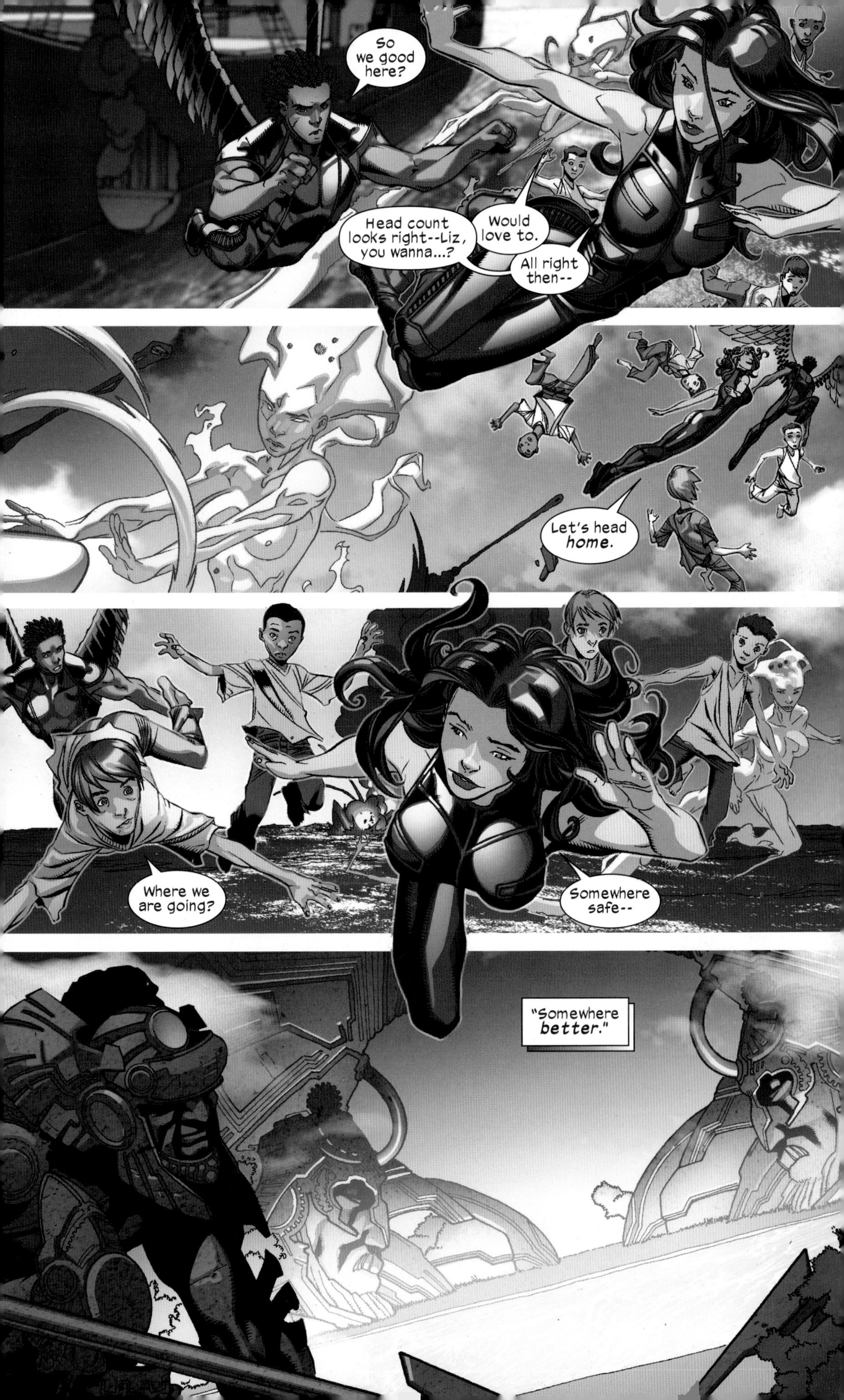
So we good here?
Head count looks right--Liz, you wanna...?
Would love to.
All right then--
Let's head home.
Where we are going?
Somewhere safe--
"Somewhere better."

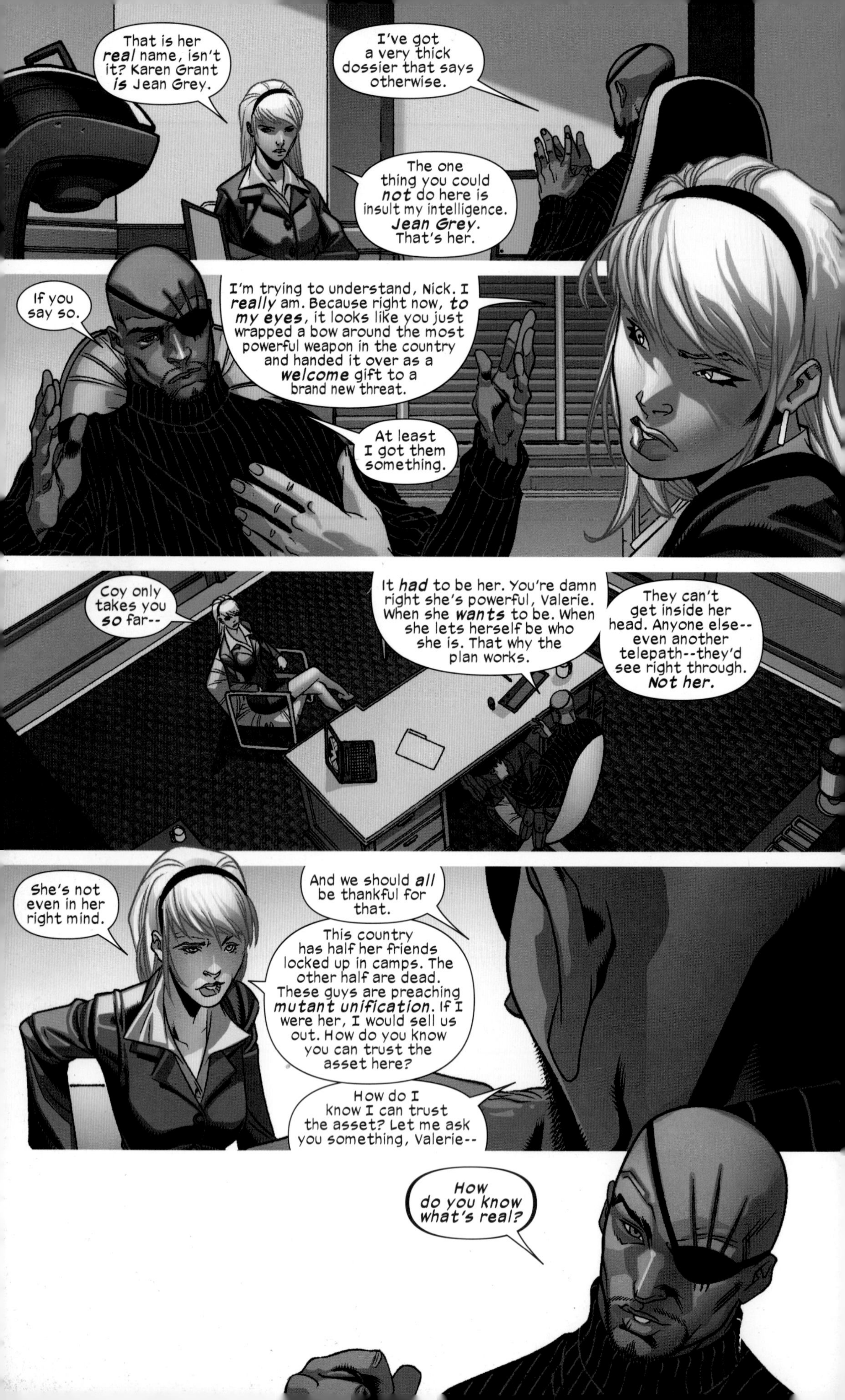

That is her real name, isn't it? Karen Grant is Jean Grey.
I've got a very thick dossier that says otherwise.
The one thing you could not do here is insult my intelligence. Jean Grey. That's her.
If you say so.
I'm trying to understand, Nick. I really am. Because right now, to my eyes, it looks like you just wrapped a bow around the most powerful weapon in the country and handed it over as a welcome gift to a brand new threat.
At least I got them something.
Coy only takes you so far--
It had to be her. You're damn right she's powerful, Valerie. When she wants to be. When she lets herself be who she is. That why the plan works.
They can't get inside her head. Anyone else--even another telepath--they'd see right through. Not her.
She's not even in her right mind.
And we should all be thankful for that.
This country has half her friends locked up in camps. The other half are dead. These guys are preaching mutant unification. If I were her, I would sell us out. How do you know you can trust the asset here?
How do I know I can trust the asset? Let me ask you something, Valerie--
How do you know what's real?

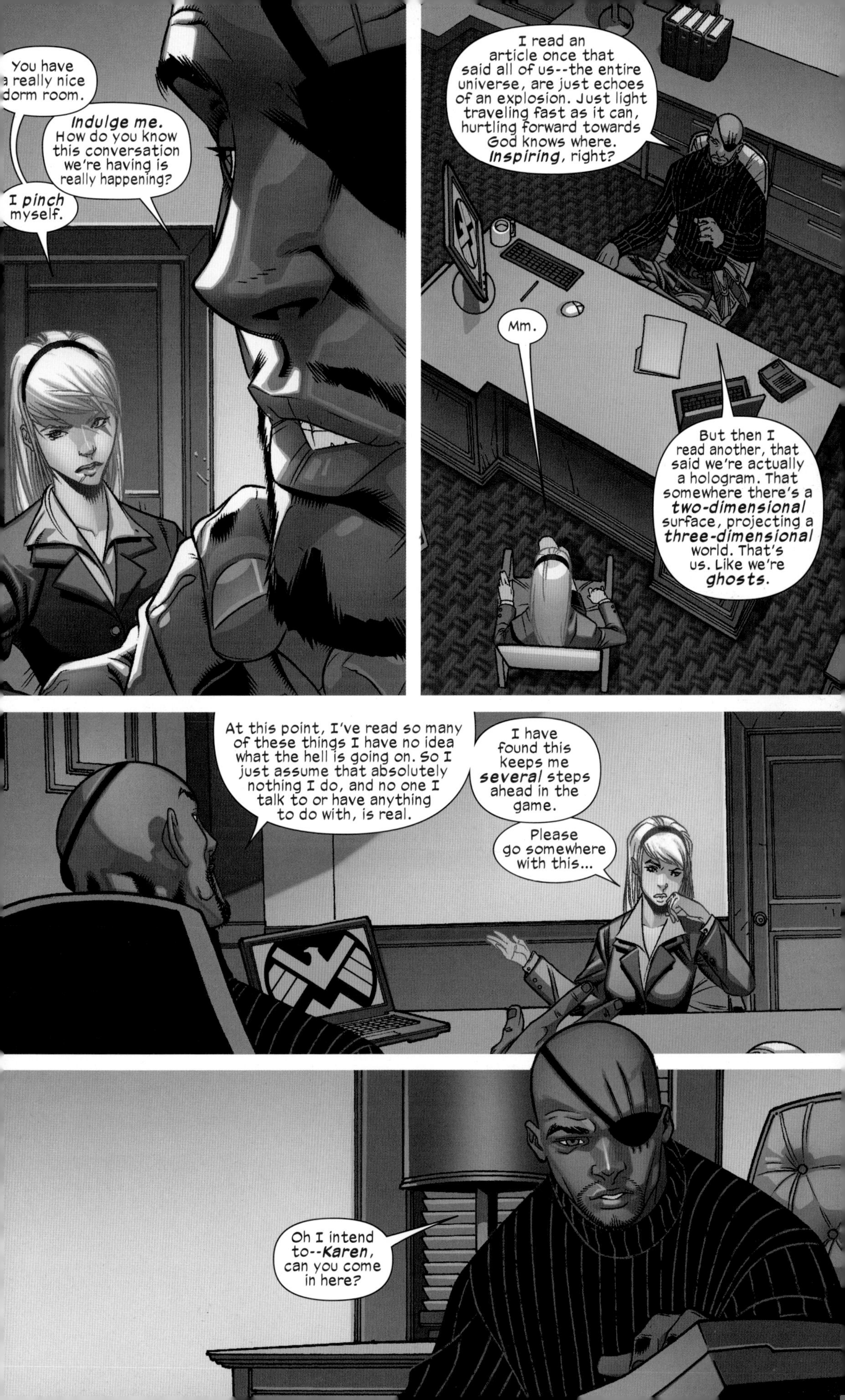

You have a really nice dorm room.
Indulge me. How do you know this conversation we're having is really happening?
I pinch myself.
I read an article once that said all of us--the entire universe, are just echoes of an explosion. Just light traveling fast as it can, hurtling forward towards God knows where. Inspiring, right?
Mm.
But then I read another, that said we're actually a hologram. That somewhere there's a two-dimensional surface, projecting a three-dimensional world. That's us. Like we're ghosts.
At this point, I've read so many of these things I have no idea what the hell is going on. So I just assume that absolutely nothing I do, and no one I talk to or have anything to do with, is real.
I have found this keeps me several steps ahead in the game.
Please go somewhere with this...
Oh I intend to--Karen, can you come in here?

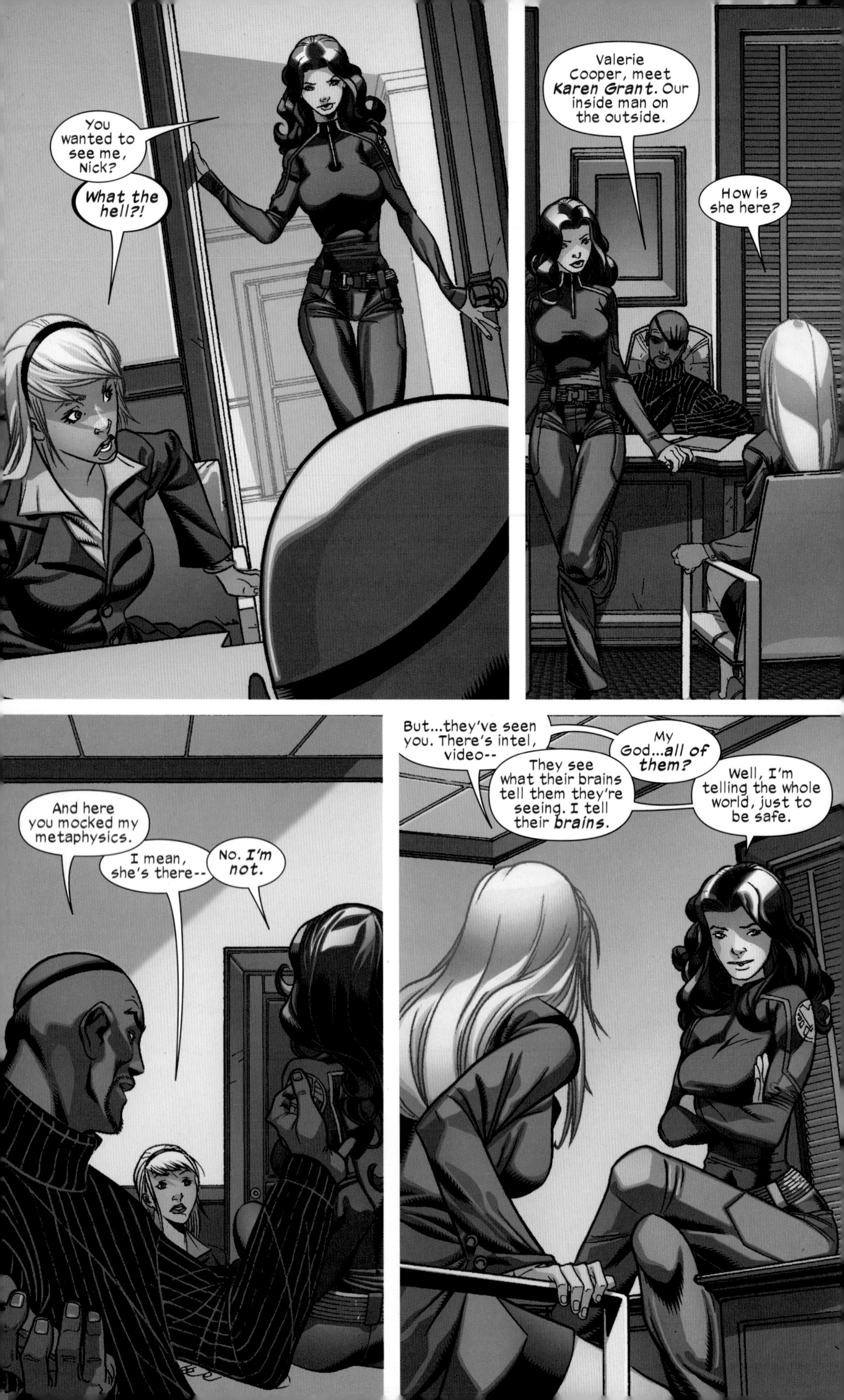
You wanted to see me, Nick?
What the hell?!
Valerie Cooper, meet Karen Grant. Our inside man on the outside.
How is she here?
And here you mocked my metaphysics.
I mean, she's there--
No. I'm not.
But...they've seen you. There's intel, video--
They see what their brains tell them they're seeing. I tell their brains.
My God...all of them?
Well, I'm telling the whole world, just to be safe.

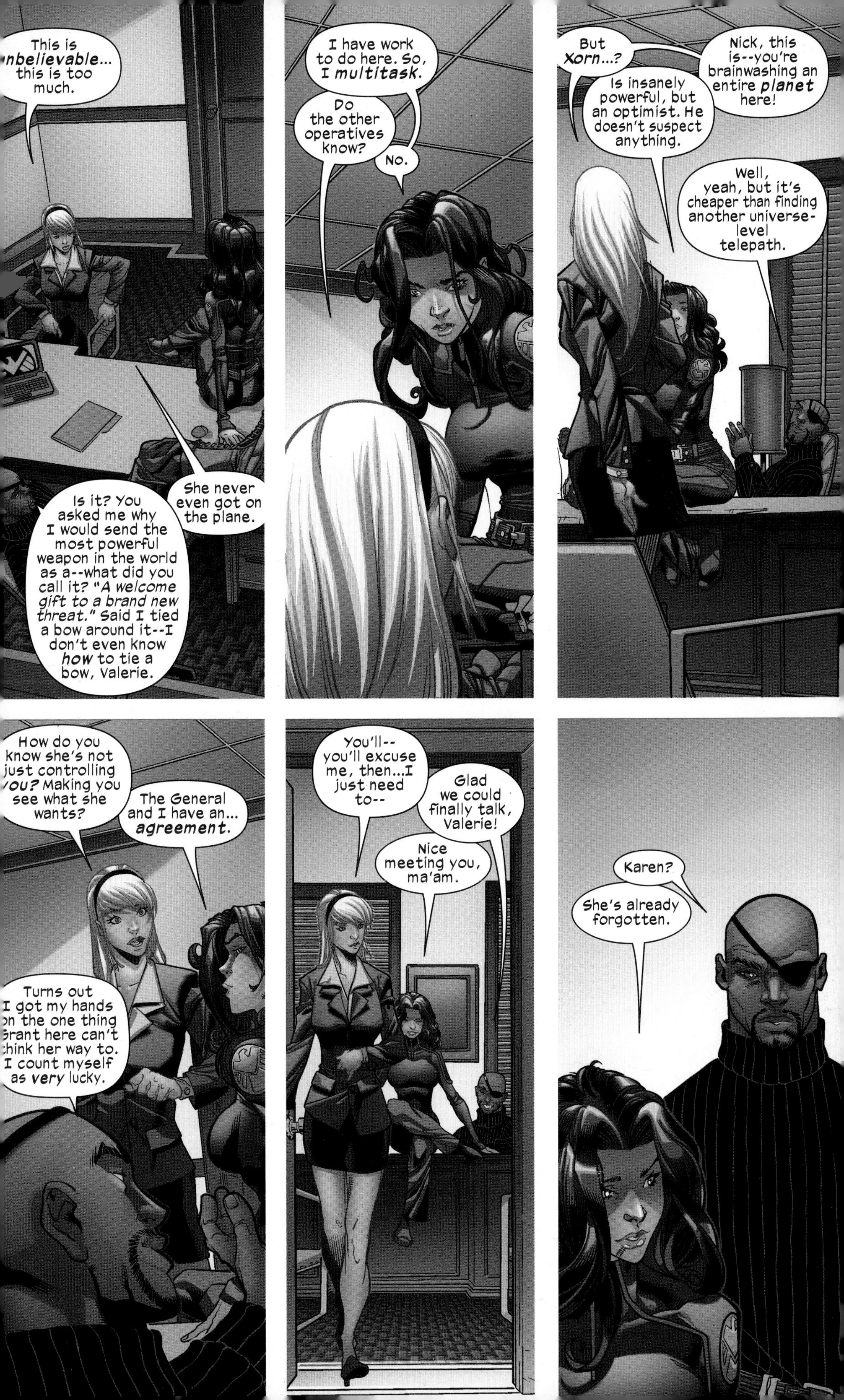
This is nbelievable... this is too much.
Is it? You asked me why I would send the most powerful weapon in the world as a--what did you call it? "A welcome gift to a brand new threat." Said I tied a bow around it--I don't even know how to tie a bow, Valerie.
She never even got on the plane.
I have work to do here. So, I multitask.
Do the other operatives know?
No.
But Xorn...?
Is insanely powerful, but an optimist. He doesn't suspect anything.
Nick, this is--you're brainwashing an entire planet here!
Well, yeah, but it's cheaper than finding another universe-level telepath.
How do you know she's not just controlling you? Making you see what she wants?
The General and I have an... agreement.
Turns out I got my hands n the one thing Grant here can't hink her way to. I count myself as very lucky.
You'll-- you'll excuse me, then...I just need to--
Glad we could finally talk, Valerie!
Nice meeting you, ma'am.
Karen?
She's already forgotten.

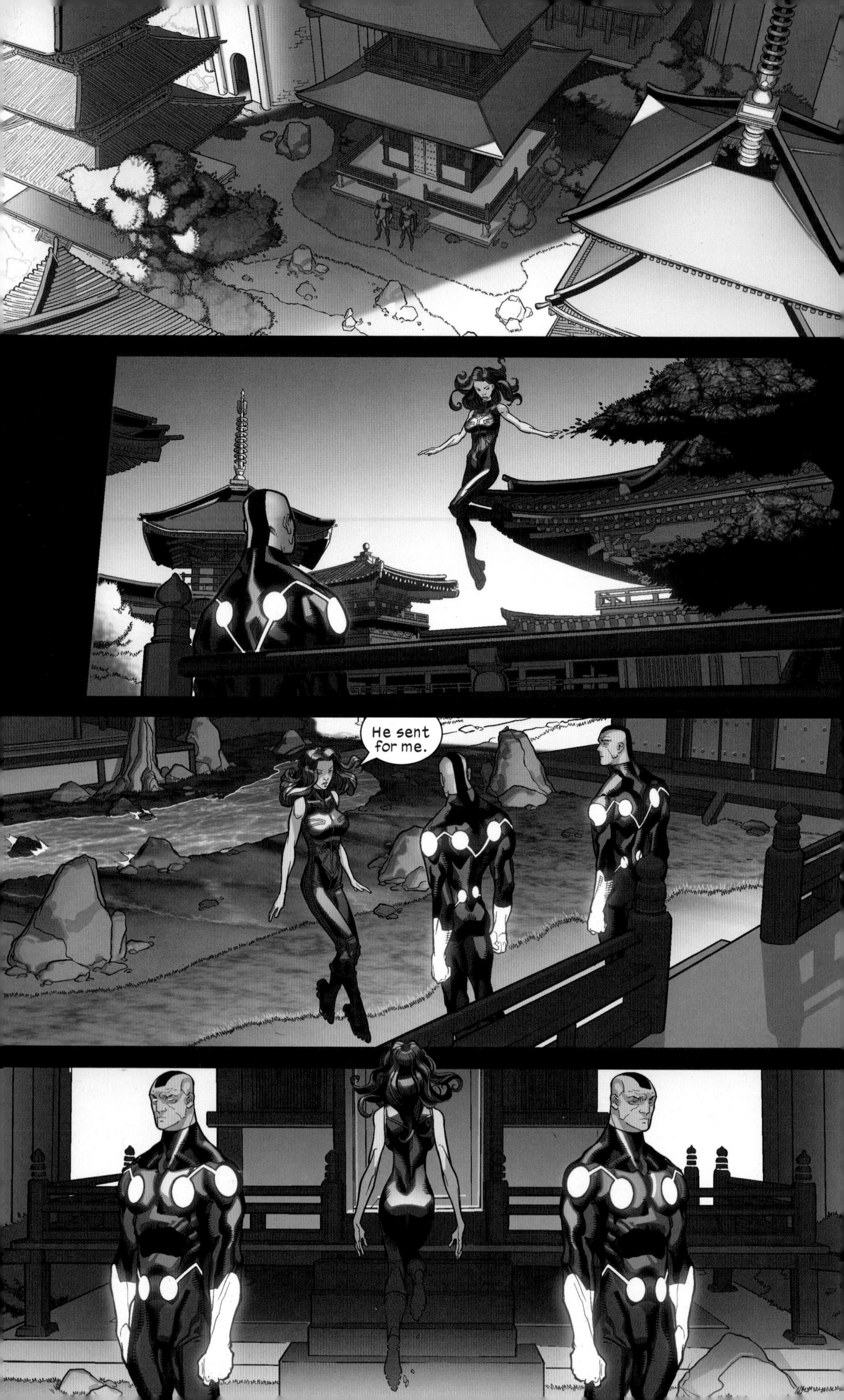
He sent for me.

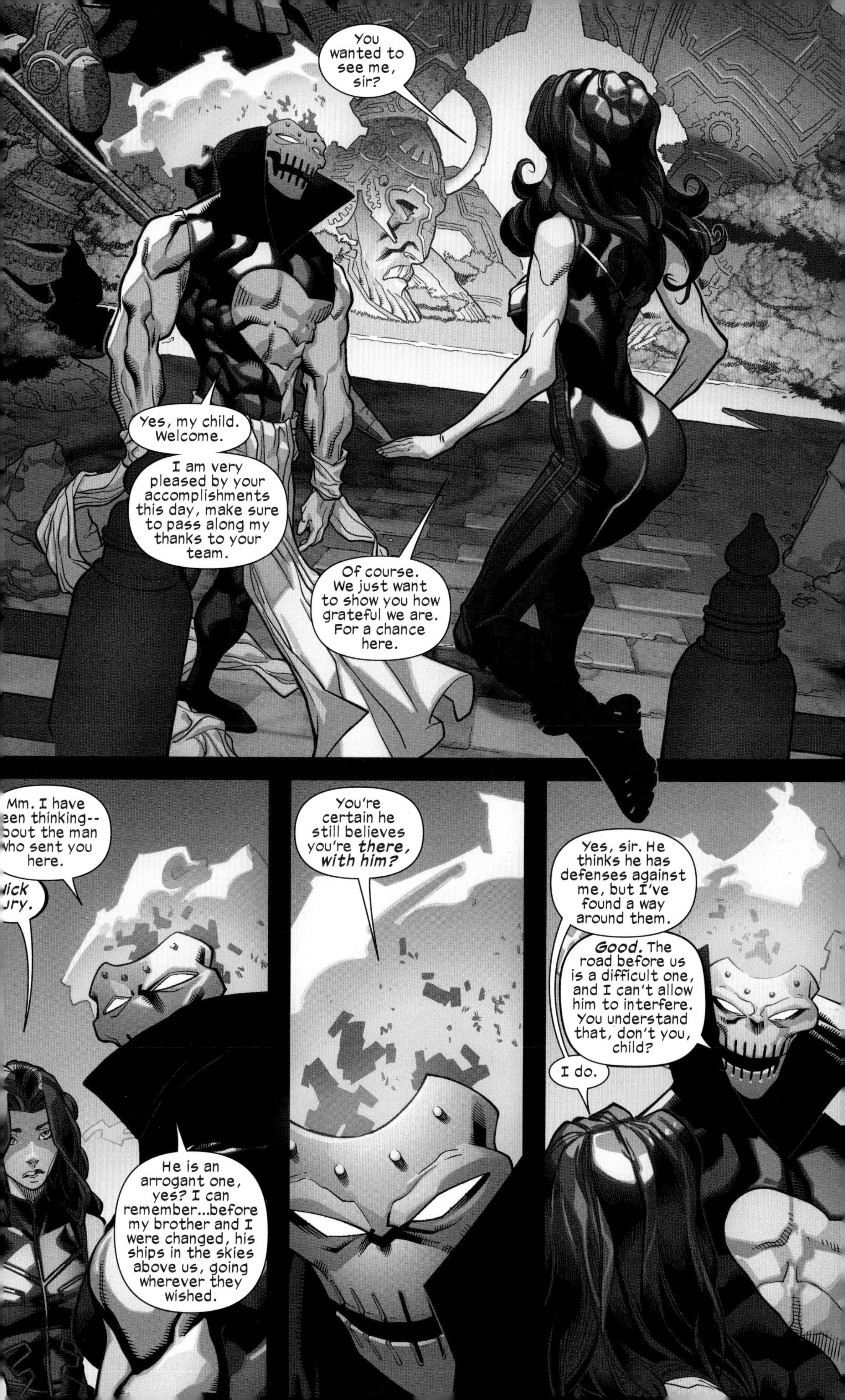

You wanted to see me, sir?
Yes, my child. Welcome.
I am very pleased by your accomplishments this day, make sure to pass along my thanks to your team.
Of course. We just want to show you how grateful we are. For a chance here.
Mm. I have een thinking-- bout the man who sent you here.
lick ury.
He is an arrogant one, yes? I can remember...before my brother and I were changed, his ships in the skies above us, going wherever they wished.
You're certain he still believes you're *there, with him?*
Yes, sir. He thinks he has defenses against me, but I've found a way around them.
Good. The road before us is a difficult one, and I can't allow him to interfere. You understand that, don't you, child?
I do.

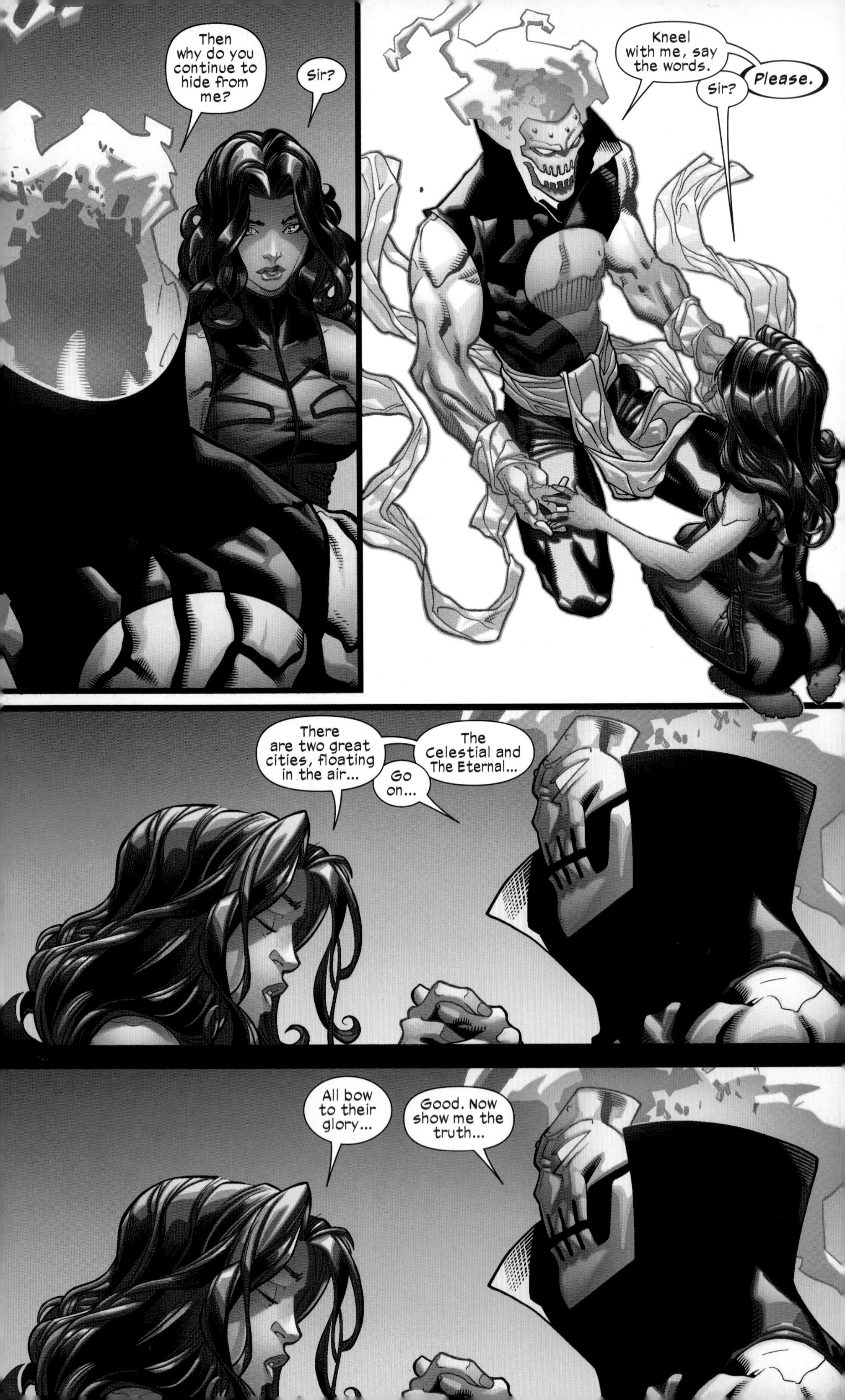
Then why do you continue to hide from me?
Sir?
Kneel with me, say the words.
Please.
Sir?
There are two great cities, floating in the air...
The Celestial and The Eternal...
Go on...
All bow to their glory...
Good. Now show me the truth...

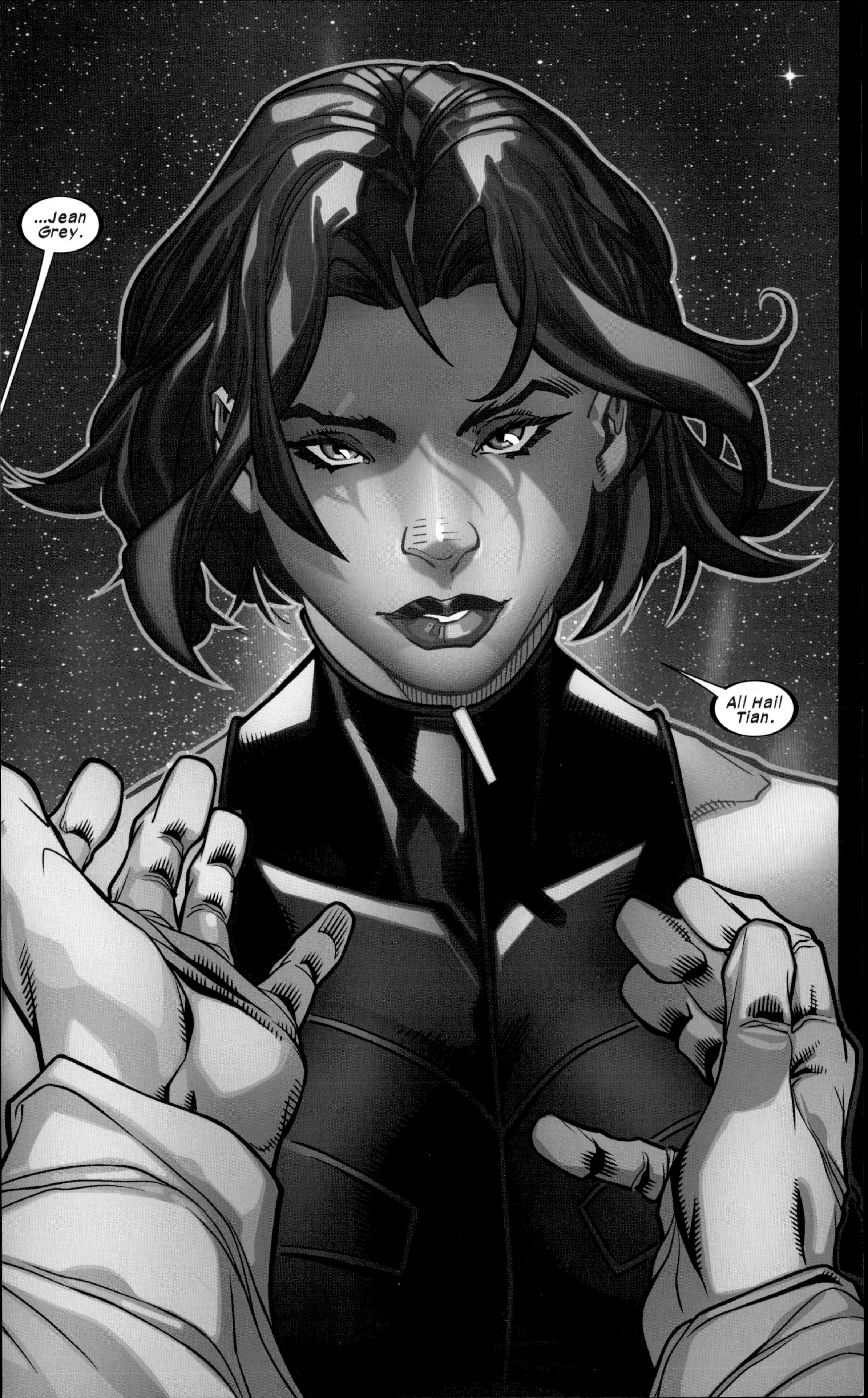
...Jean Grey.
All Hail Tian.

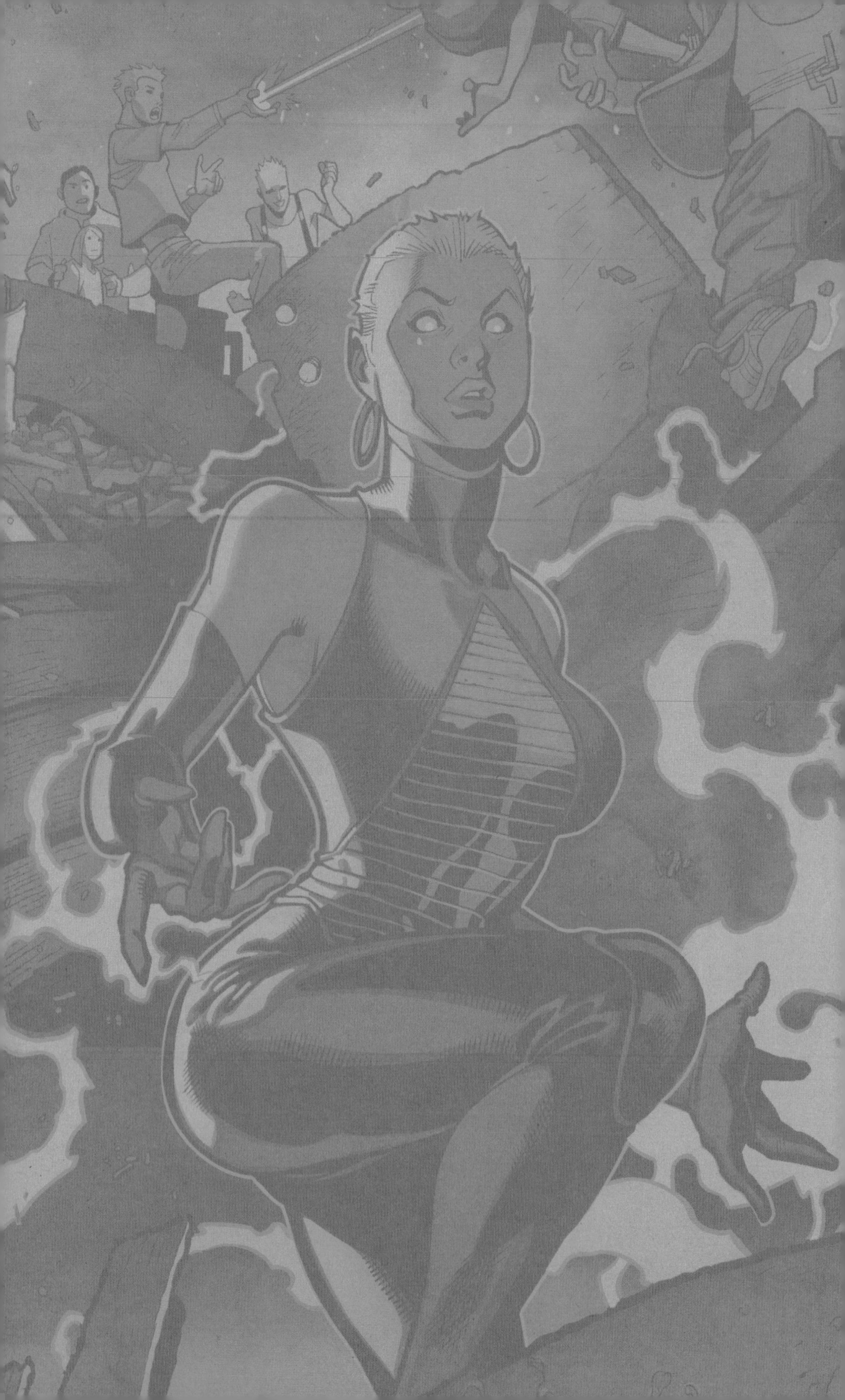

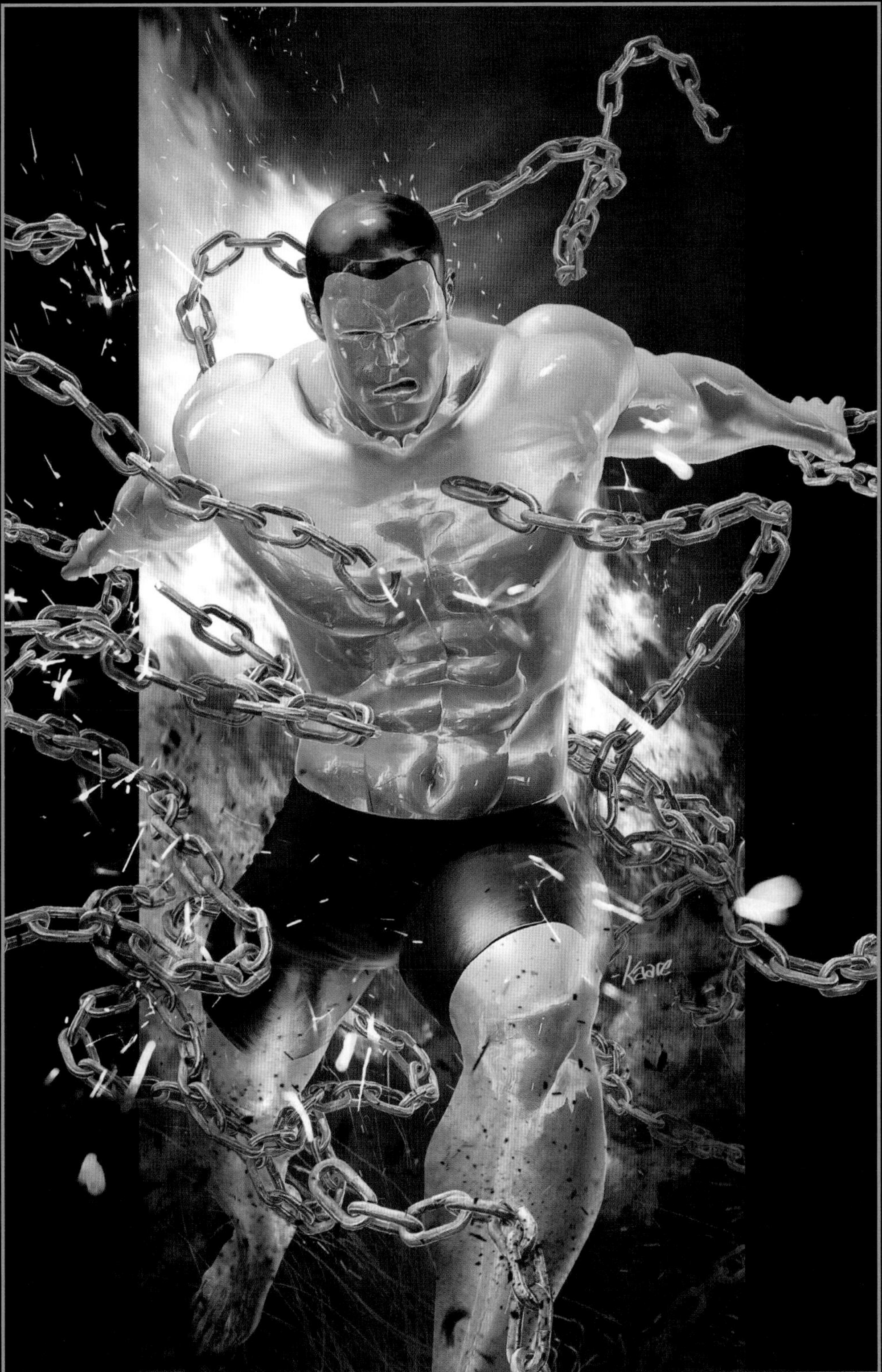
Kaare

ISSUE 09 COVER

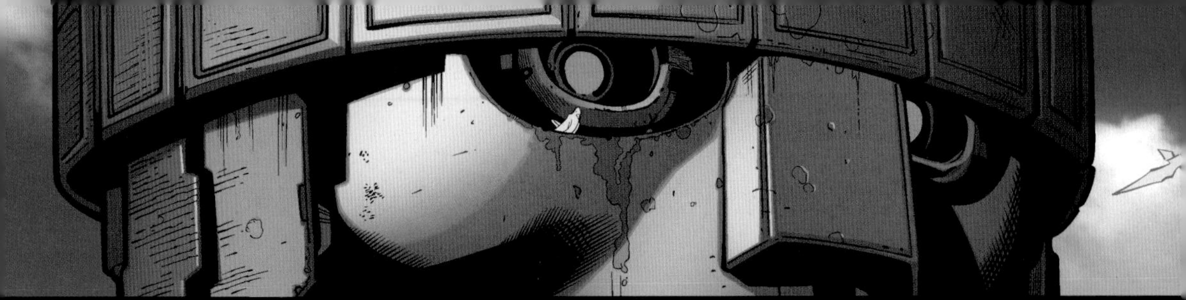

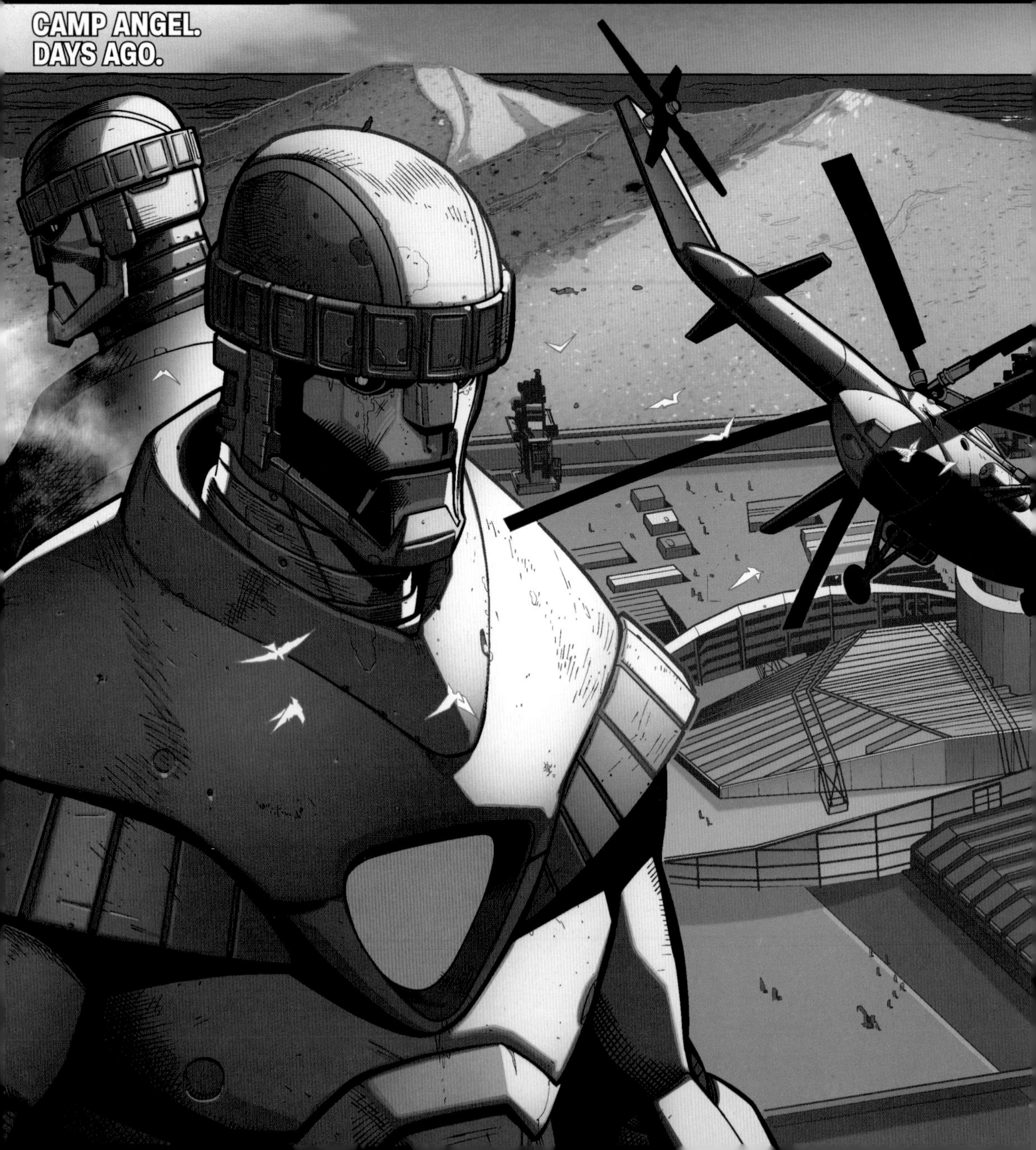
CAMP ANGEL.
DAYS AGO.

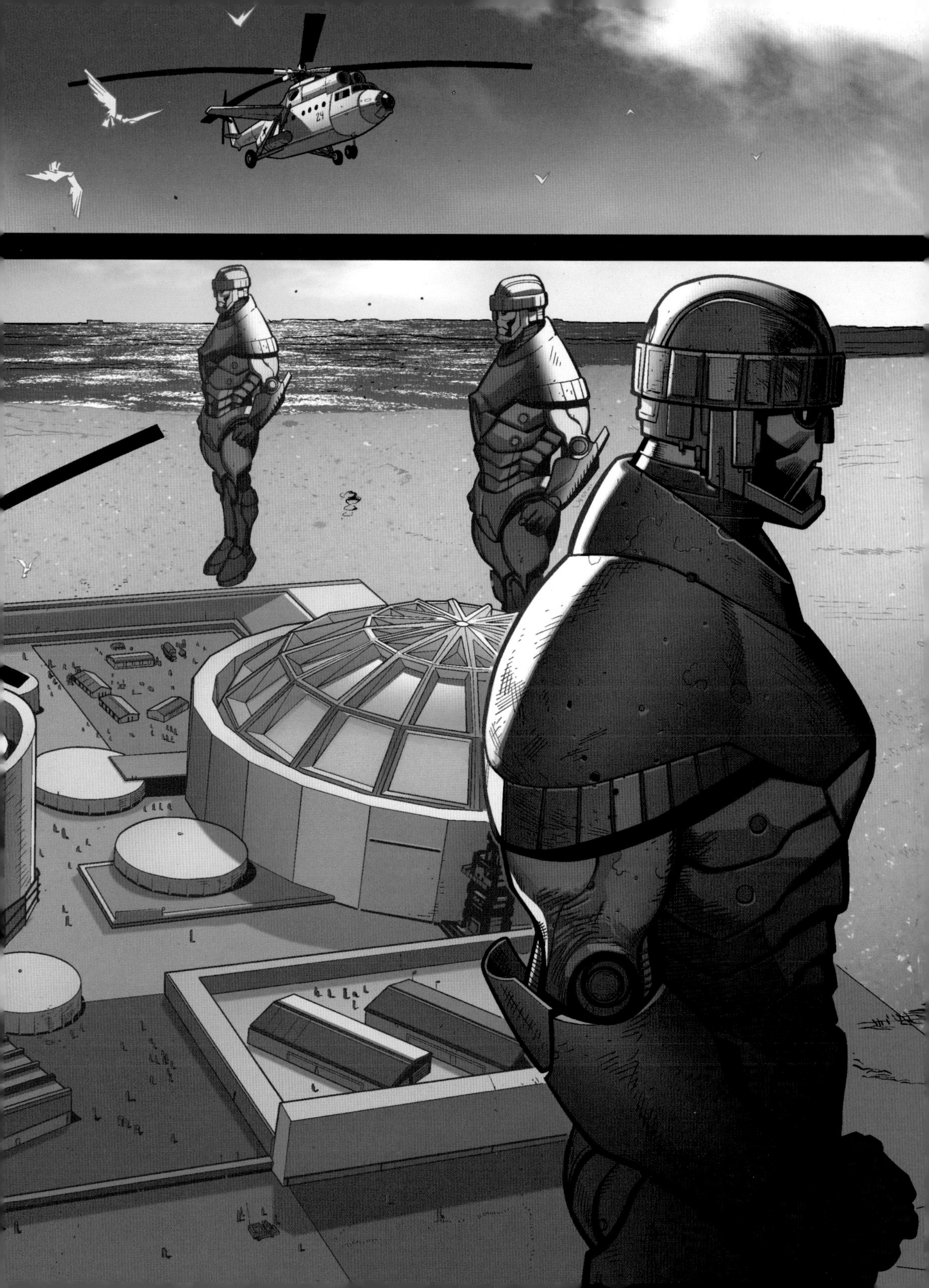

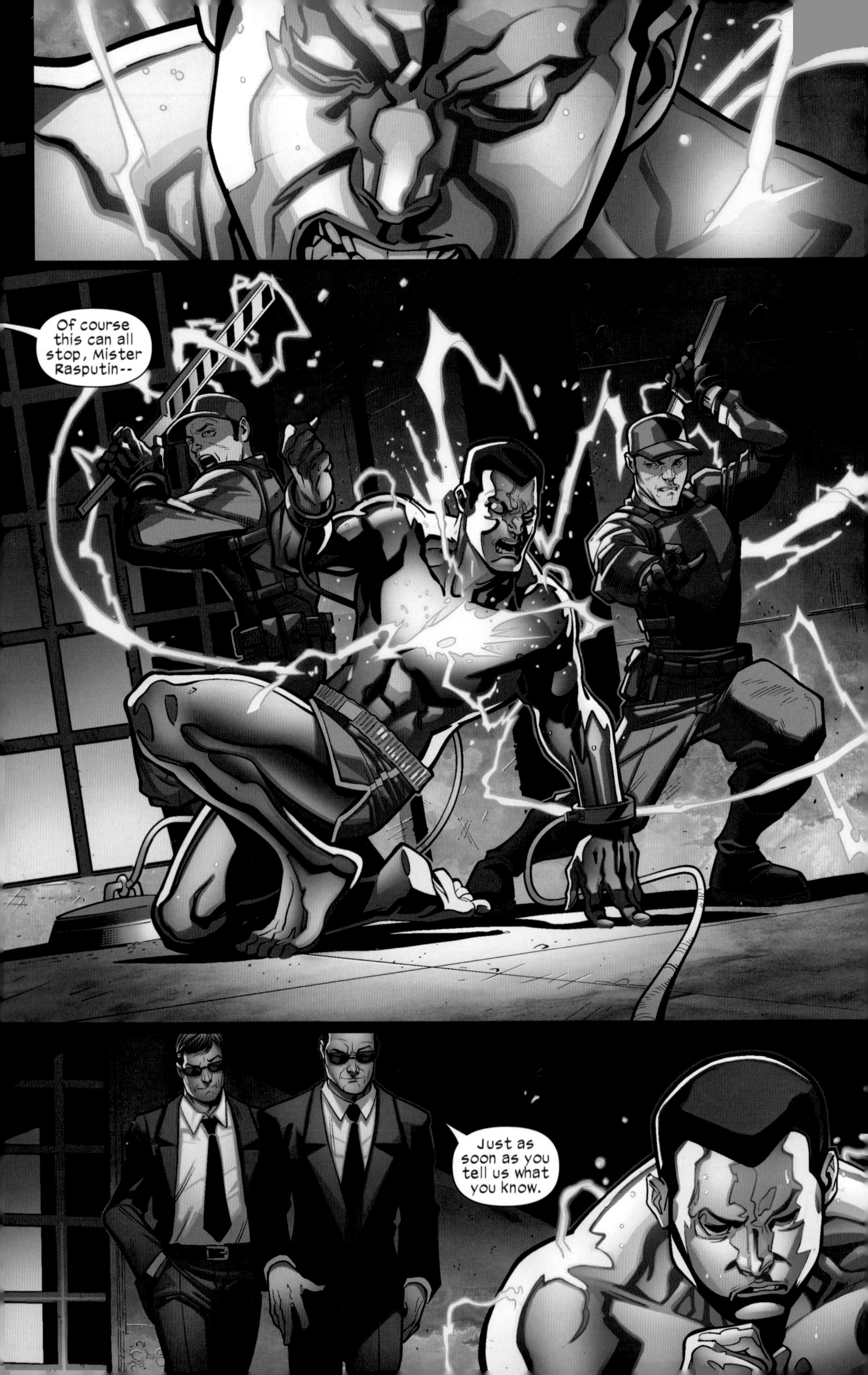

Of course this can all stop, Mister Rasputin--
Just as soon as you tell us what you know.

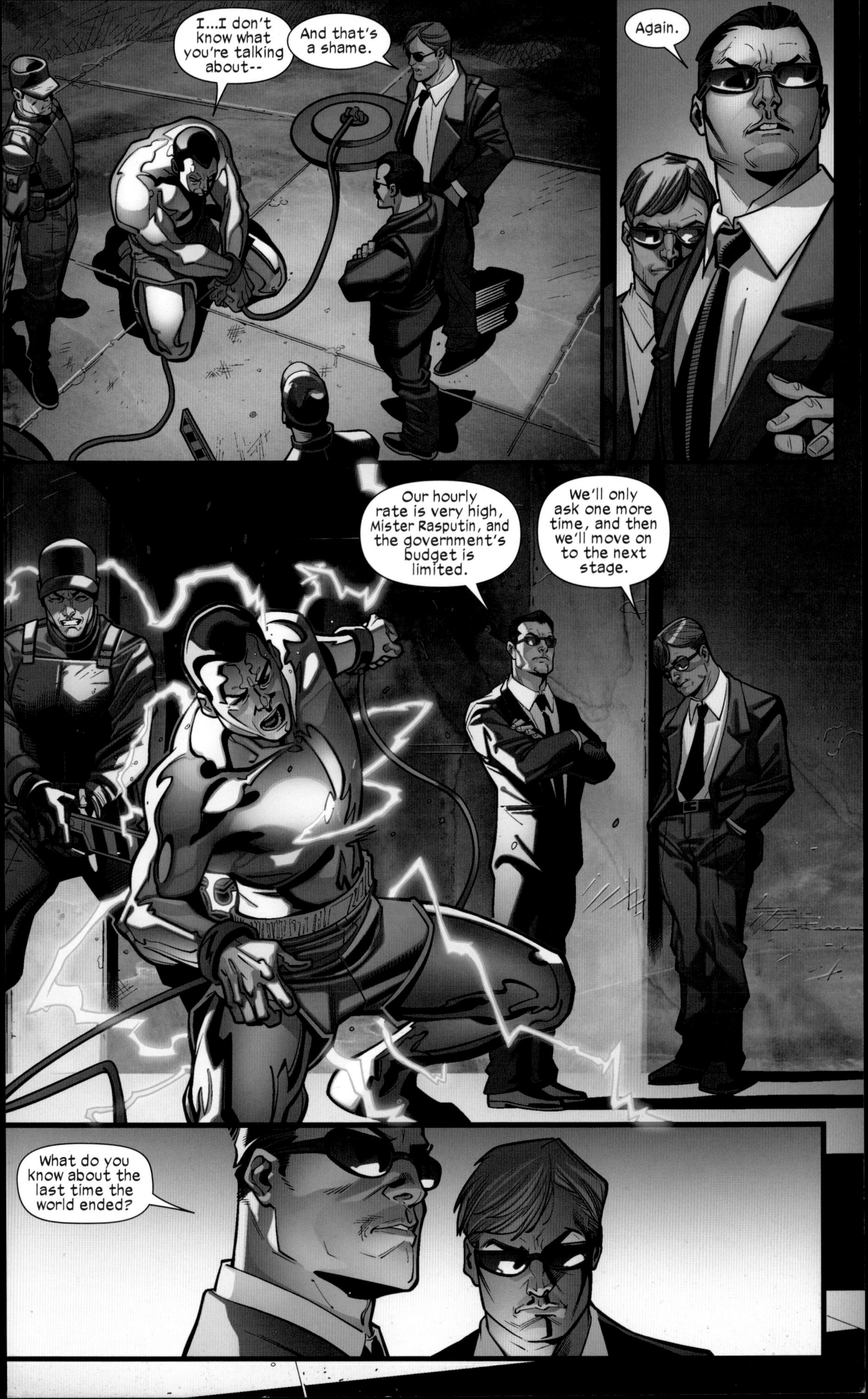
I...I don't know what you're talking about--
And that's a shame.
Again.
Our hourly rate is very high, Mister Rasputin, and the government's budget is limited.
We'll only ask one more time, and then we'll move on to the next stage.
What do you know about the last time the world ended?

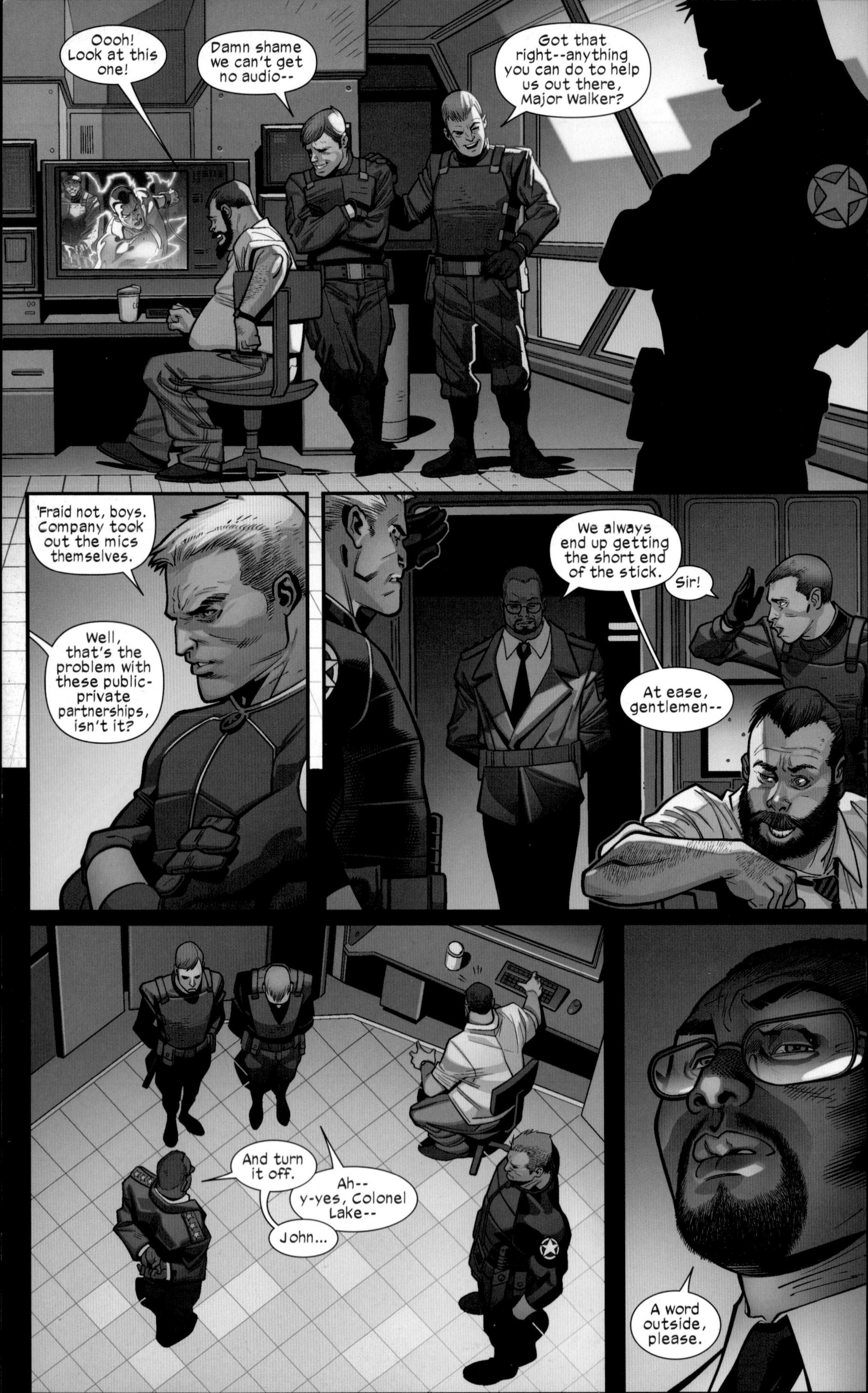
Oooh! Look at this one!
Damn shame we can't get no audio--
Got that right--anything you can do to help us out there, Major Walker?
'Fraid not, boys. Company took out the mics themselves.
Well, that's the problem with these public-private partnerships, isn't it?
We always end up getting the short end of the stick.
Sir!
At ease, gentlemen--
And turn it off.
Ah-- y-yes, Colonel Lake--
John...
A word outside, please.

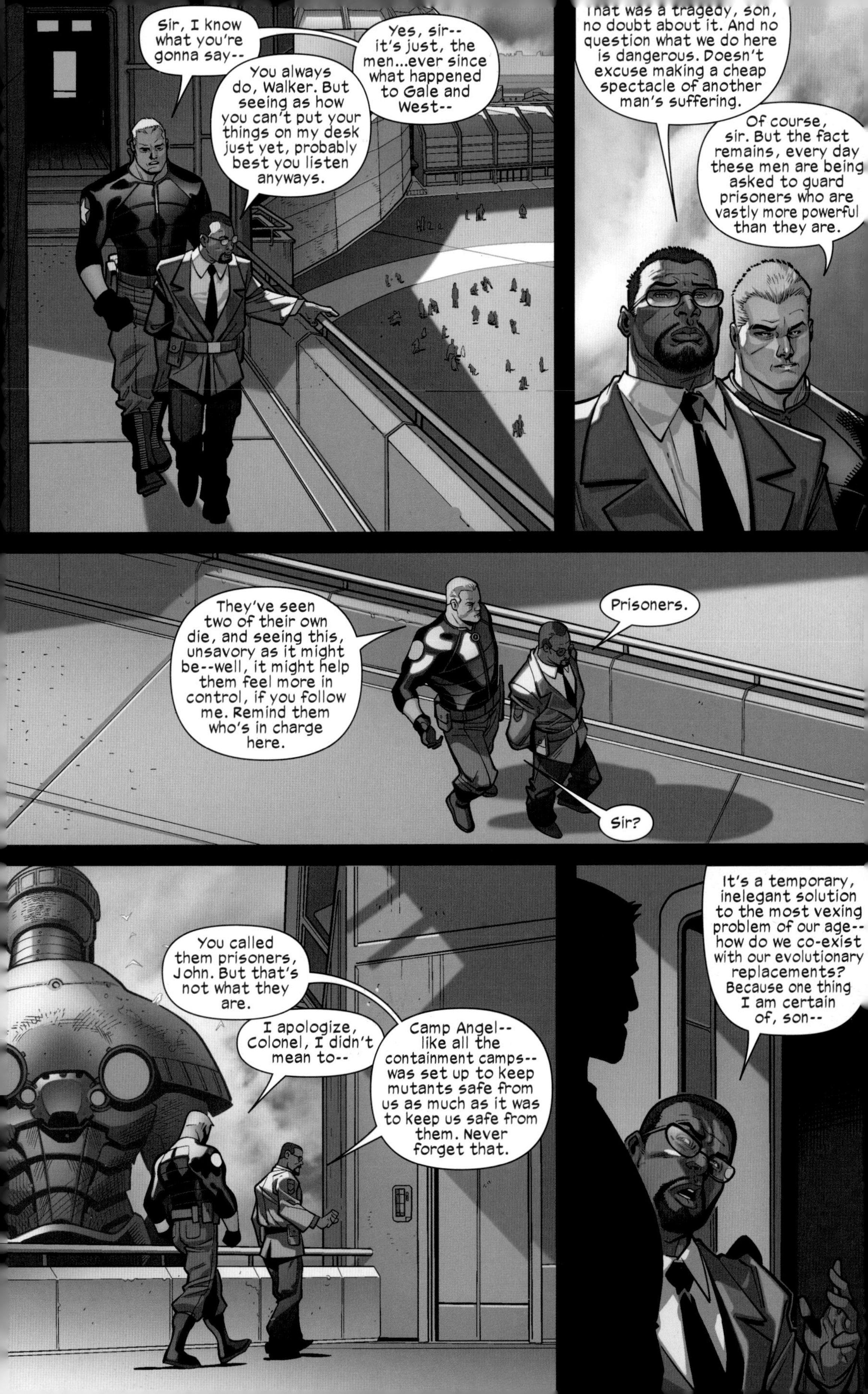
Sir, I know what you're gonna say--
You always do, Walker. But seeing as how you can't put your things on my desk just yet, probably best you listen anyways.
Yes, sir-- it's just, the men...ever since what happened to Gale and West--
That was a tragedy, son, no doubt about it. And no question what we do here is dangerous. Doesn't excuse making a cheap spectacle of another man's suffering.
Of course, sir. But the fact remains, every day these men are being asked to guard prisoners who are vastly more powerful than they are.
They've seen two of their own die, and seeing this, unsavory as it might be--well, it might help them feel more in control, if you follow me. Remind them who's in charge here.
Prisoners.
Sir?
You called them prisoners, John. But that's not what they are.
I apologize, Colonel, I didn't mean to--
Camp Angel-- like all the containment camps-- was set up to keep mutants safe from us as much as it was to keep us safe from them. Never forget that.
It's a temporary, inelegant solution to the most vexing problem of our age-- how do we co-exist with our evolutionary replacements? Because one thing I am certain of, son--

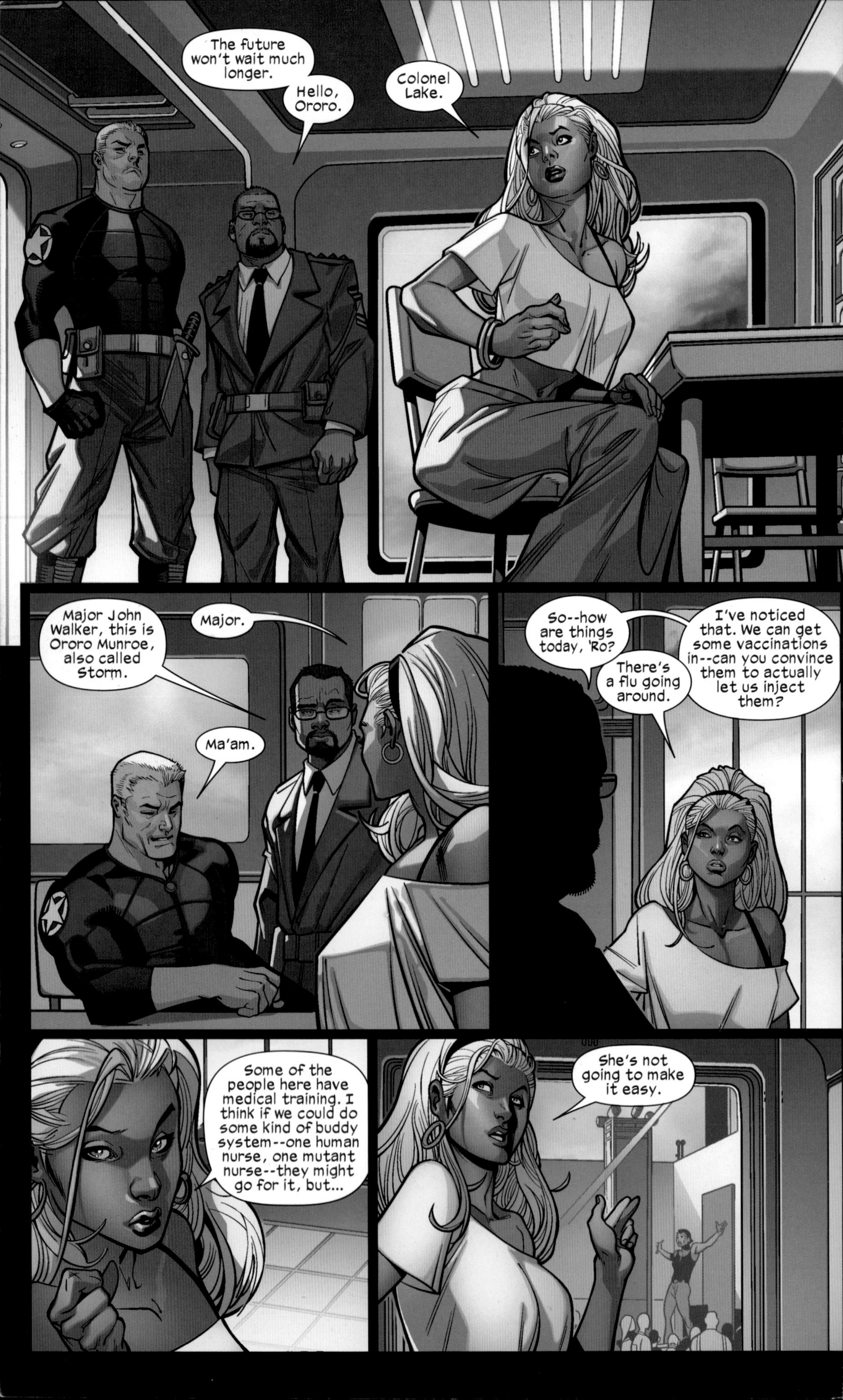
The future won't wait much longer.
Hello, Ororo.
Colonel Lake.
Major John Walker, this is Ororo Munroe, also called Storm.
Major.
Ma'am.
So--how are things today, 'Ro?
There's a flu going around.
I've noticed that. We can get some vaccinations in--can you convince them to actually let us inject them?
Some of the people here have medical training. I think if we could do some kind of buddy system--one human nurse, one mutant nurse--they might go for it, but...
She's not going to make it easy.

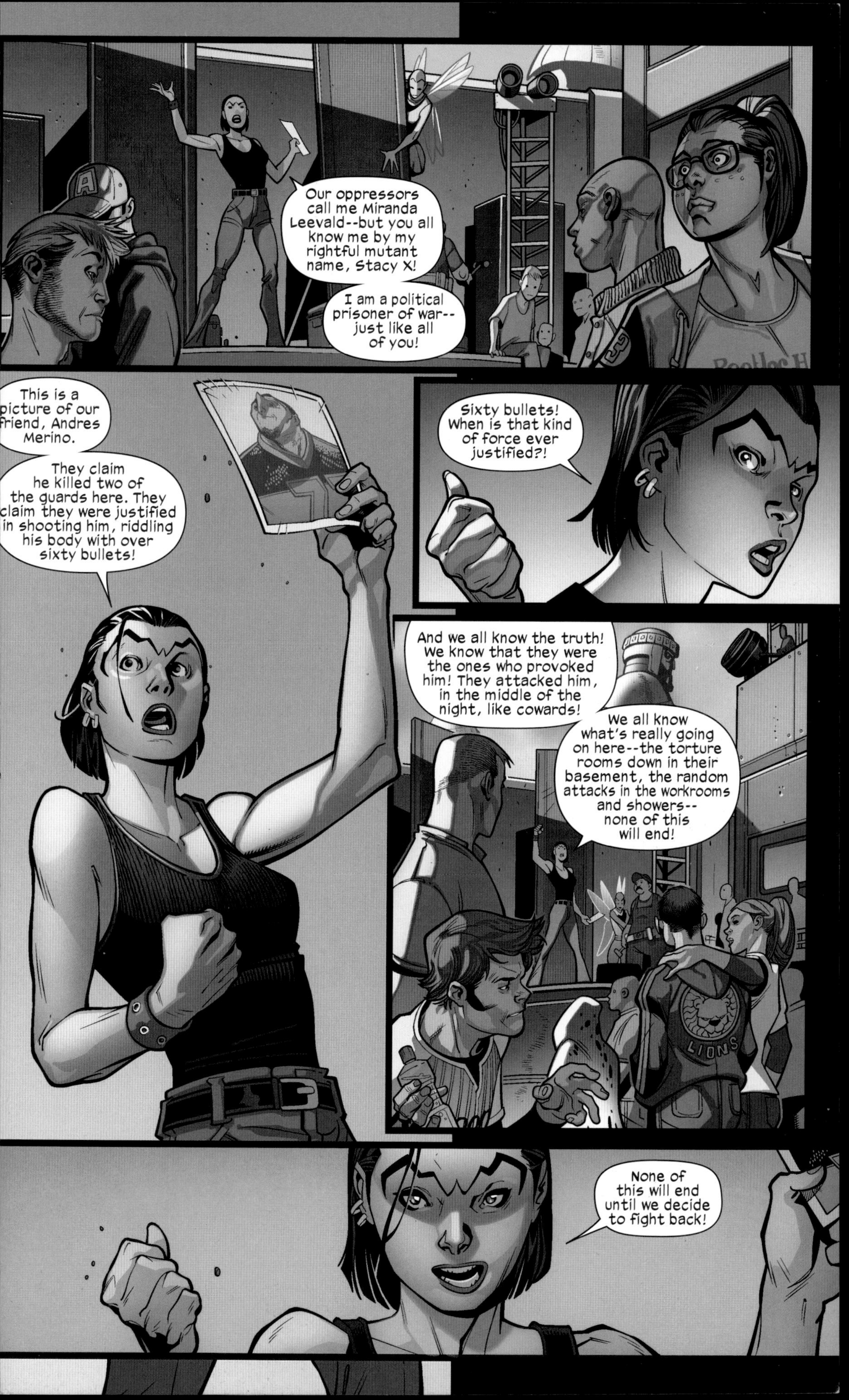
Our oppressors call me Miranda Leevald--but you all know me by my rightful mutant name, Stacy X!
I am a political prisoner of war--just like all of you!
This is a picture of our friend, Andres Merino.
They claim he killed two of the guards here. They claim they were justified in shooting him, riddling his body with over sixty bullets!
Sixty bullets! When is that kind of force ever justified?!
And we all know the truth! We know that they were the ones who provoked him! They attacked him, in the middle of the night, like cowards!
We all know what's really going on here--the torture rooms down in their basement, the random attacks in the workrooms and showers--none of this will end!
LIONS
None of this will end until we decide to fight back!

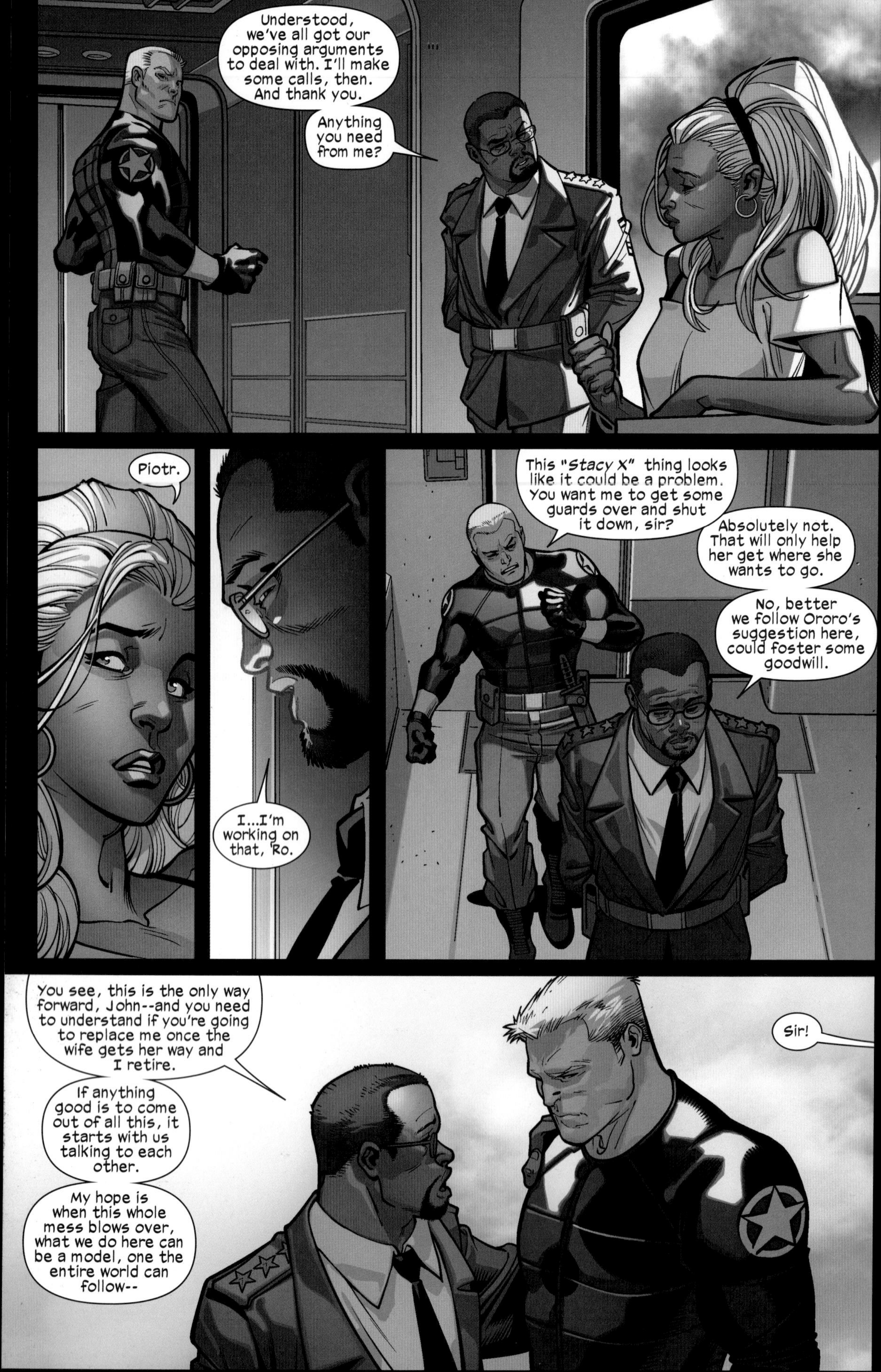
Understood, we've all got our opposing arguments to deal with. I'll make some calls, then. And thank you.
Anything you need from me?
Piotr.
I...I'm working on that, 'Ro.
This "Stacy X" thing looks like it could be a problem. You want me to get some guards over and shut it down, sir?
Absolutely not. That will only help her get where she wants to go.
No, better we follow Ororo's suggestion here, could foster some goodwill.
You see, this is the only way forward, John--and you need to understand if you're going to replace me once the wife gets her way and I retire.
If anything good is to come out of all this, it starts with us talking to each other.
My hope is when this whole mess blows over, what we do here can be a model, one the entire world can follow--
Sir!

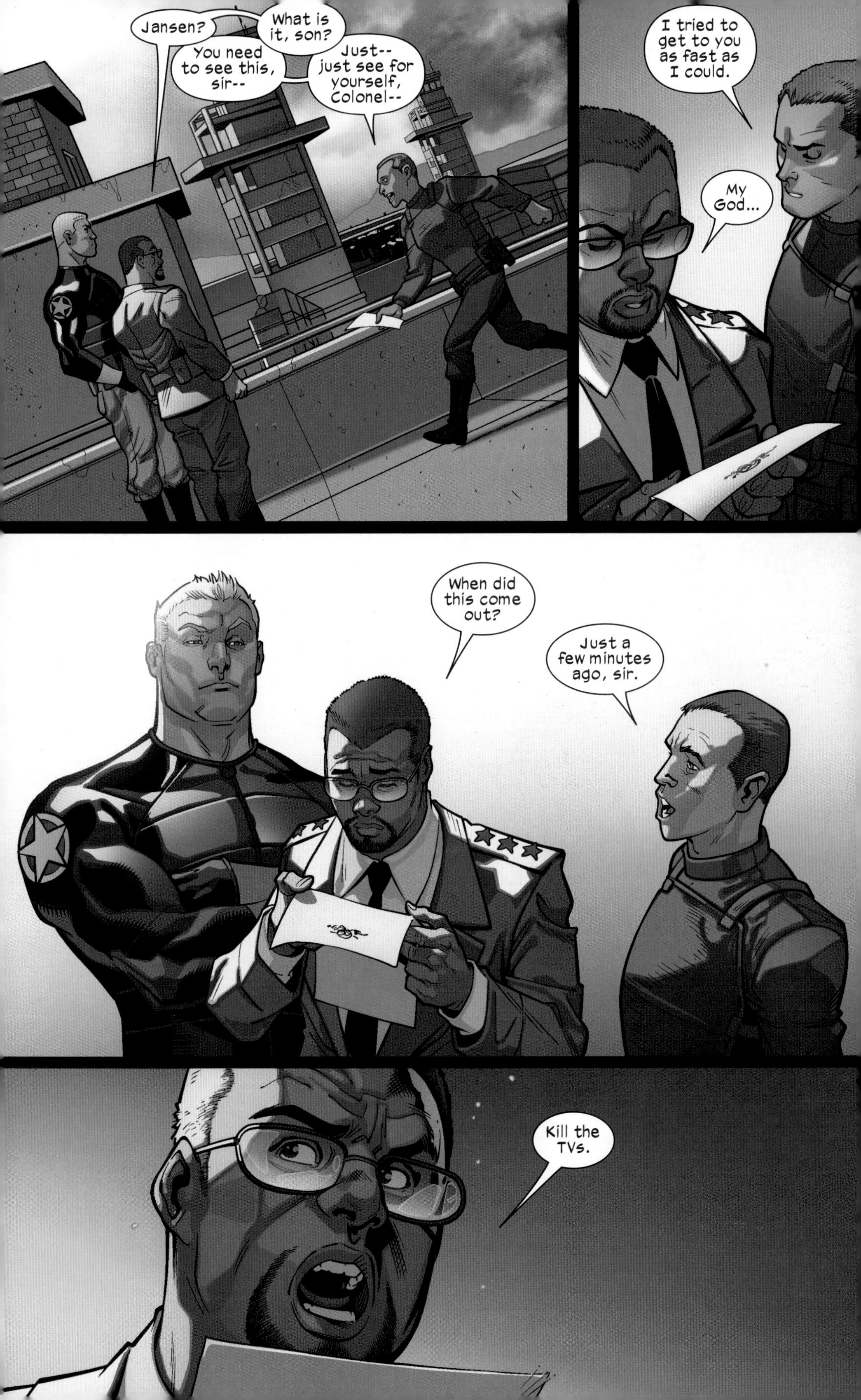
Jansen?
What is it, son?
You need to see this, sir--
Just-- just see for yourself, Colonel--
I tried to get to you as fast as I could.
My God...
When did this come out?
Just a few minutes ago, sir.
Kill the TVs.

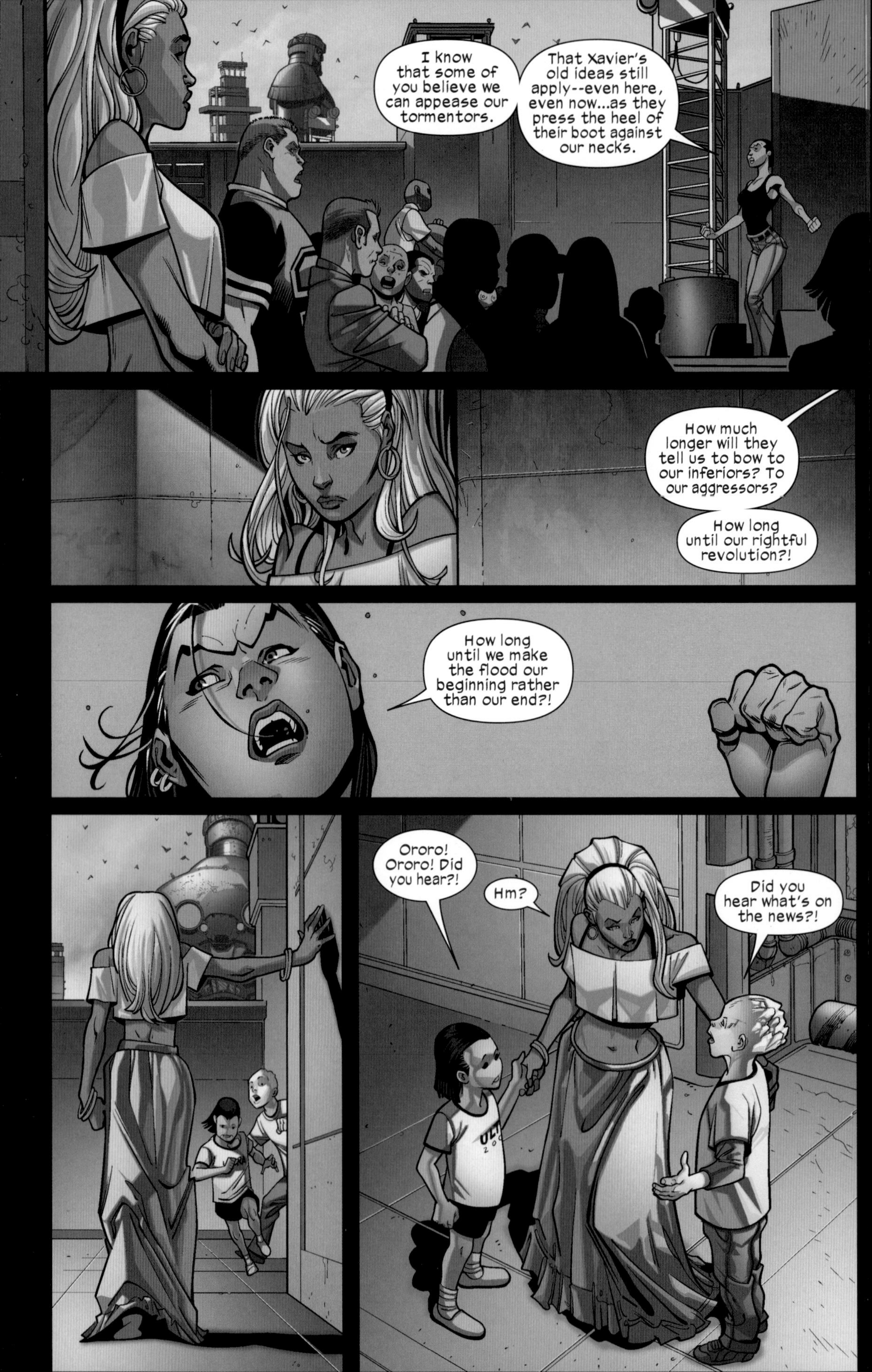
I know that some of you believe we can appease our tormentors.
That Xavier's old ideas still apply--even here, even now...as they press the heel of their boot against our necks.
How much longer will they tell us to bow to our inferiors? To our aggressors?
How long until our rightful revolution?!
How long until we make the flood our beginning rather than our end?!
Ororo! Ororo! Did you hear?!
Hm?
Did you hear what's on the news?!

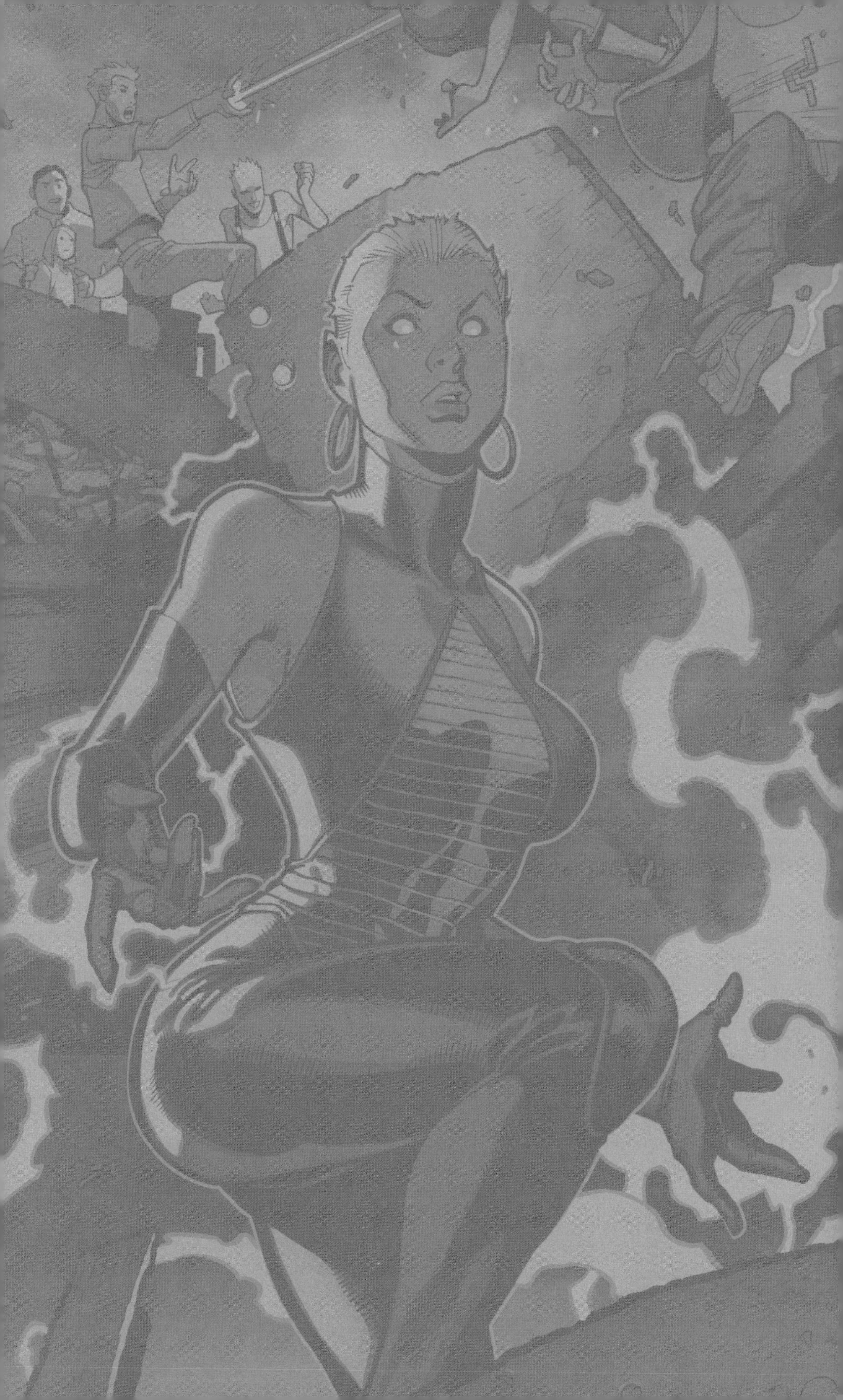

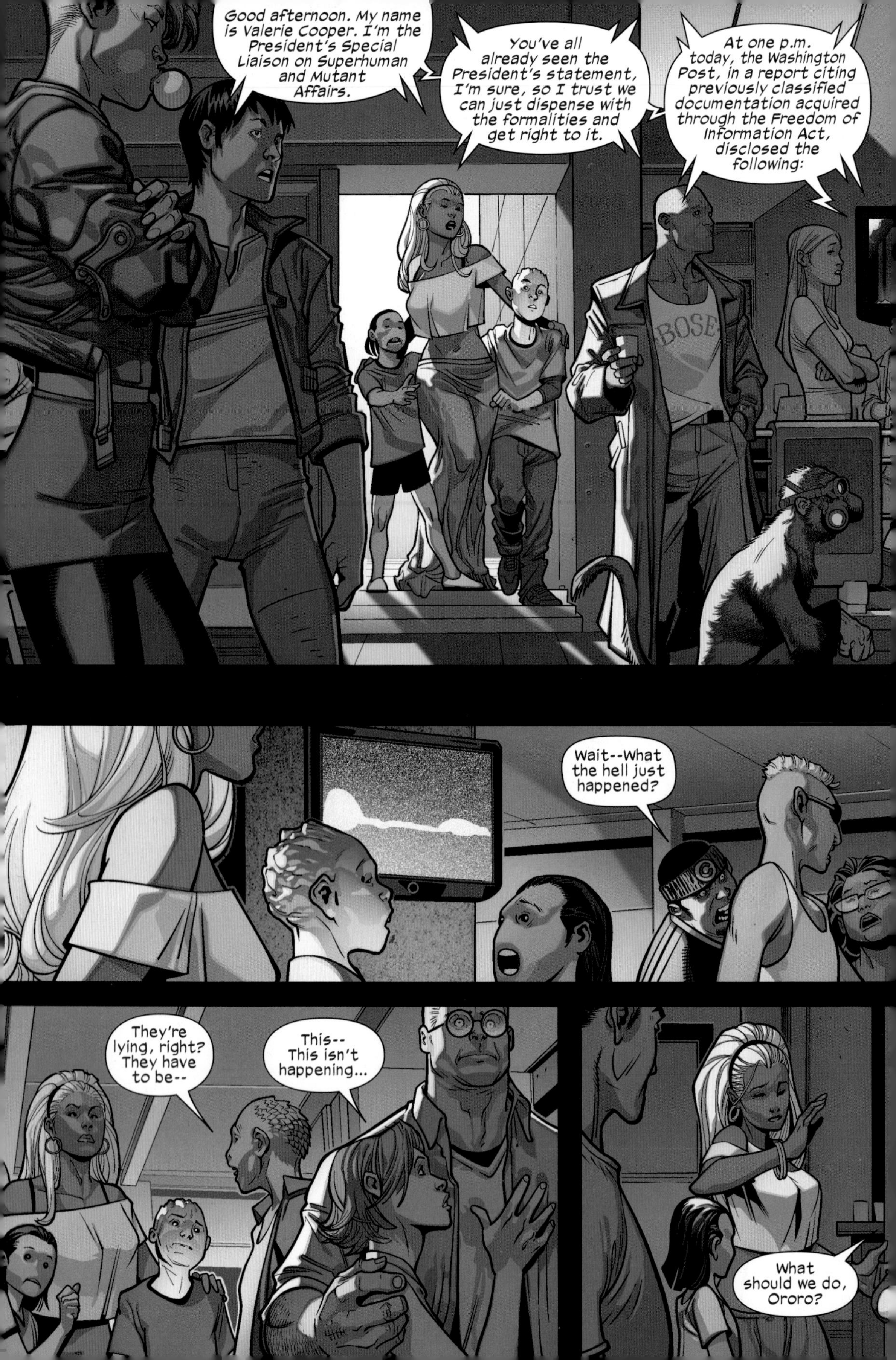
Good afternoon. My name is Valerie Cooper. I'm the President's Special Liaison on Superhuman and Mutant Affairs.
You've all already seen the President's statement, I'm sure, so I trust we can just dispense with the formalities and get right to it.
At one p.m. today, the Washington Post, in a report citing previously classified documentation acquired through the Freedom of Information Act, disclosed the following:
BOSE
Wait--What the hell just happened?
They're lying, right? They have to be--
This-- This isn't happening...
What should we do, Ororo?

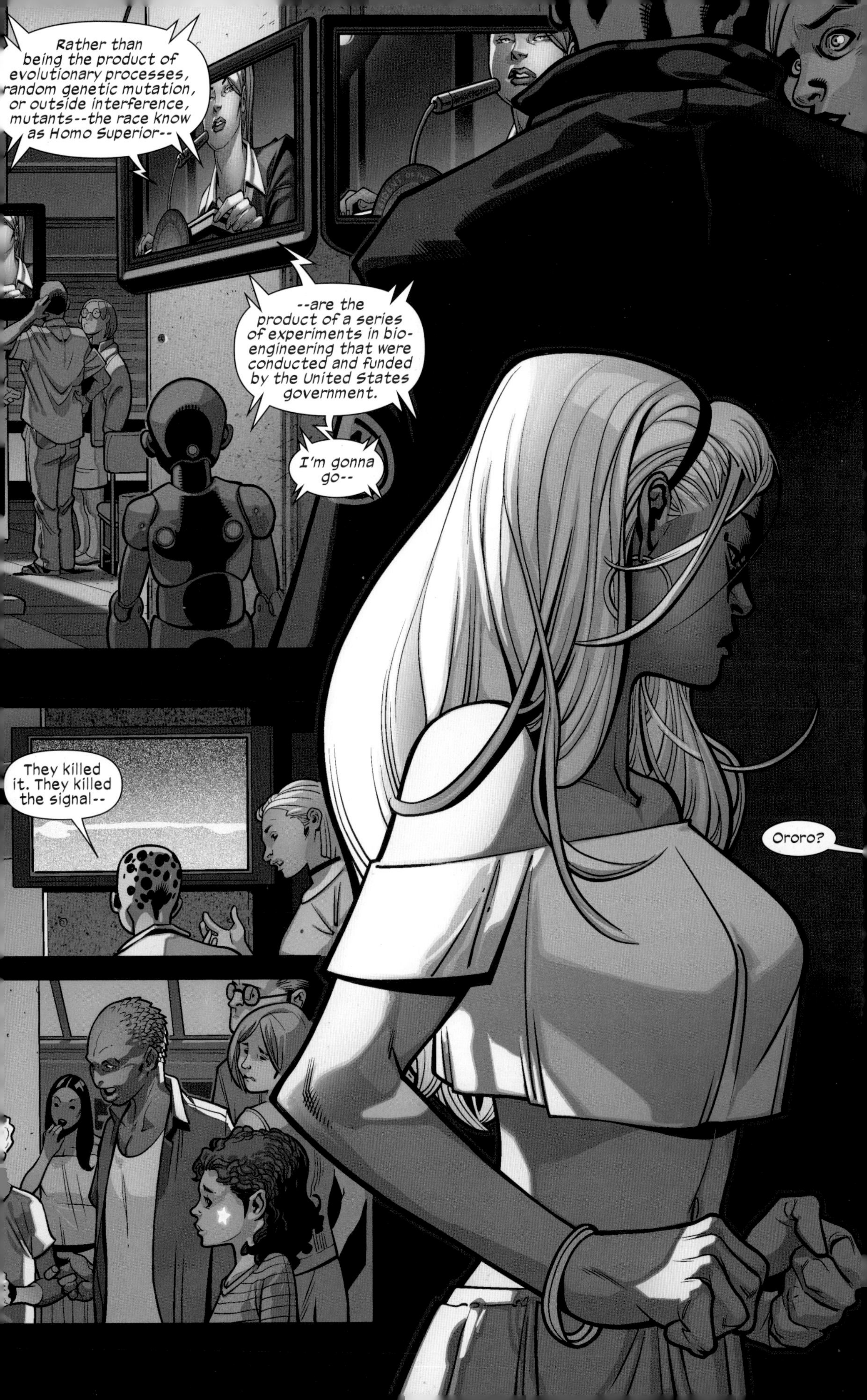
Rather than being the product of evolutionary processes, random genetic mutation, or outside interference, mutants--the race know as Homo Superior--
--are the product of a series of experiments in bio-engineering that were conducted and funded by the United States government.
I'm gonna go--
They killed it. They killed the signal--
Ororo?

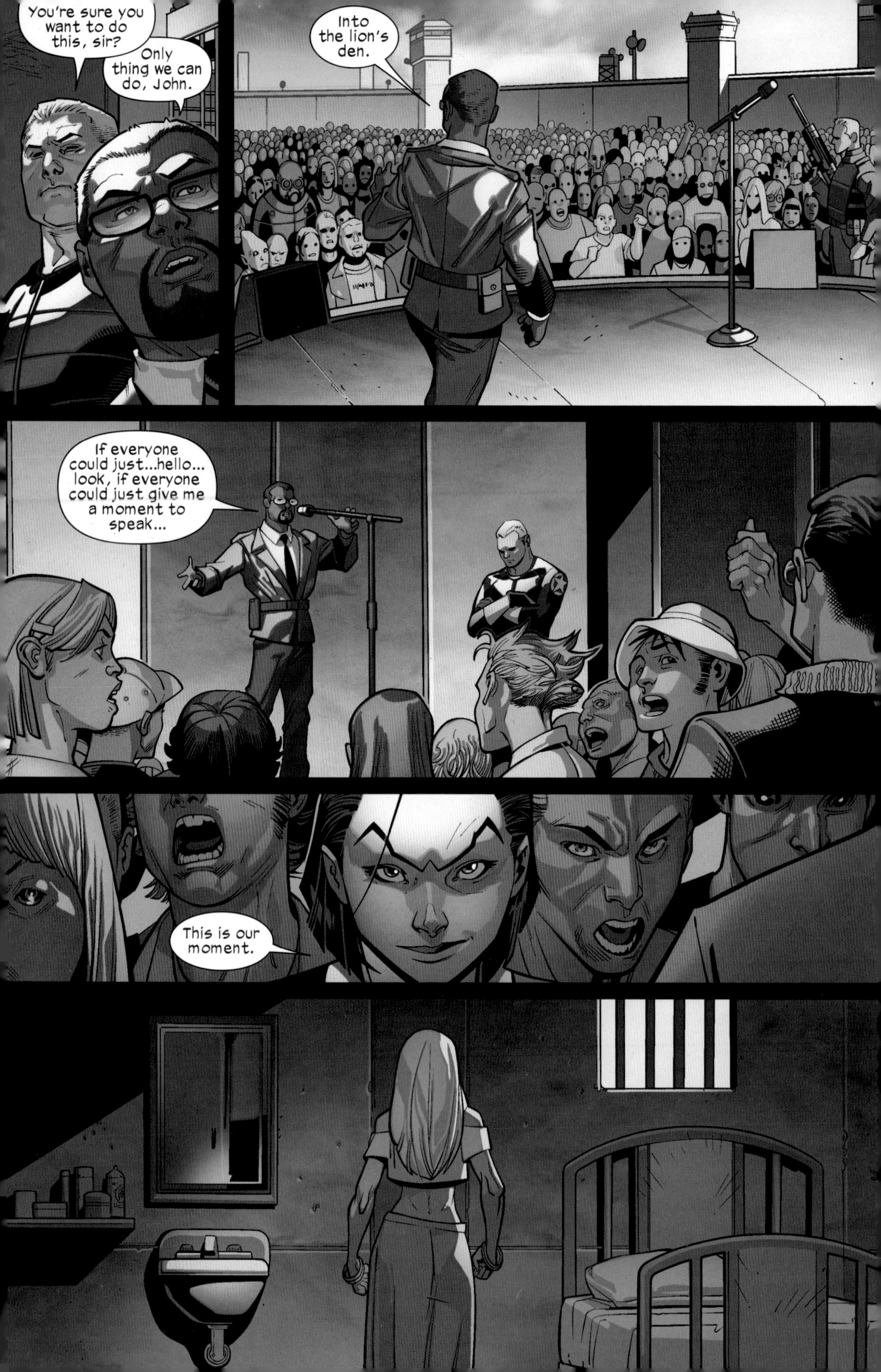
You're sure you want to do this, sir?
Only thing we can do, John.
Into the lion's den.
If everyone could just...hello... look, if everyone could just give me a moment to speak...
This is our moment.

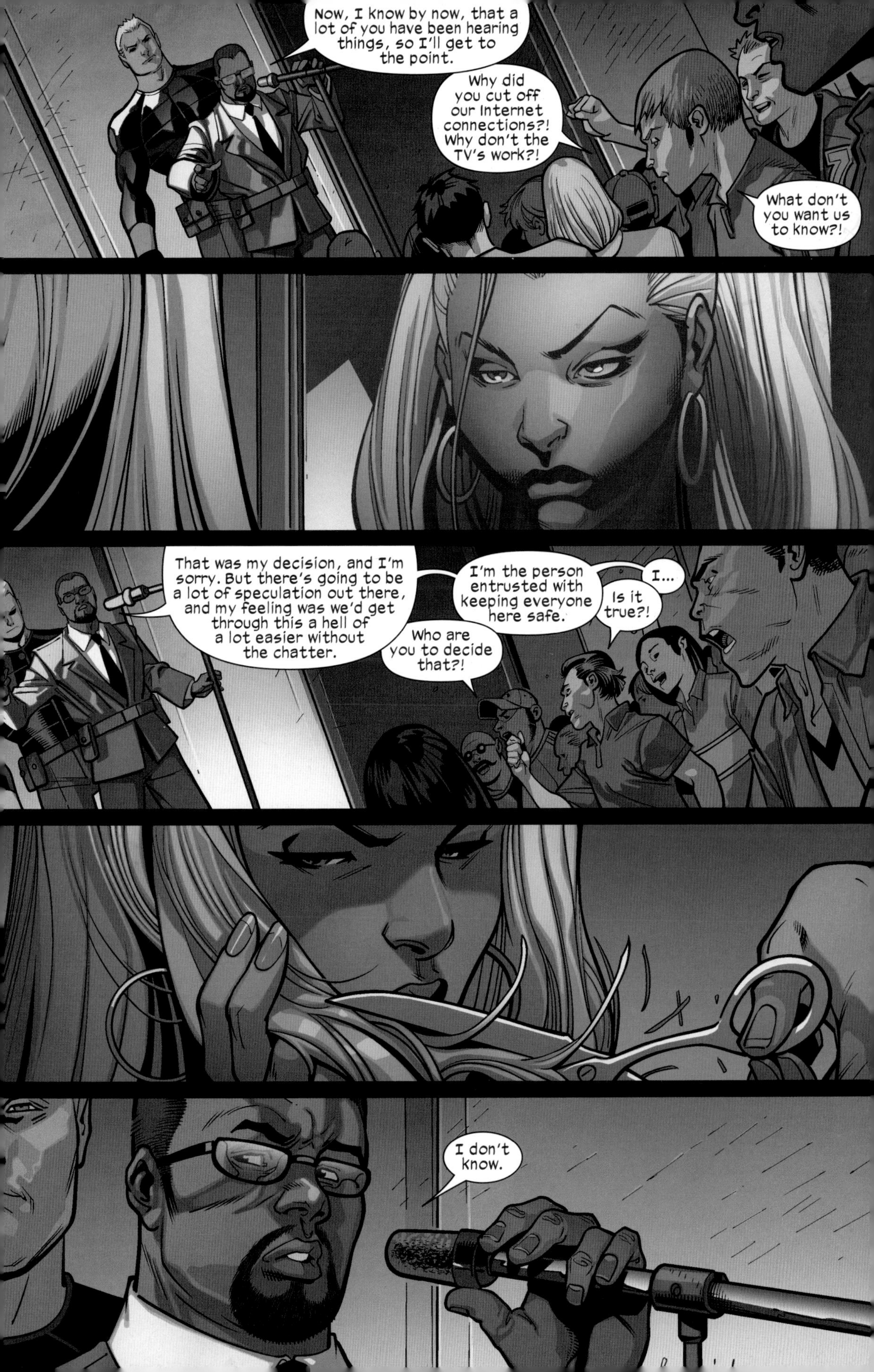
Now, I know by now, that a lot of you have been hearing things, so I'll get to the point.
Why did you cut off our Internet connections?! Why don't the TV's work?!
What don't you want us to know?!
That was my decision, and I'm sorry. But there's going to be a lot of speculation out there, and my feeling was we'd get through this a hell of a lot easier without the chatter.
I'm the person entrusted with keeping everyone here safe.
I...
Is it true?!
Who are you to decide that?!
I don't know.

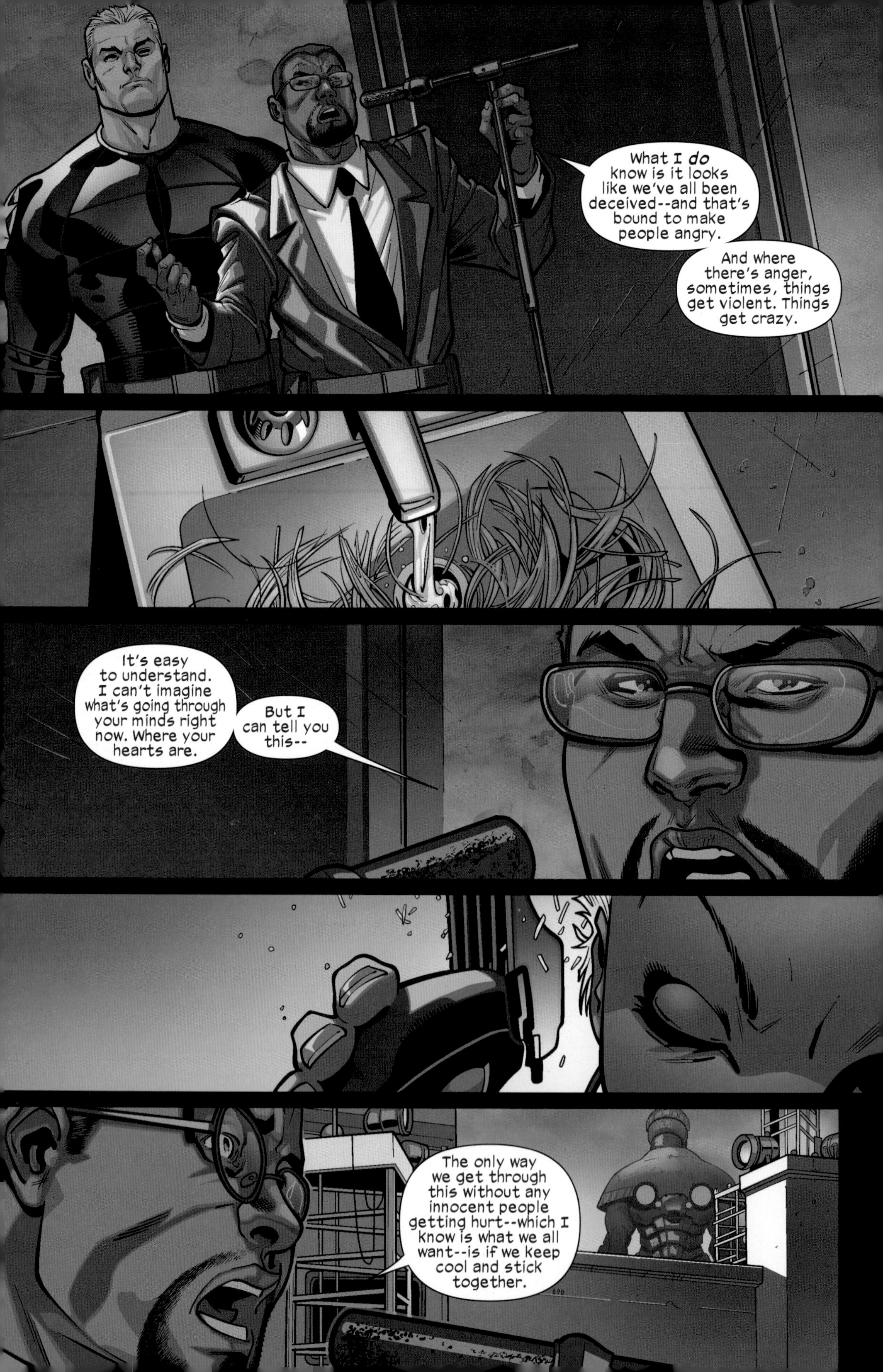
What I *do* know is it looks like we've all been deceived--and that's bound to make people angry.
And where there's anger, sometimes, things get violent. Things get crazy.
It's easy to understand. I can't imagine what's going through your minds right now. Where your hearts are.
But I can tell you this--
The only way we get through this without any innocent people getting hurt--which I know is what we all want--is if we keep cool and stick together.

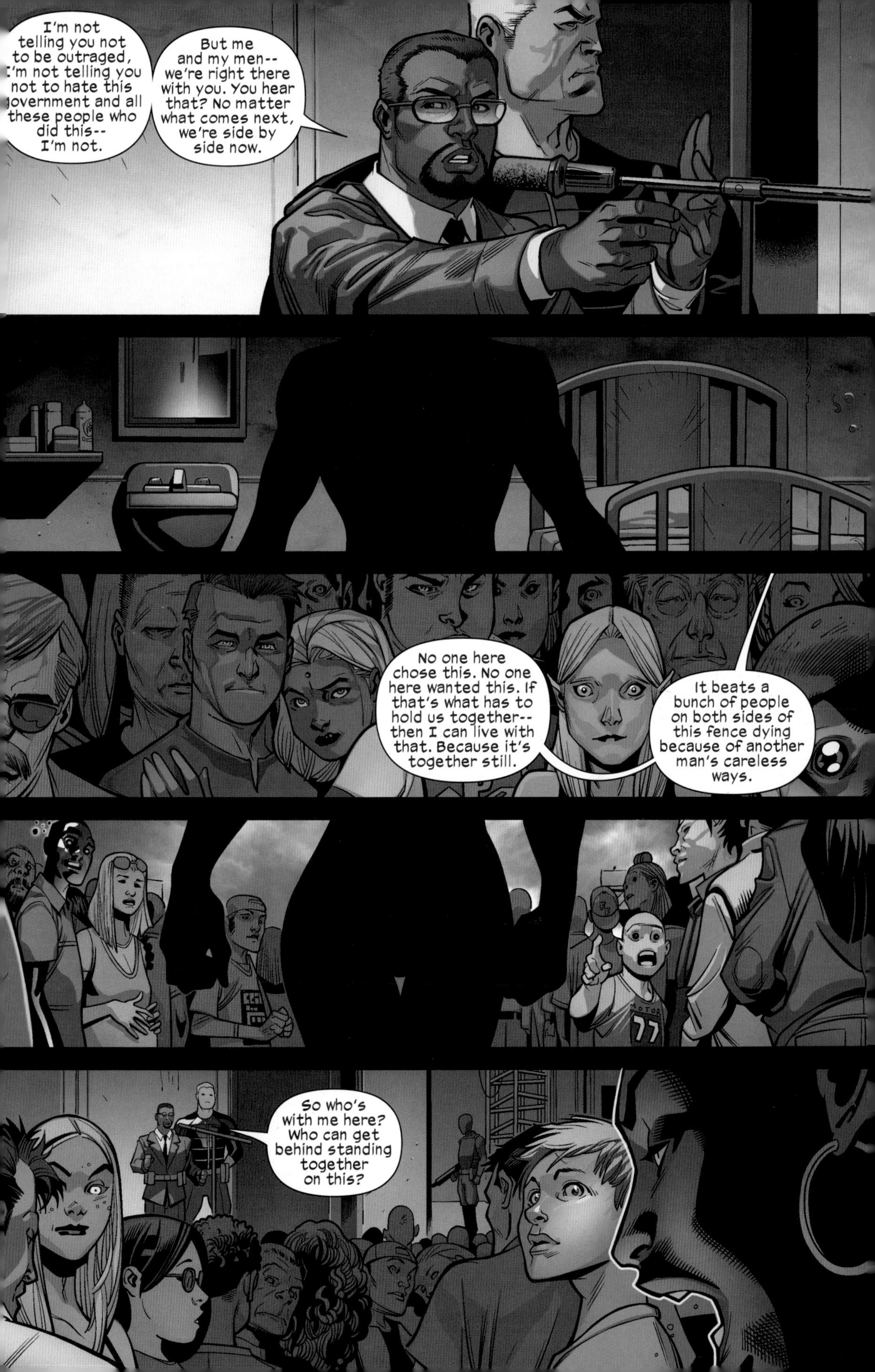
I'm not telling you not to be outraged, I'm not telling you not to hate this government and all these people who did this-- I'm not.
But me and my men-- we're right there with you. You hear that? No matter what comes next, we're side by side now.
No one here chose this. No one here wanted this. If that's what has to hold us together-- then I can live with that. Because it's together still.
It beats a bunch of people on both sides of this fence dying because of another man's careless ways.
So who's with me here? Who can get behind standing together on this?

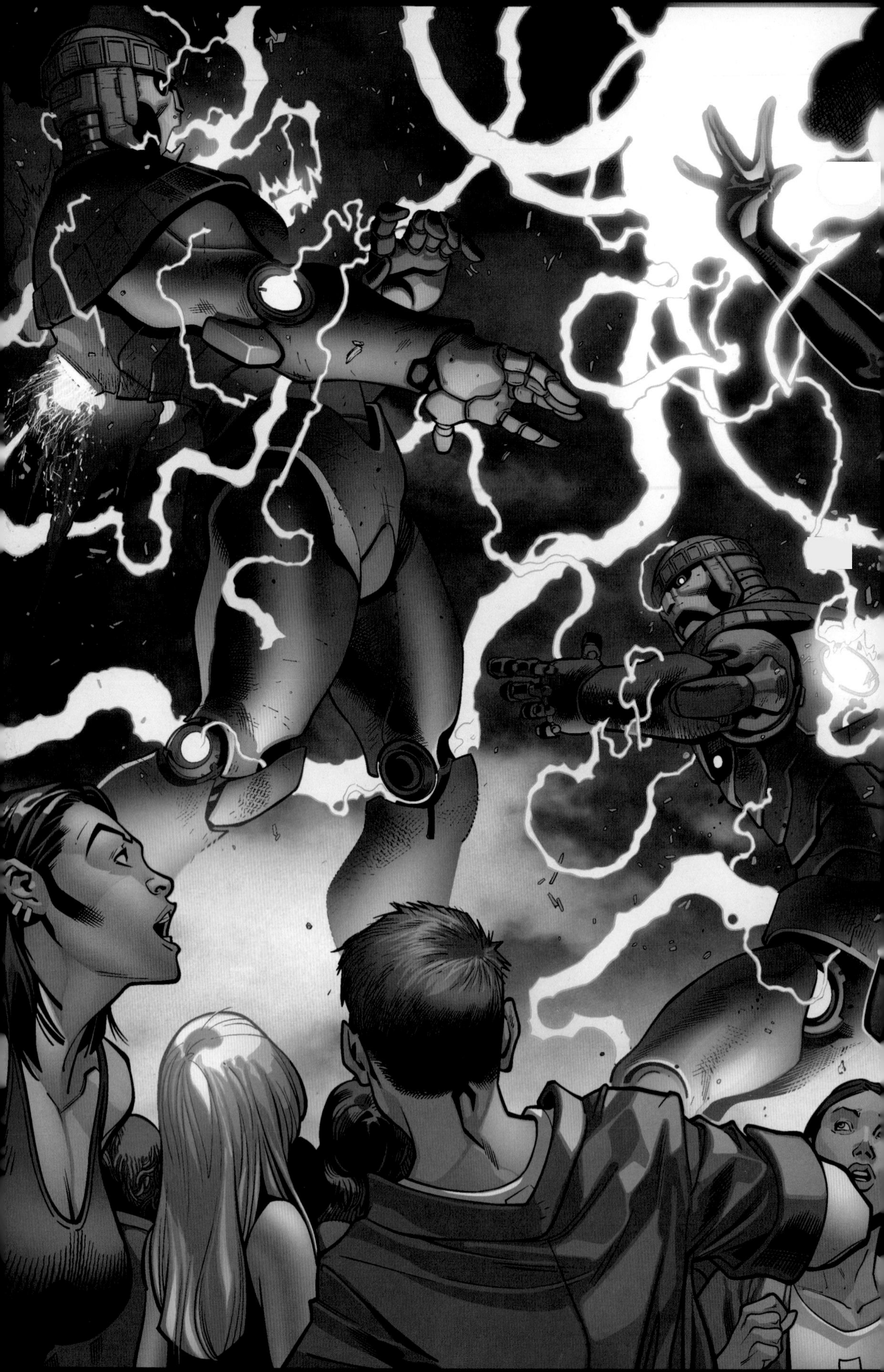

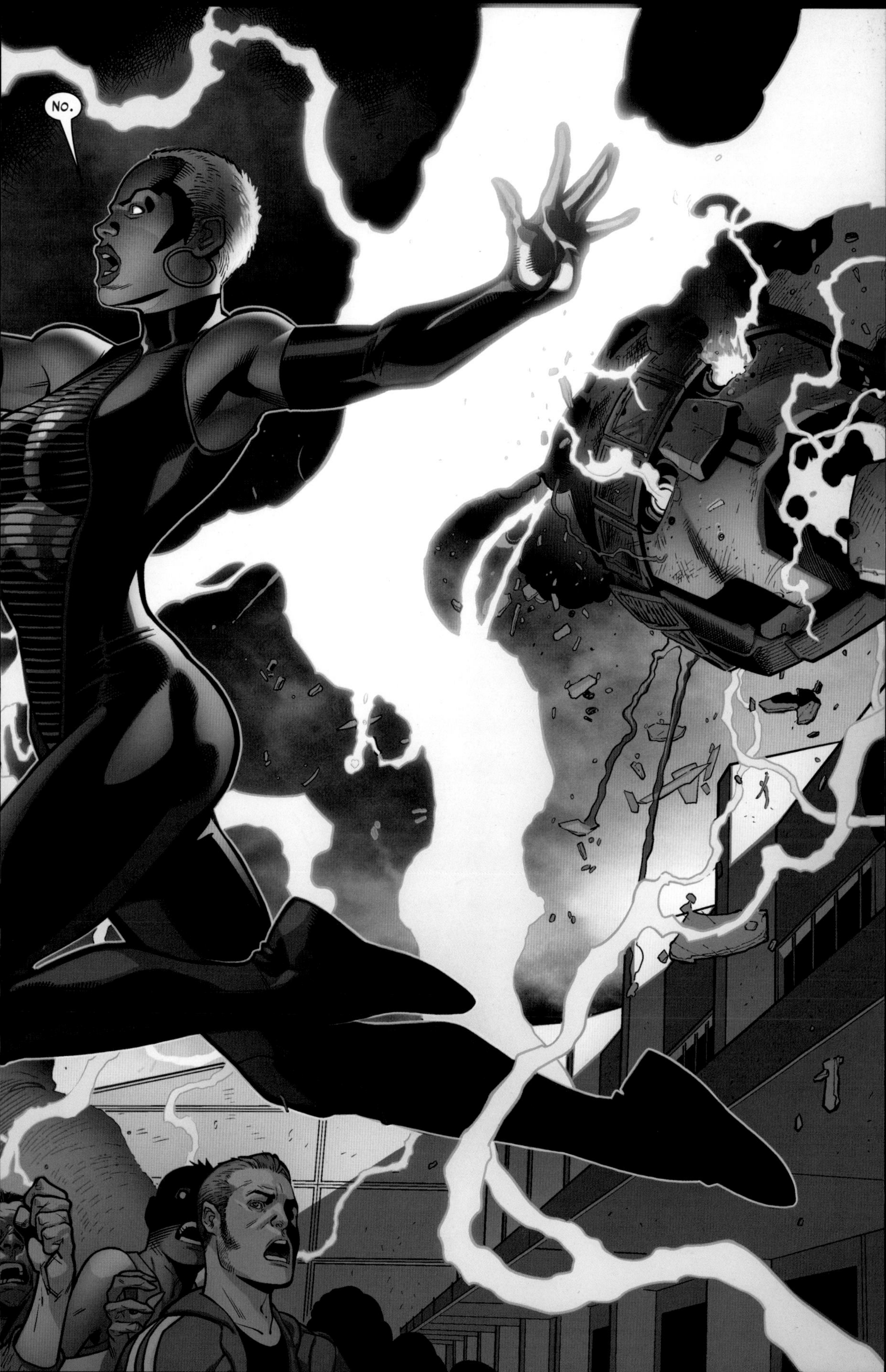
NO.

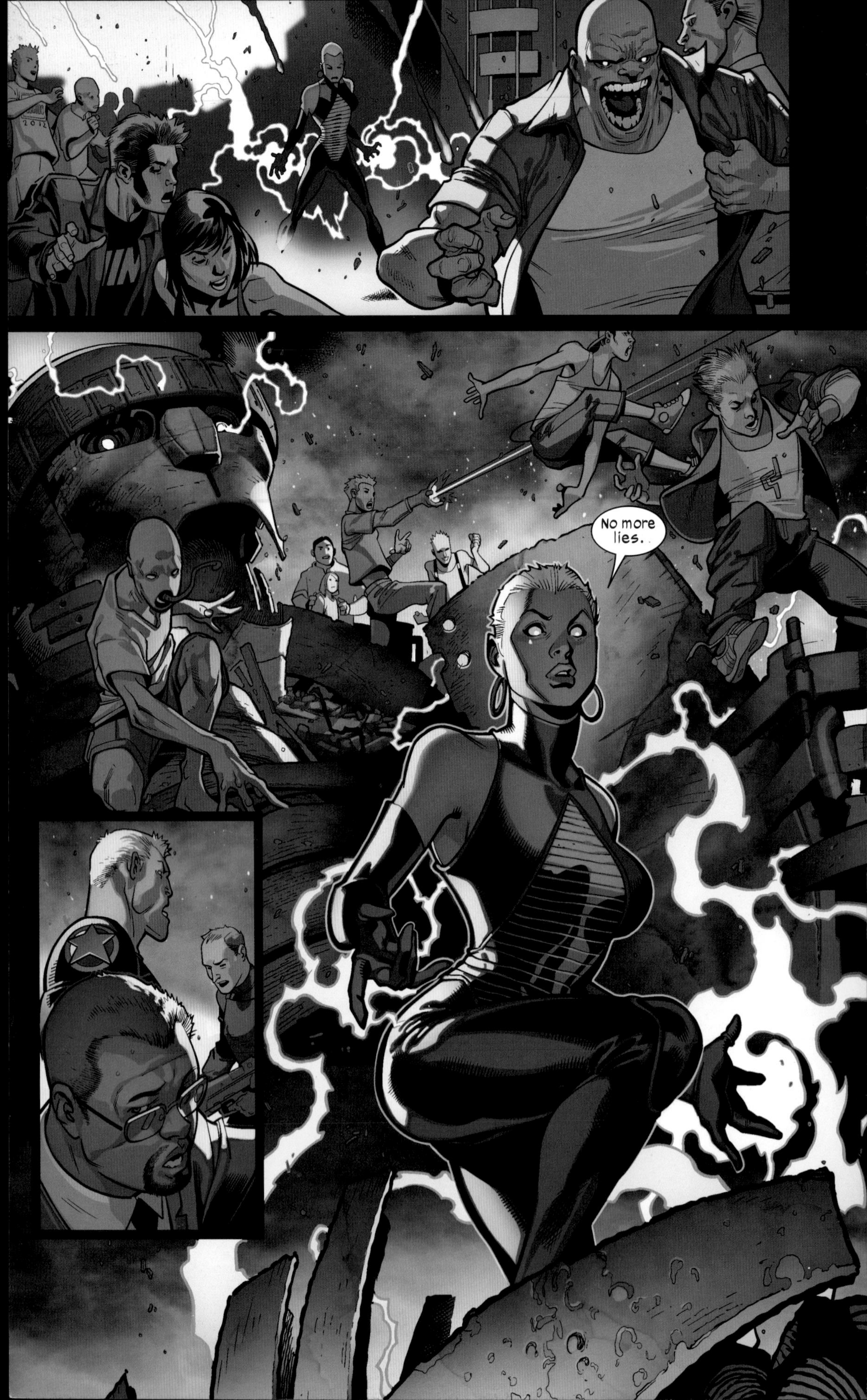
No more lies.

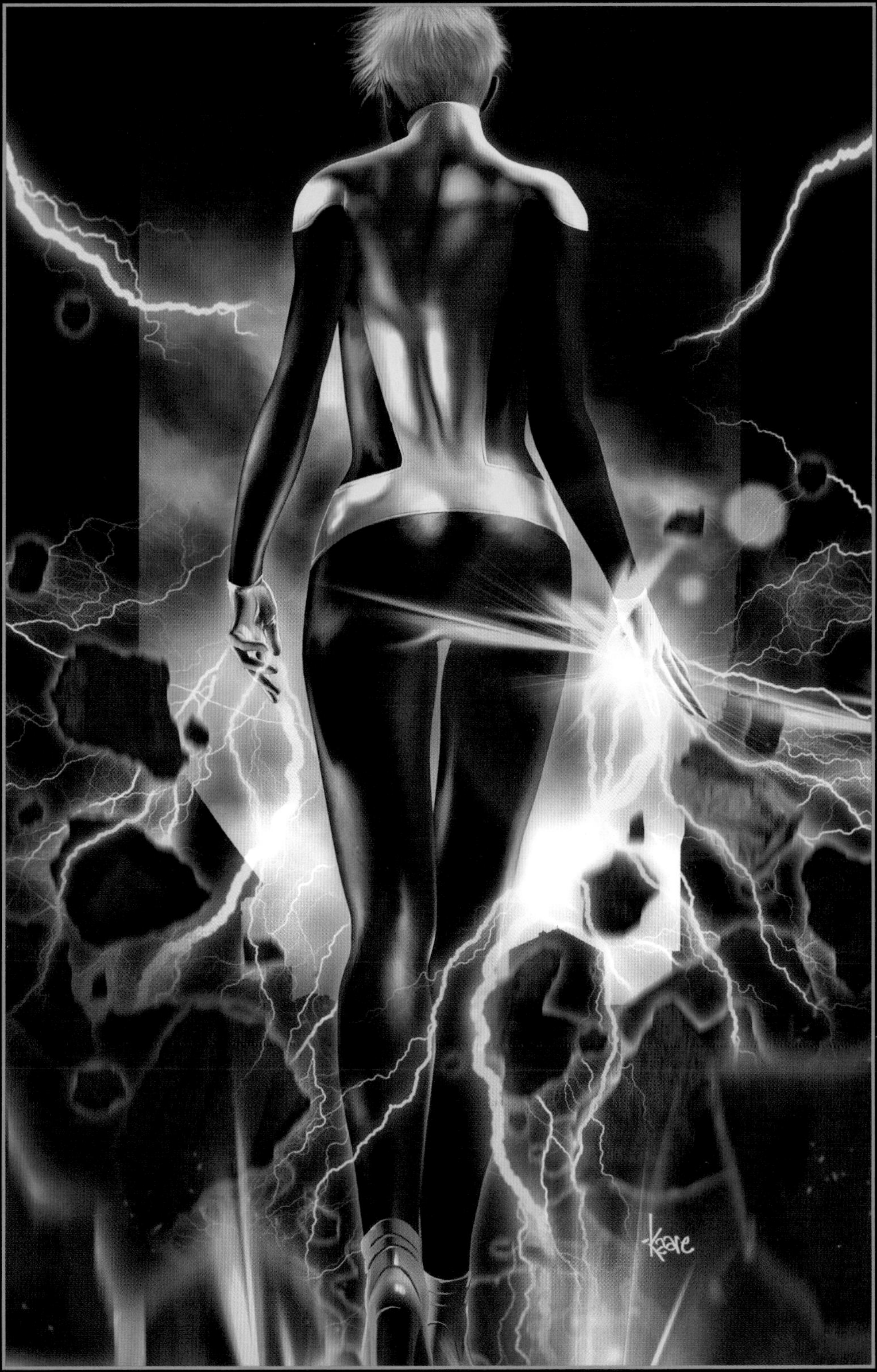
Kaare

ISSUE 010 COVER

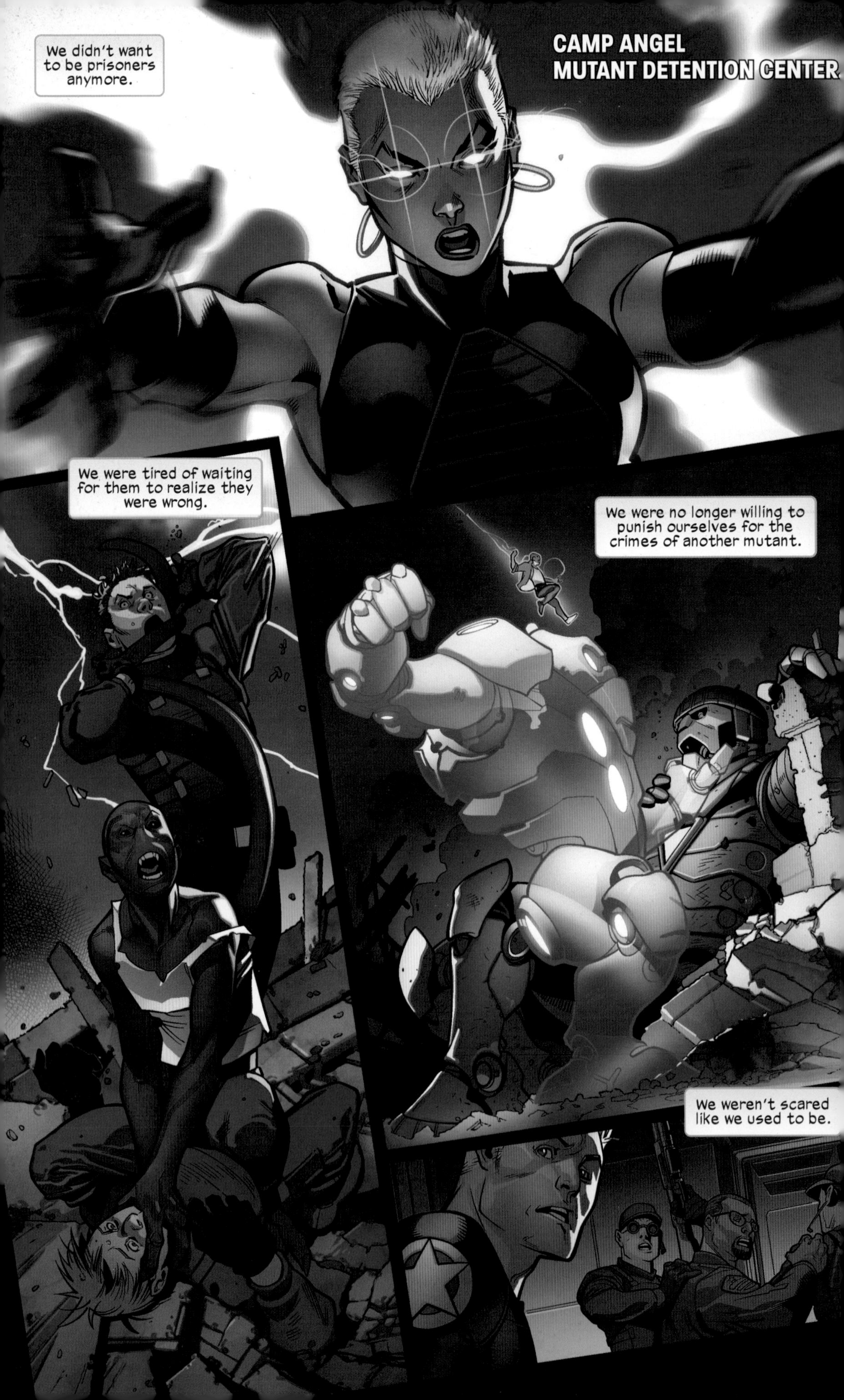
CAMP ANGEL
MUTANT DETENTION CENTER
We didn't want to be prisoners anymore.
We were tired of waiting for them to realize they were wrong.
We were no longer willing to punish ourselves for the crimes of another mutant.
We weren't scared like we used to be.

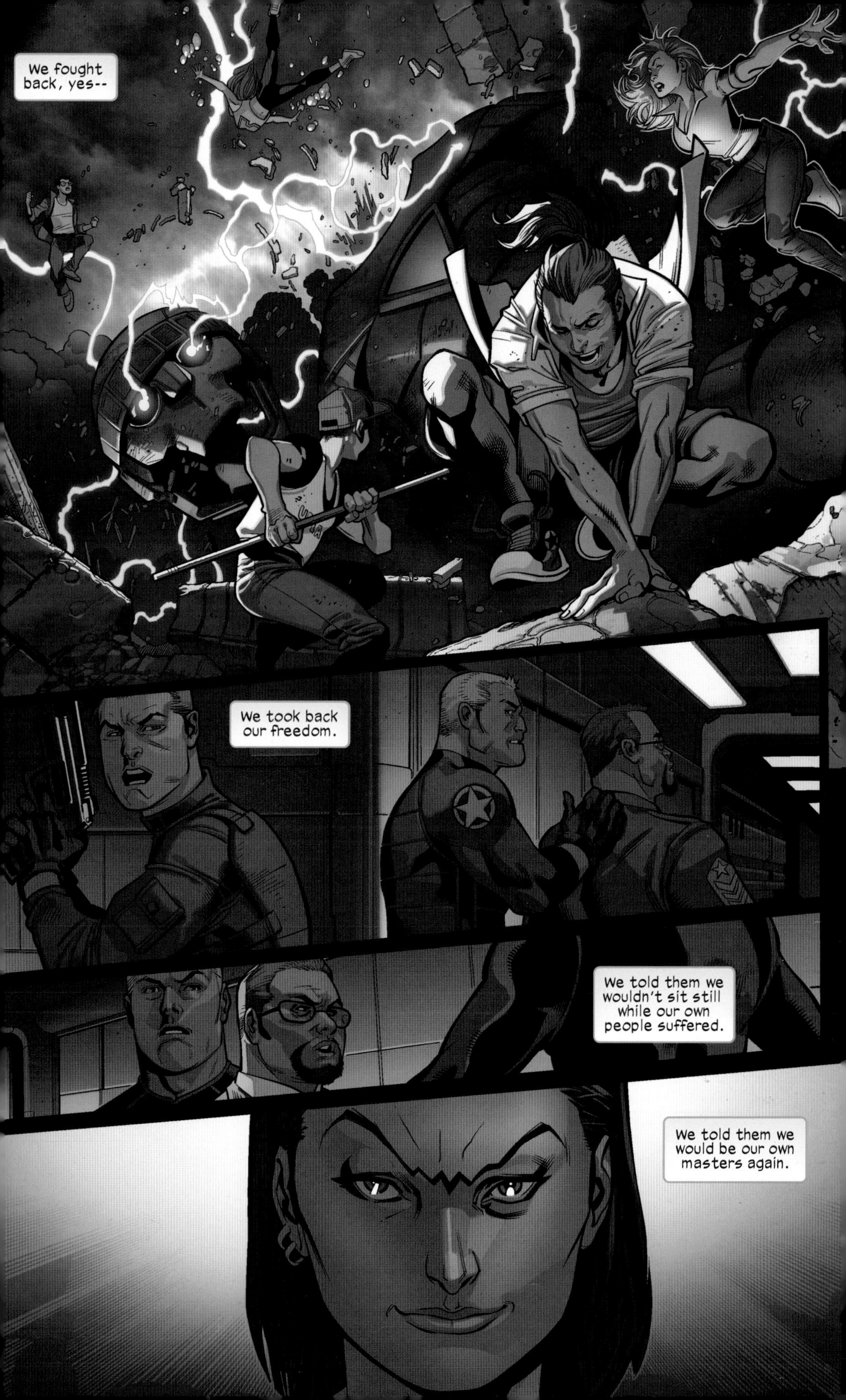
We fought back, yes--
We took back our freedom.
We told them we wouldn't sit still while our own people suffered.
We told them we would be our own masters again.

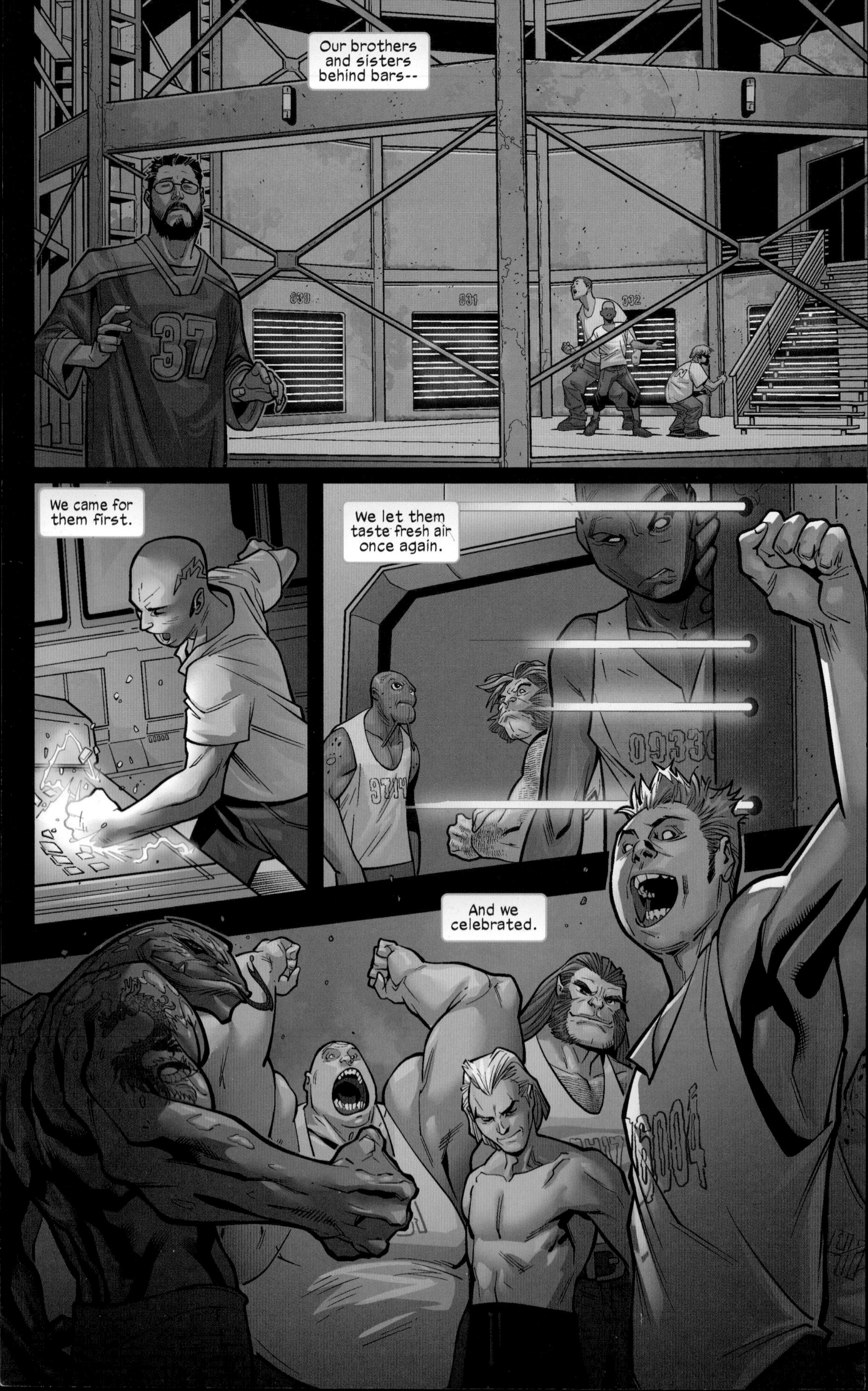
Our brothers and sisters behind bars--
We came for them first.
We let them taste fresh air once again.
And we celebrated.

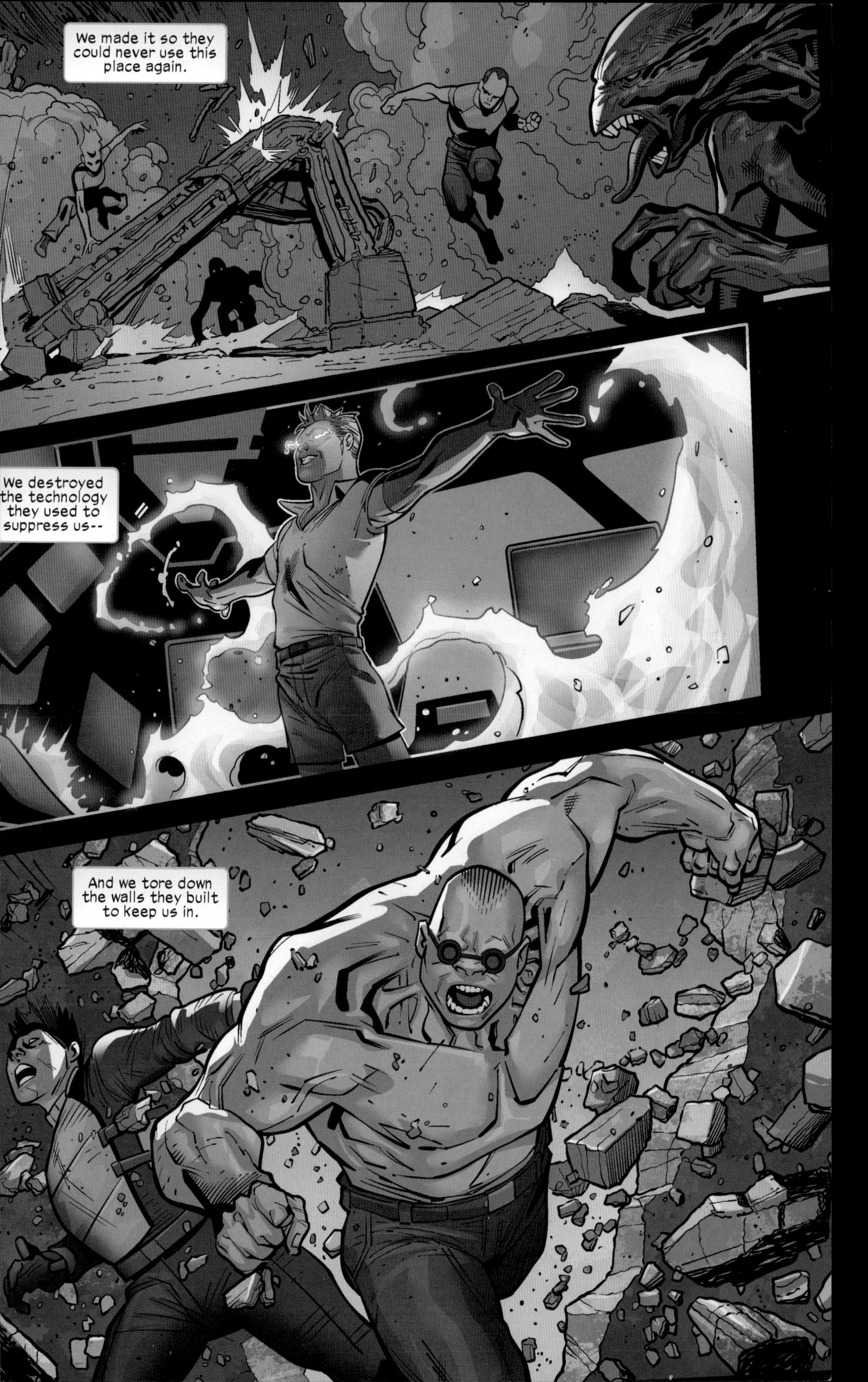
We made it so they could never use this place again.
We destroyed the technology they used to suppress us--
And we tore down the walls they built to keep us in.

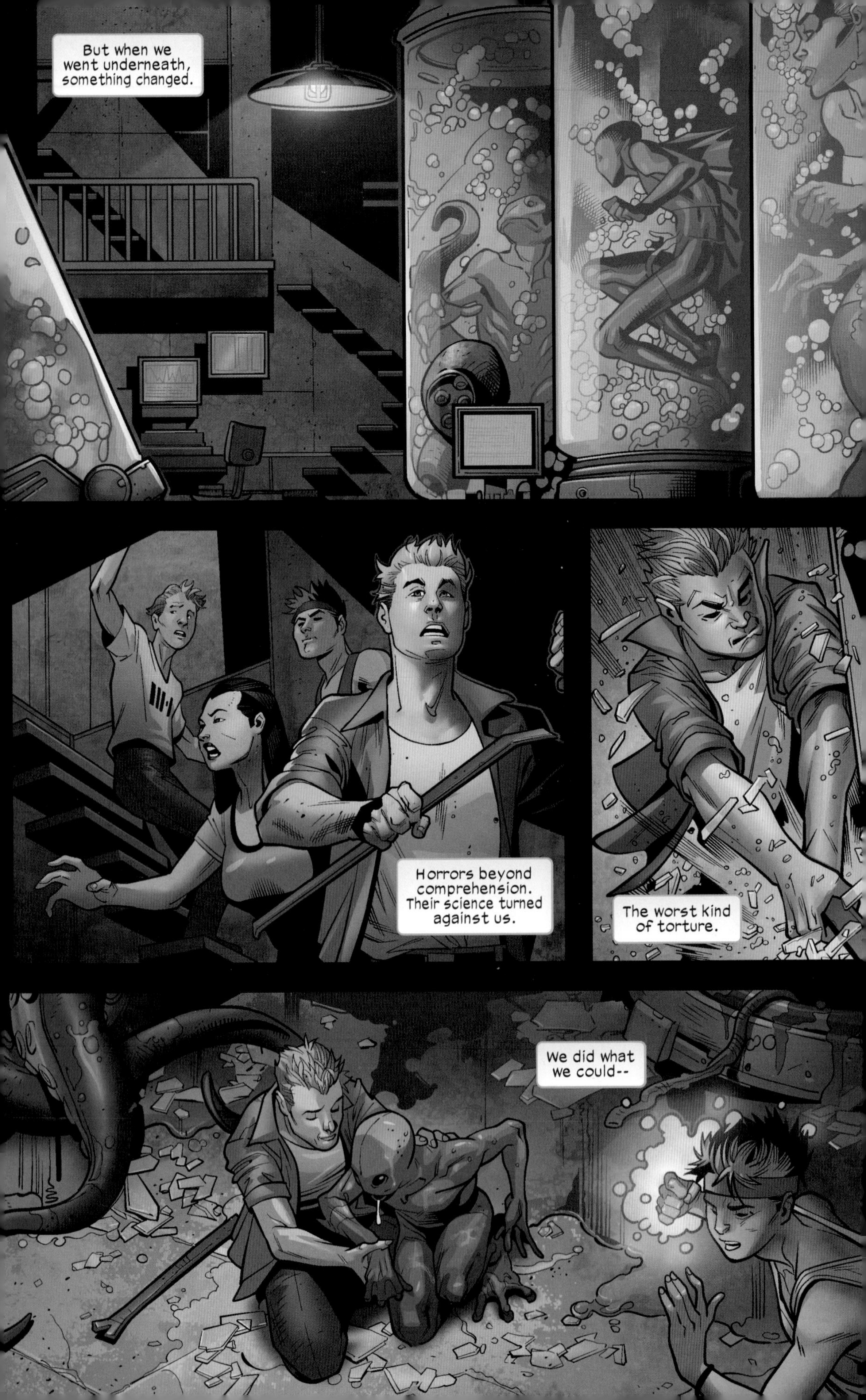
But when we went underneath, something changed.
Horrors beyond comprehension. Their science turned against us.
The worst kind of torture.
We did what we could--

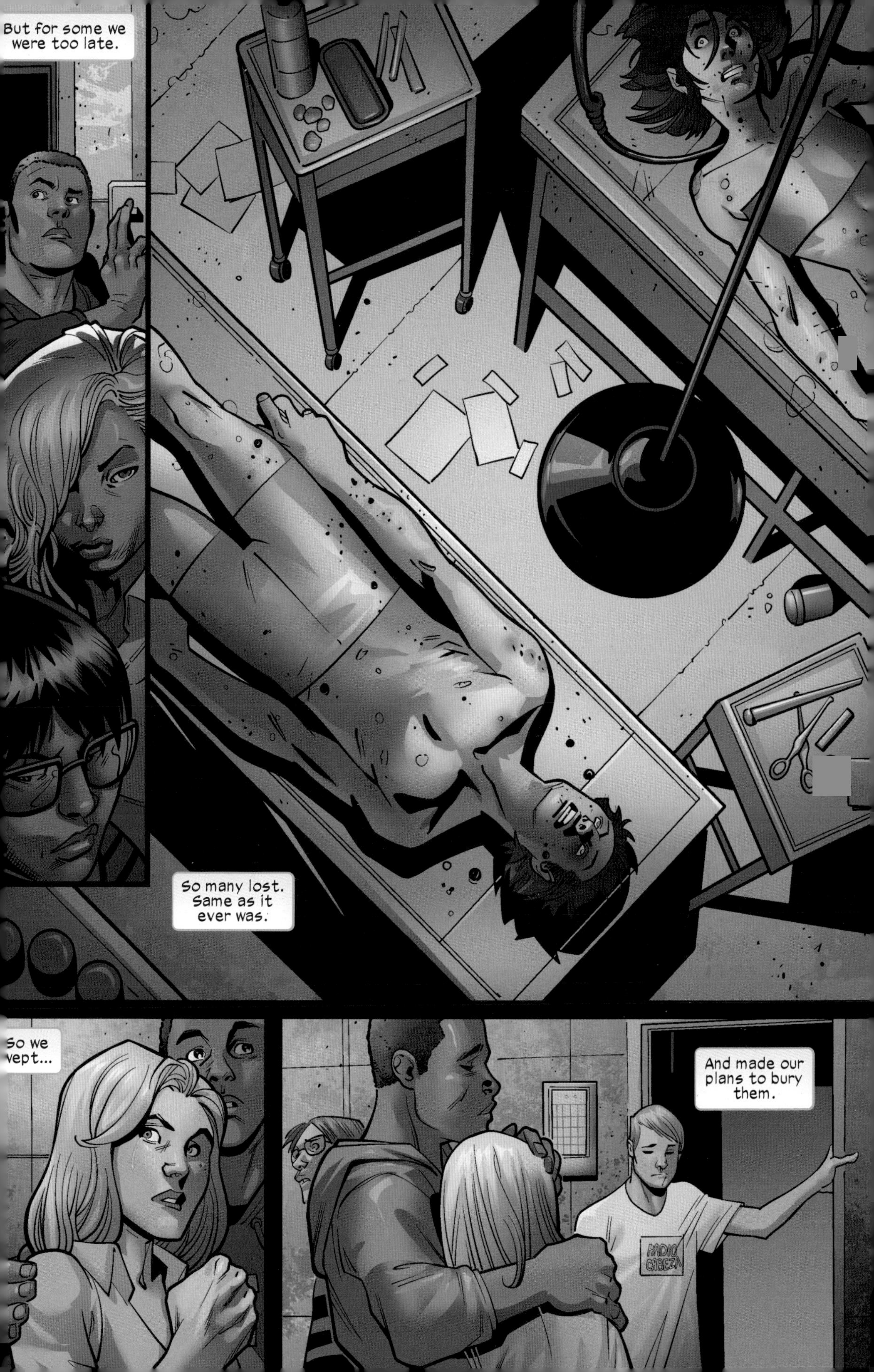
But for some we were too late.
So many lost. Same as it ever was.
So we vept...
And made our plans to bury them.
RADIO CABEZA

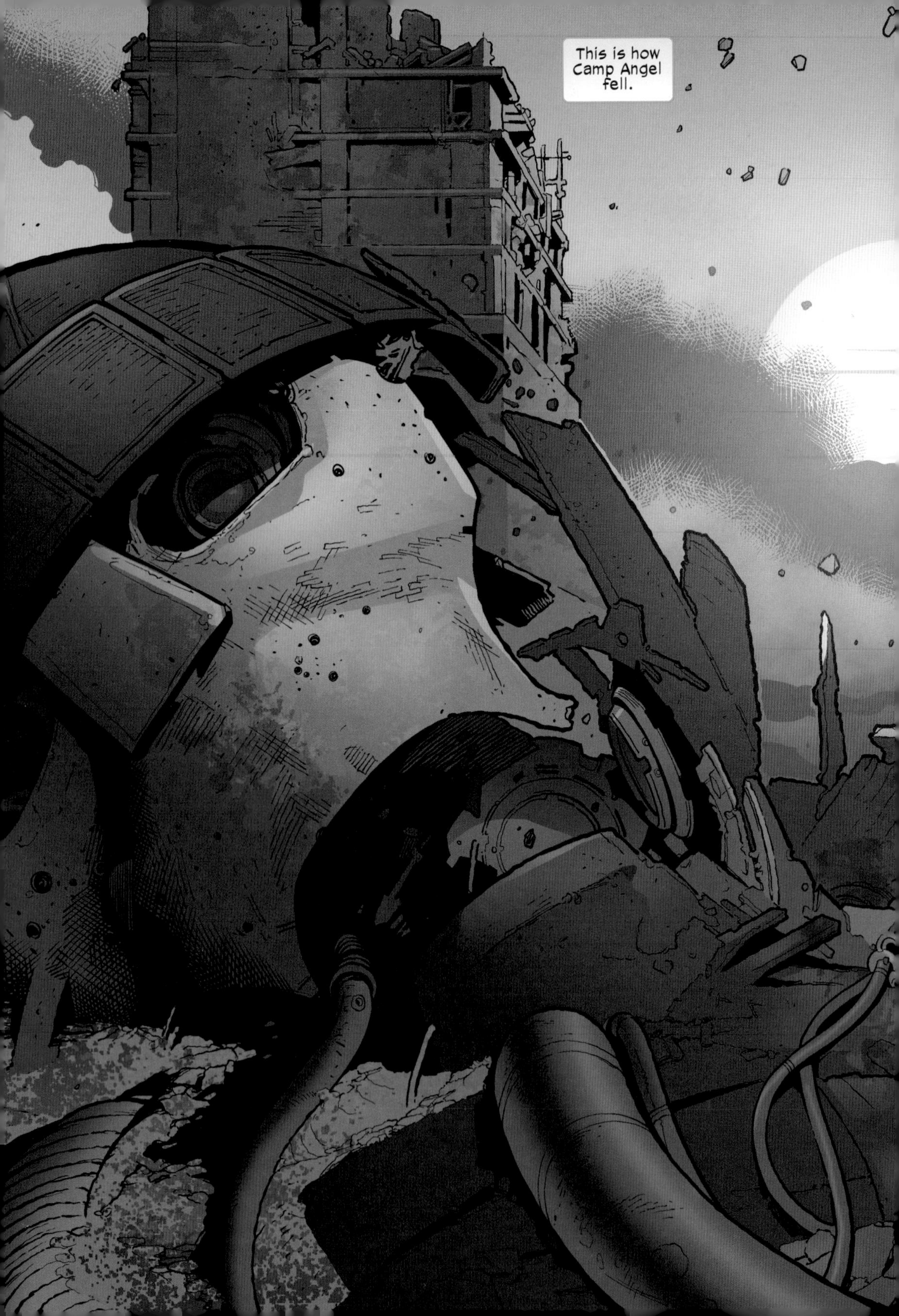
This is how Camp Angel fell.

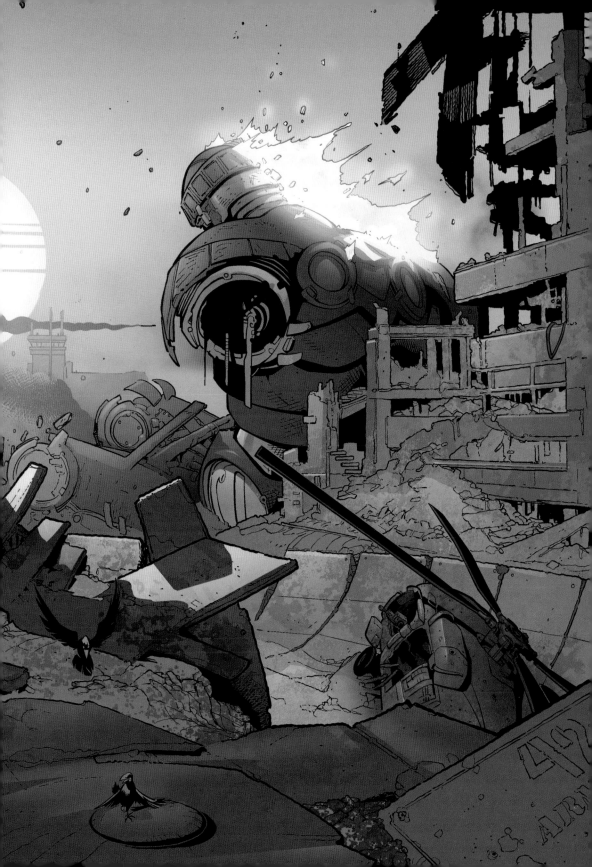

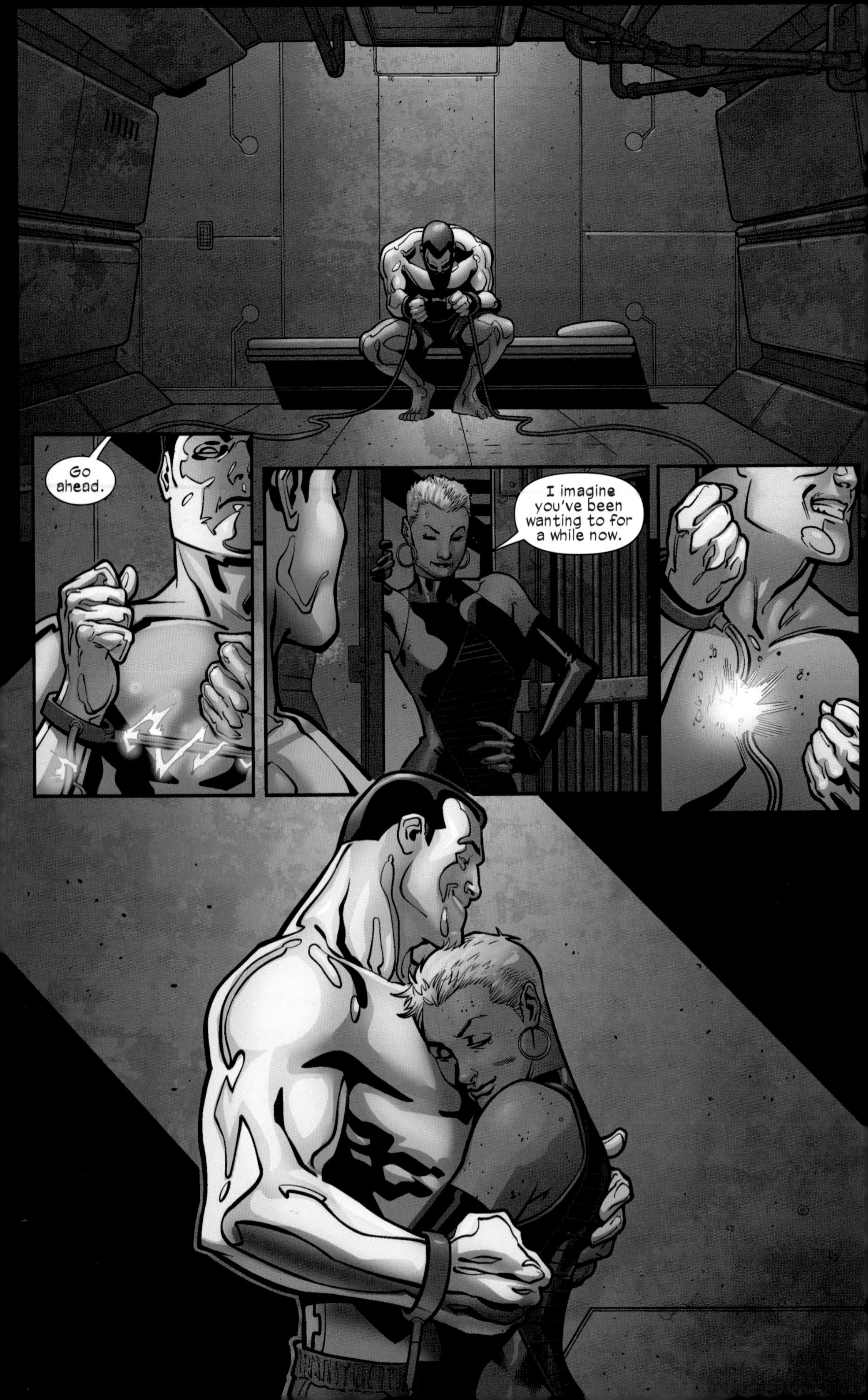
Go ahead.
I imagine you've been wanting to for a while now.

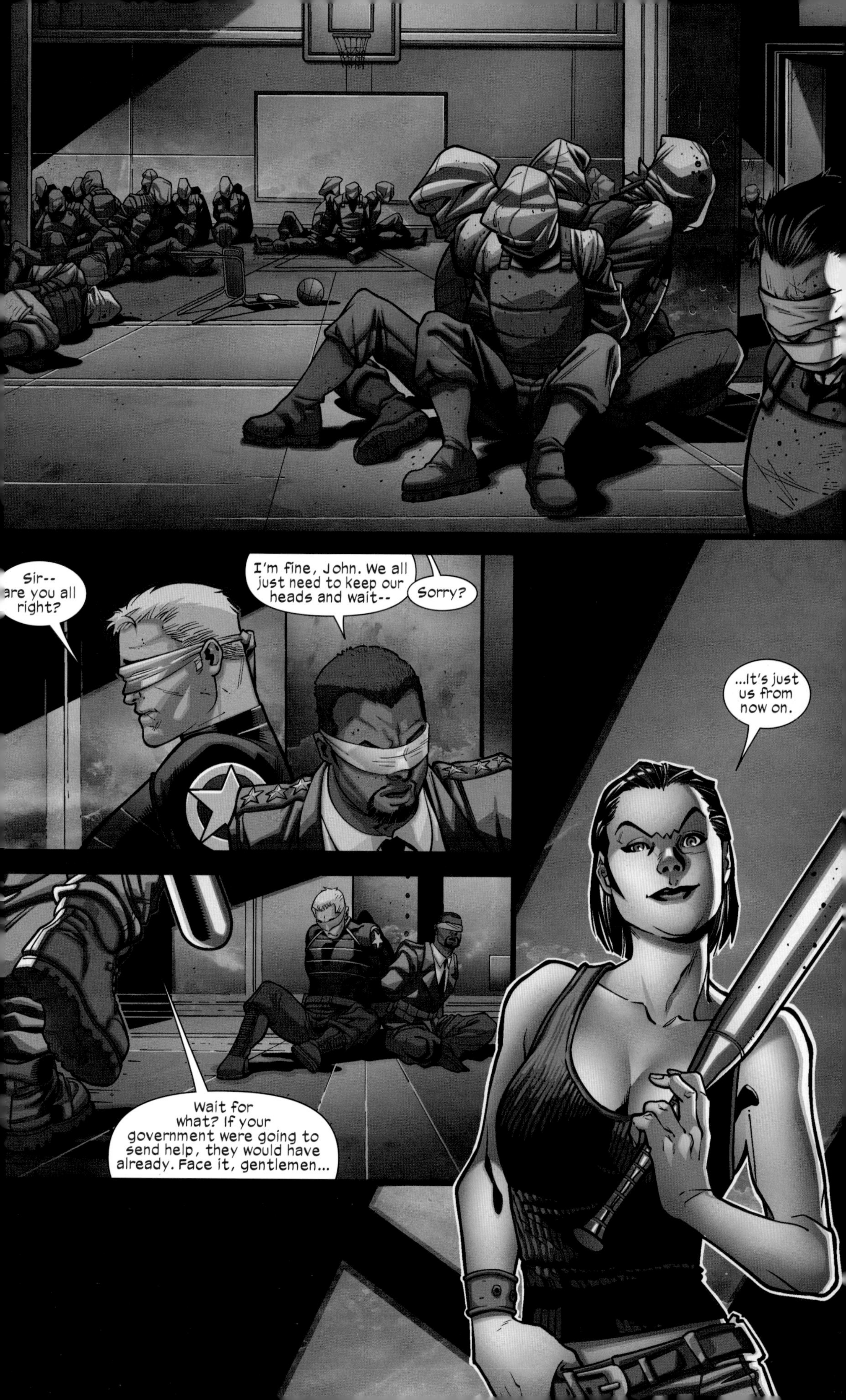

Sir-- are you all right?
I'm fine, John. We all just need to keep our heads and wait--
Sorry?
Wait for what? If your government were going to send help, they would have already. Face it, gentlemen...
...It's just us from now on.

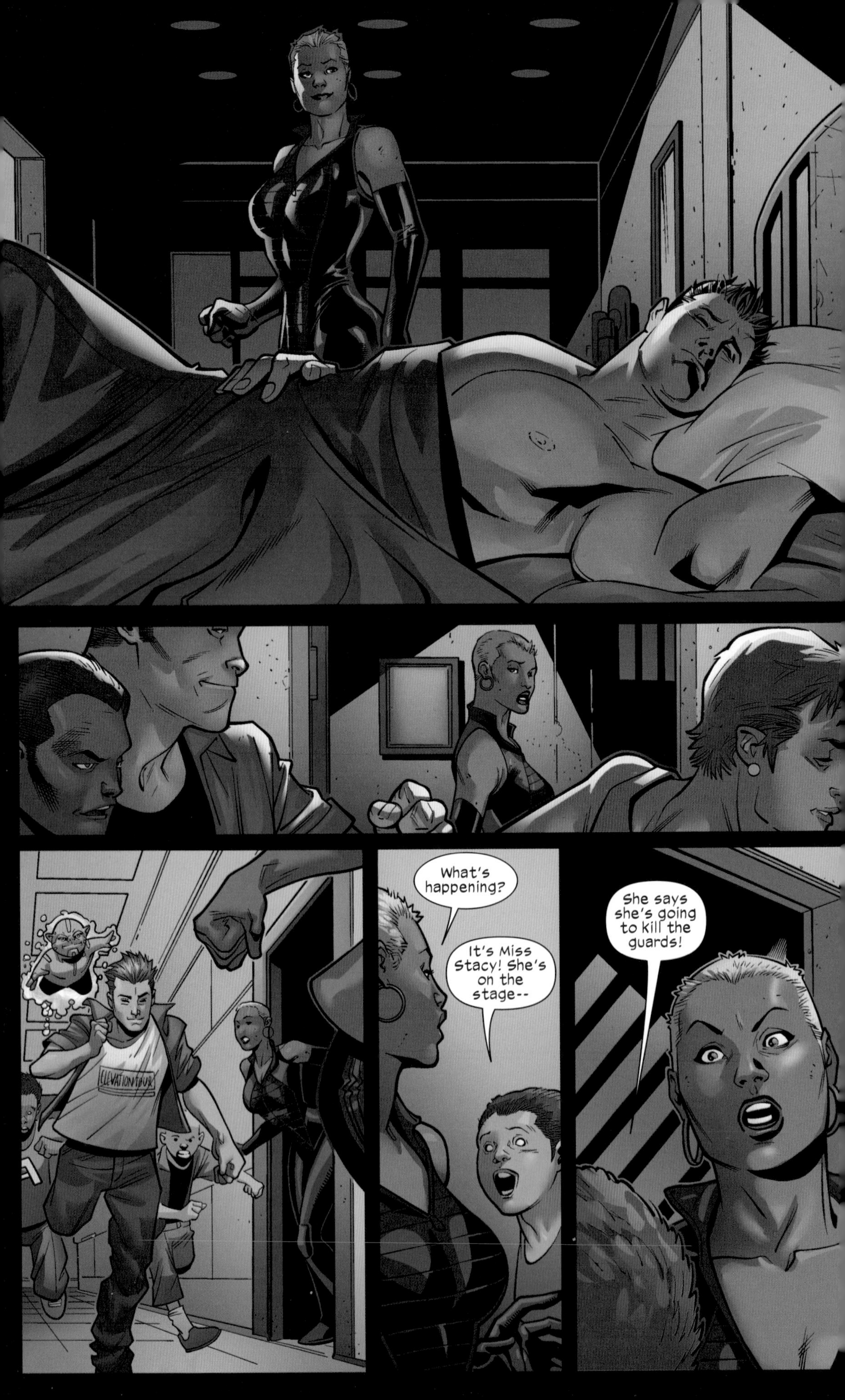
What's happening?
It's Miss Stacy! She's on the stage--
She says she's going to kill the guards!

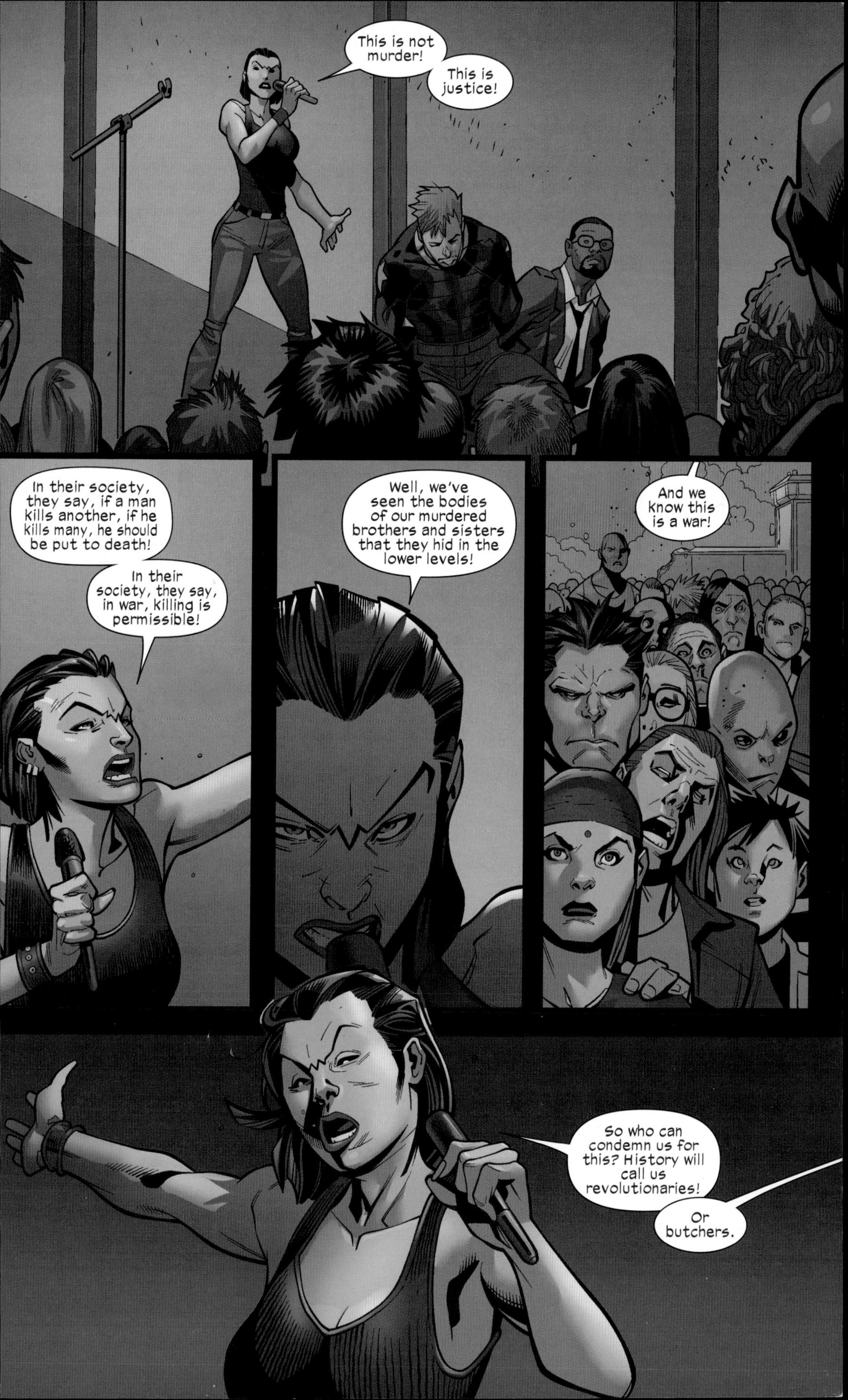
This is not murder!
This is justice!
In their society, they say, if a man kills another, if he kills many, he should be put to death!
In their society, they say, in war, killing is permissible!
Well, we've seen the bodies of our murdered brothers and sisters that they hid in the lower levels!
And we know this is a war!
So who can condemn us for this? History will call us revolutionaries!
Or butchers.

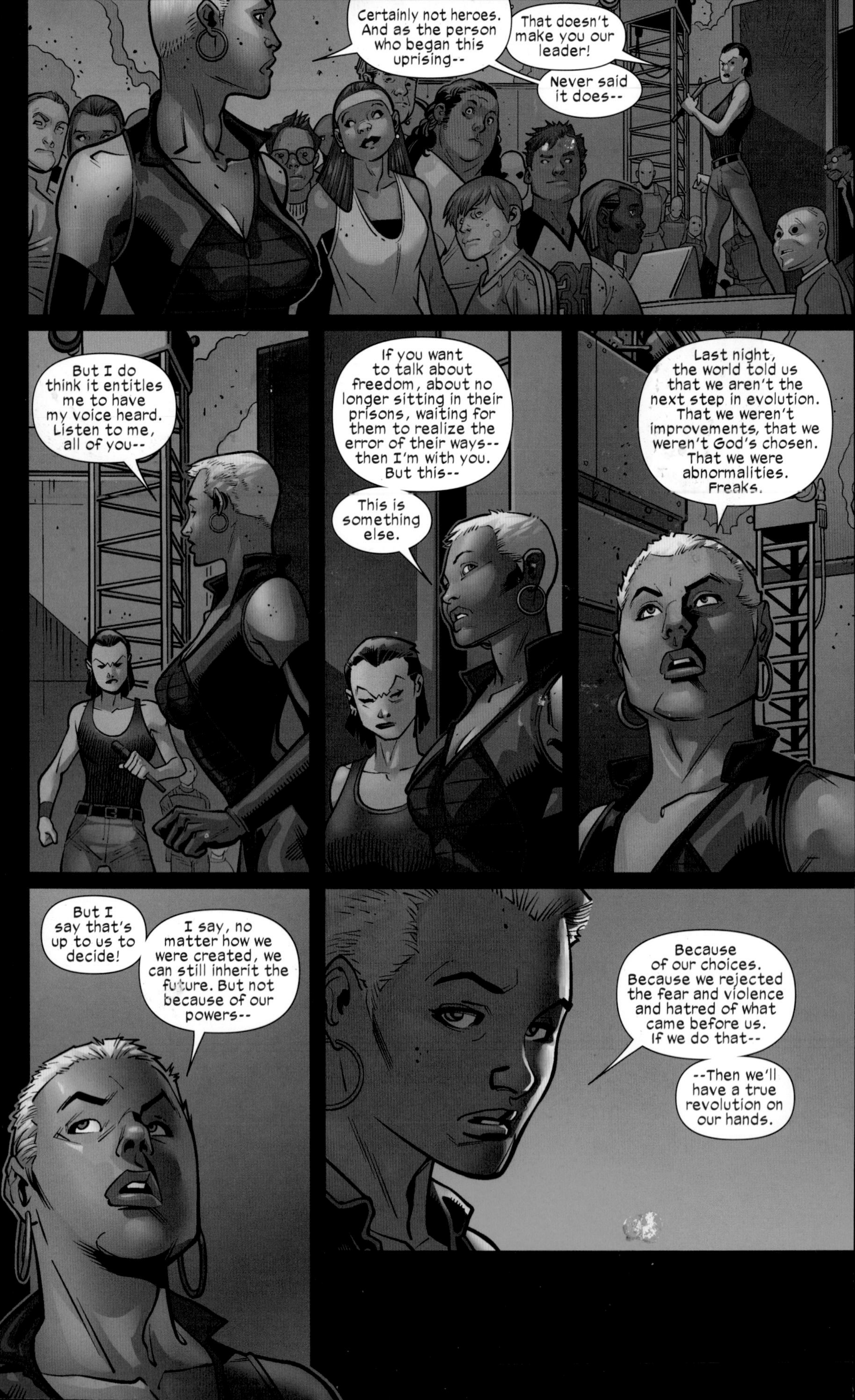
Certainly not heroes. And as the person who began this uprising--
That doesn't make you our leader!
Never said it does--
But I do think it entitles me to have my voice heard. Listen to me, all of you--
If you want to talk about freedom, about no longer sitting in their prisons, waiting for them to realize the error of their ways-- then I'm with you. But this--
This is something else.
Last night, the world told us that we aren't the next step in evolution. That we weren't improvements, that we weren't God's chosen. That we were abnormalities. Freaks.
But I say that's up to us to decide!
I say, no matter how we were created, we can still inherit the future. But not because of our powers--
Because of our choices. Because we rejected the fear and violence and hatred of what came before us. If we do that--
--Then we'll have a true revolution on our hands.

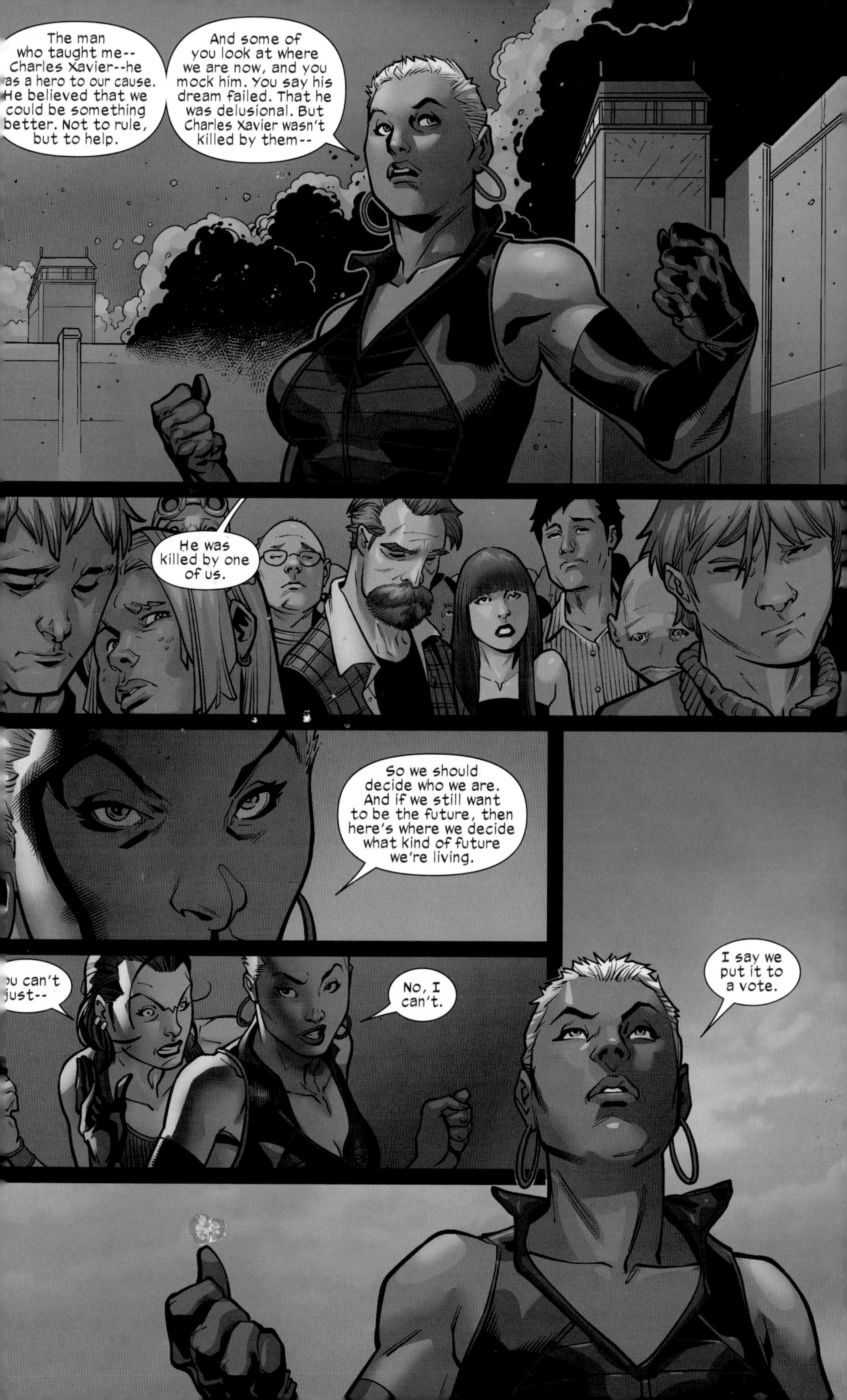
The man who taught me-- Charles Xavier--he was a hero to our cause. He believed that we could be something better. Not to rule, but to help.
And some of you look at where we are now, and you mock him. You say his dream failed. That he was delusional. But Charles Xavier wasn't killed by them--
He was killed by one of us.
So we should decide who we are. And if we still want to be the future, then here's where we decide what kind of future we're living.
u can't just--
No, I can't.
I say we put it to a vote.

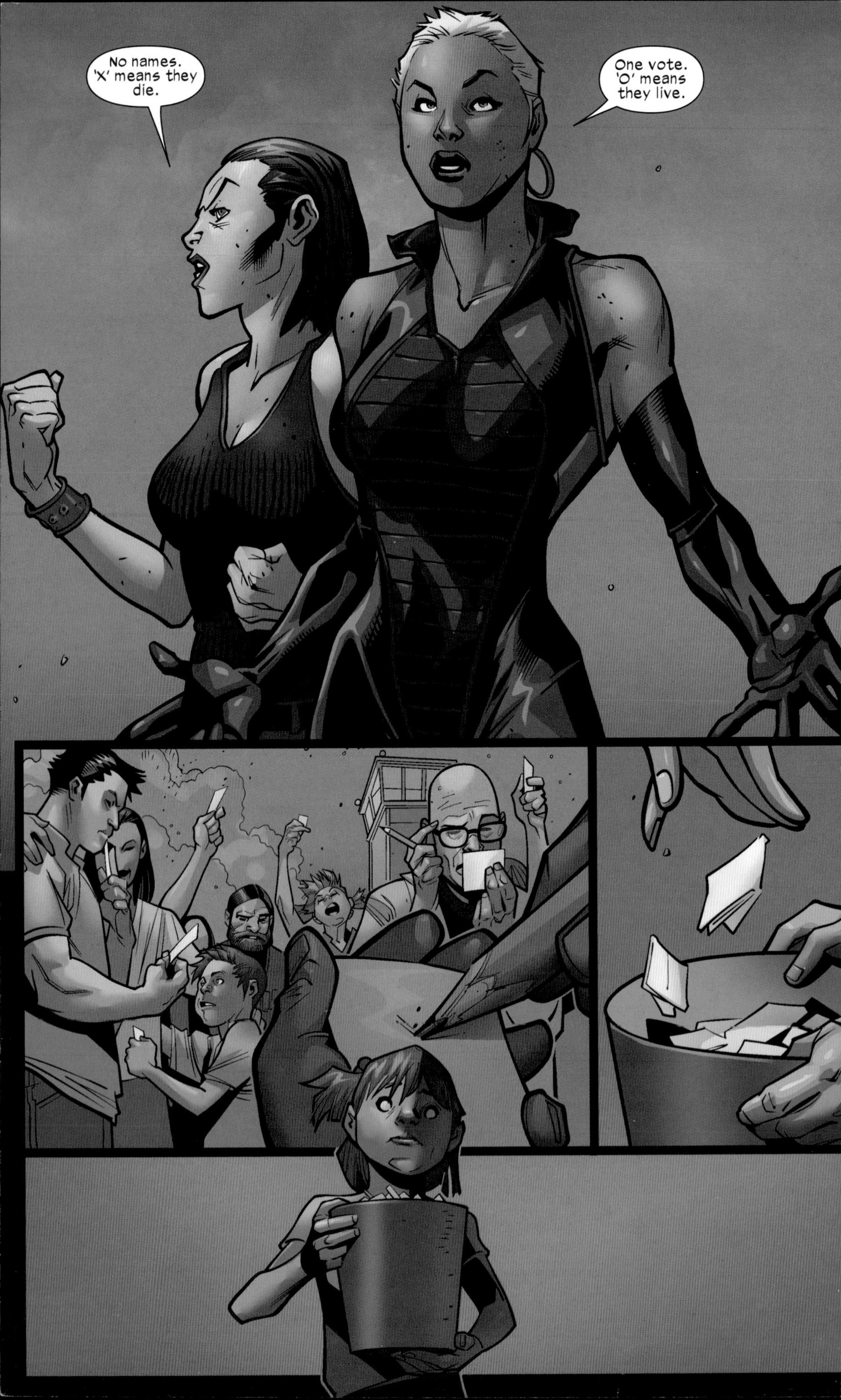
No names. 'X' means they die.
One vote. 'O' means they live.

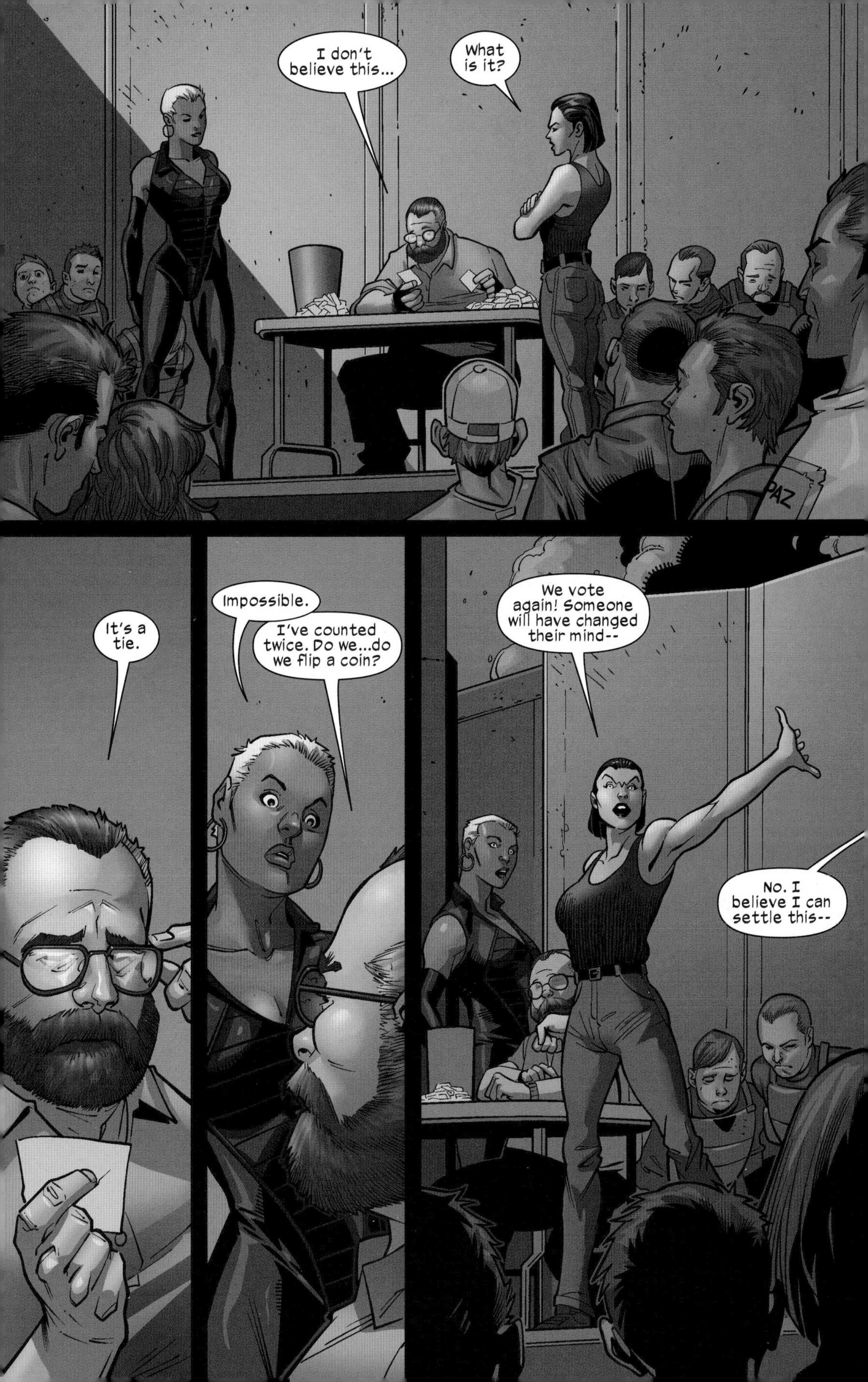
I don't believe this...
What is it?
It's a tie.
Impossible.
I've counted twice. Do we...do we flip a coin?
We vote again! Someone will have changed their mind--
No. I believe I can settle this--
PAZ

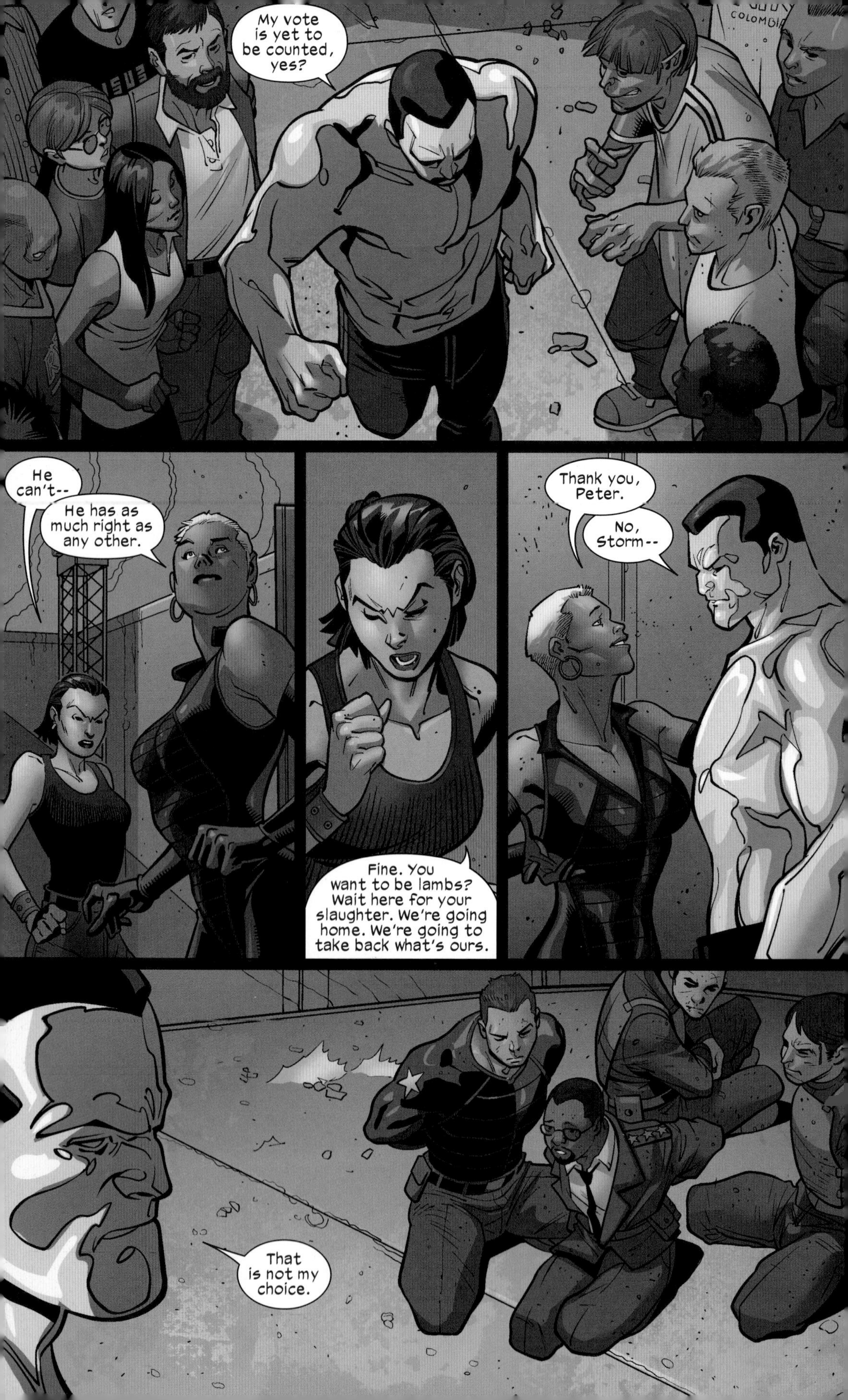
My vote is yet to be counted, yes?
He can't--
He has as much right as any other.
Fine. You want to be lambs? Wait here for your slaughter. We're going home. We're going to take back what's ours.
Thank you, Peter.
No, Storm--
That is not my choice.

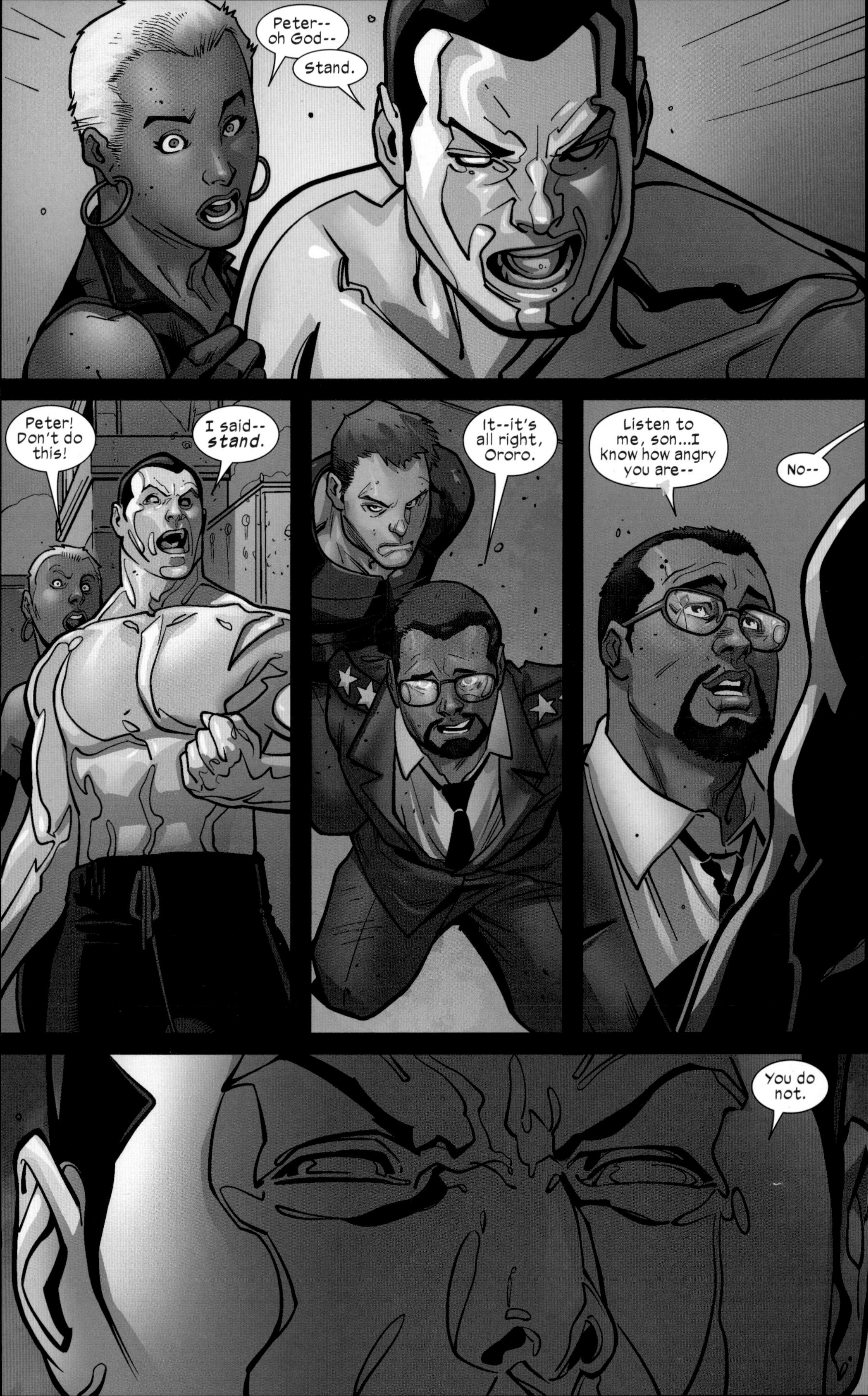
Peter-- oh God--
Stand.
Peter! Don't do this!
I said-- *stand*.
It--it's all right, Ororo.
Listen to me, son...I know how angry you are--
No--
You do not.

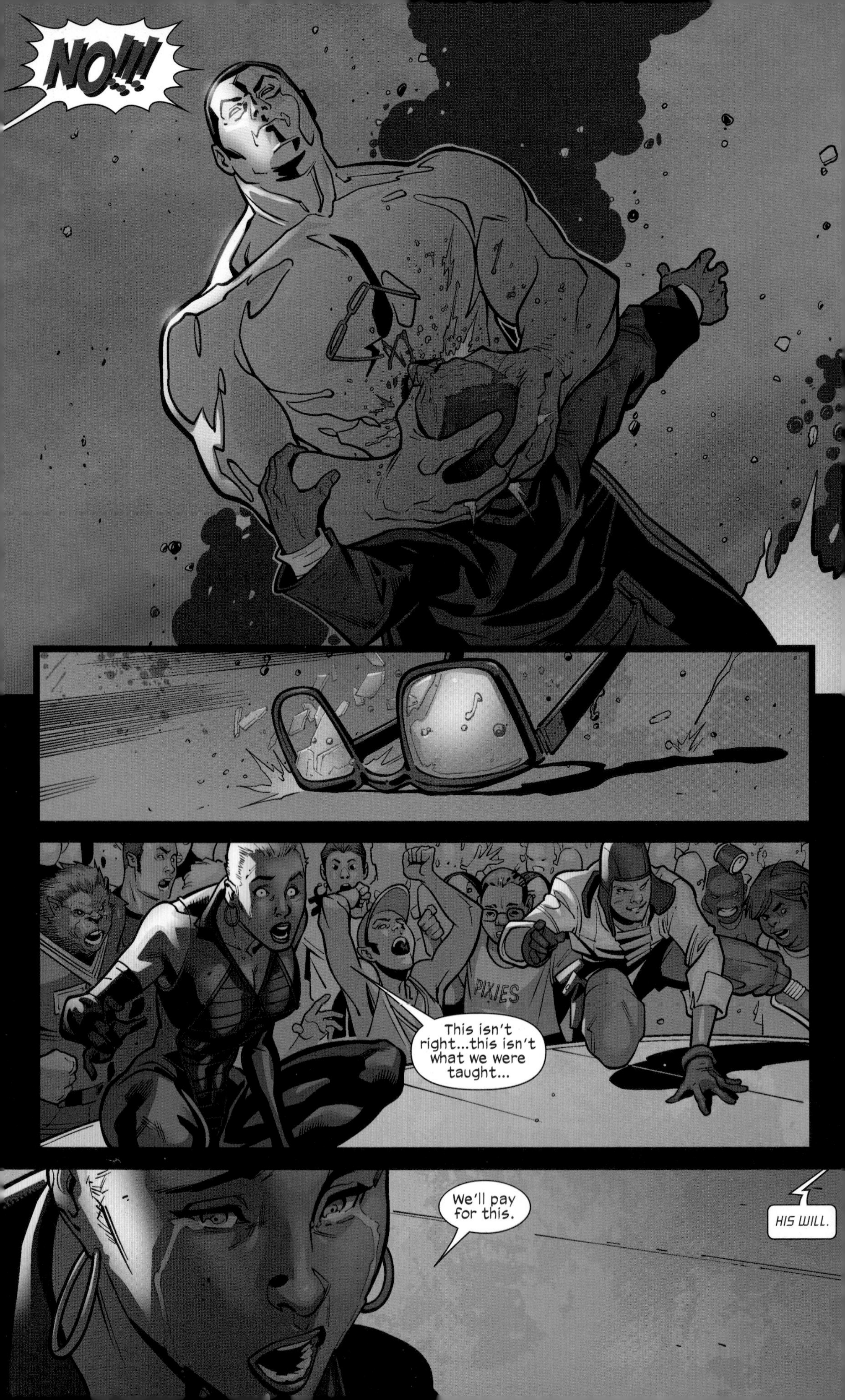
NO!!!
PIXIES
This isn't right...this isn't what we were taught...
We'll pay for this.
HIS WILL.

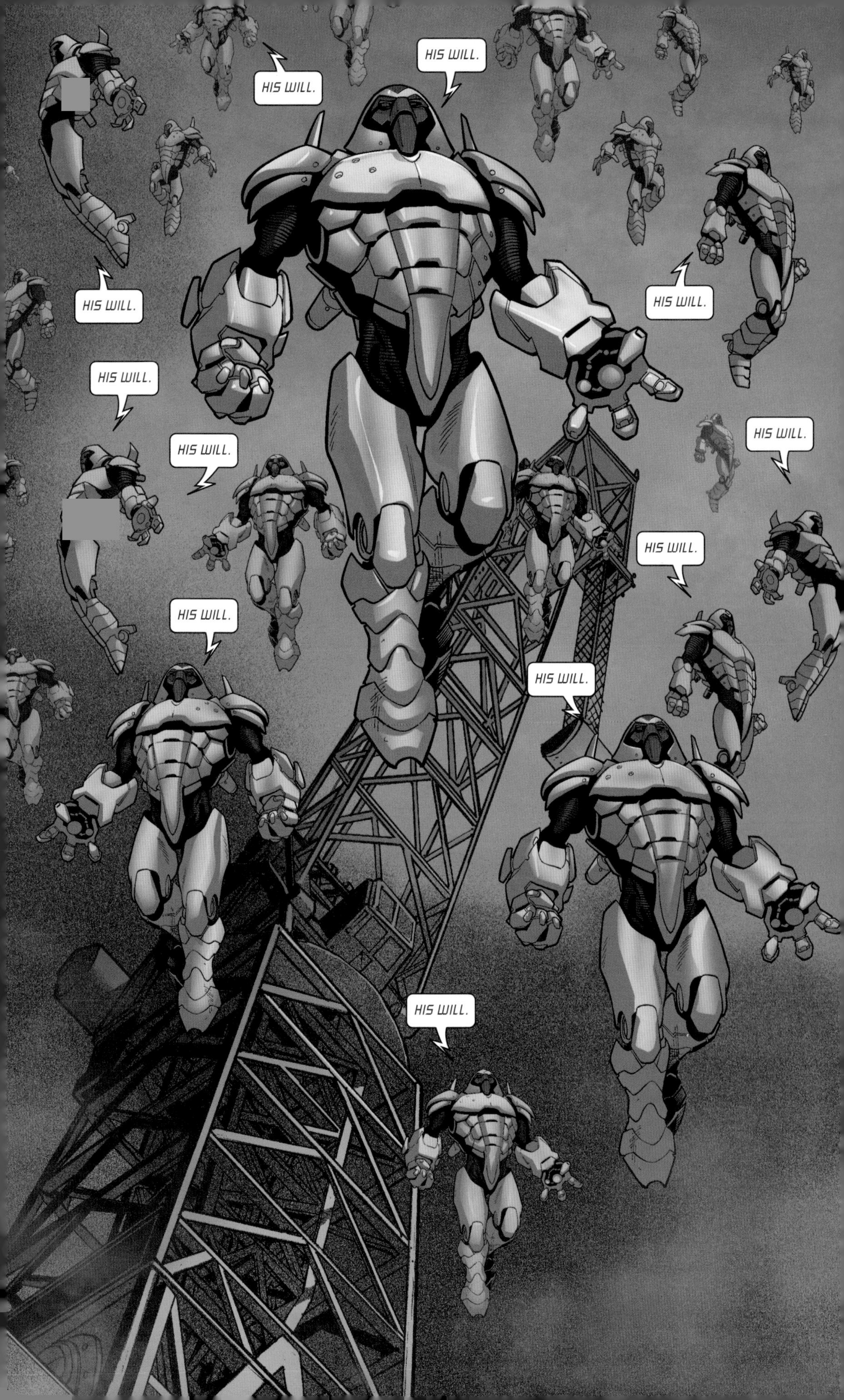
HIS WILL.
HIS WILL.
HIS WILL.
HIS WILL.
HIS WILL.
HIS WILL.
HIS WILL.
HIS WILL.
HIS WILL.
HIS WILL.
HIS WILL.

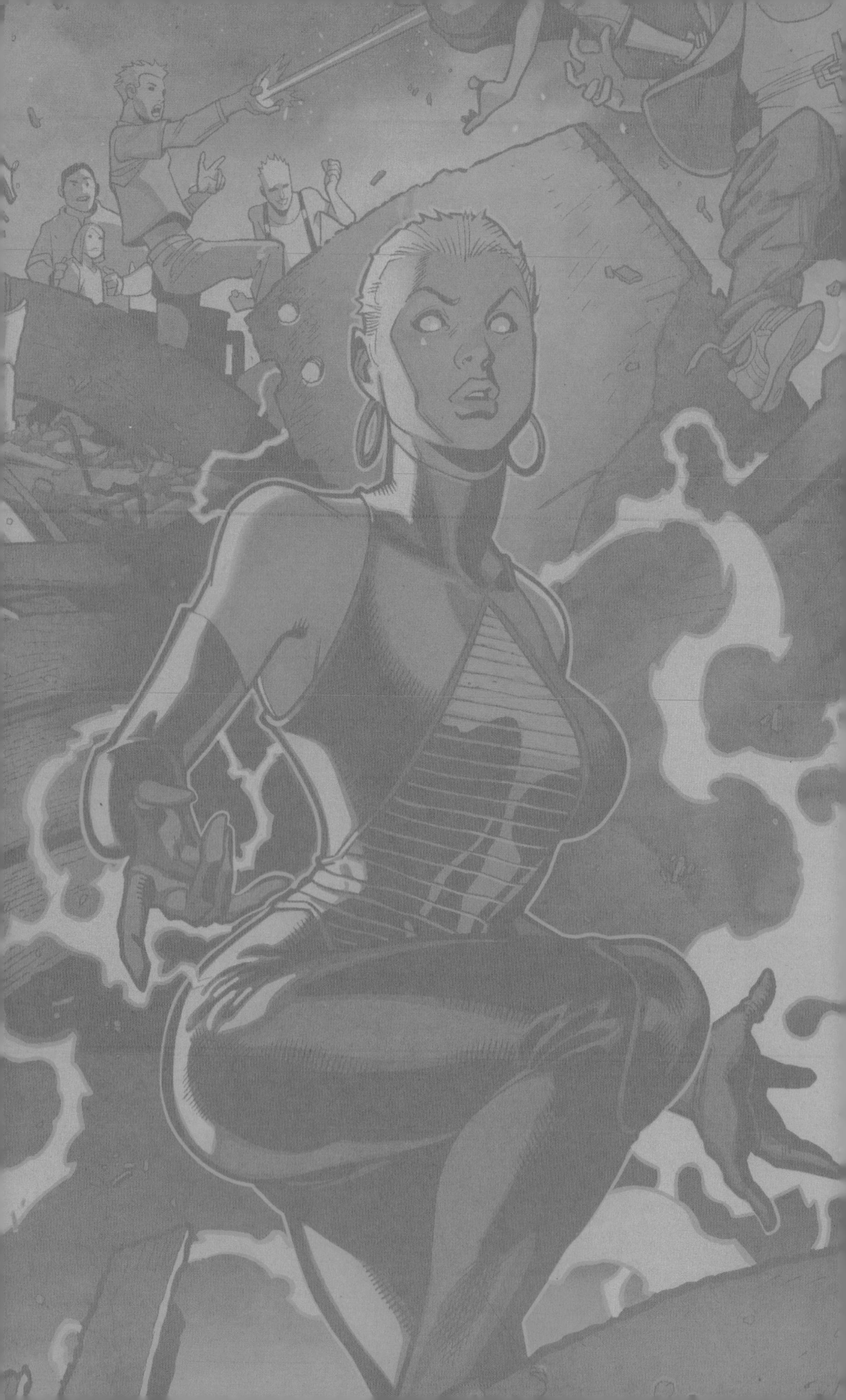

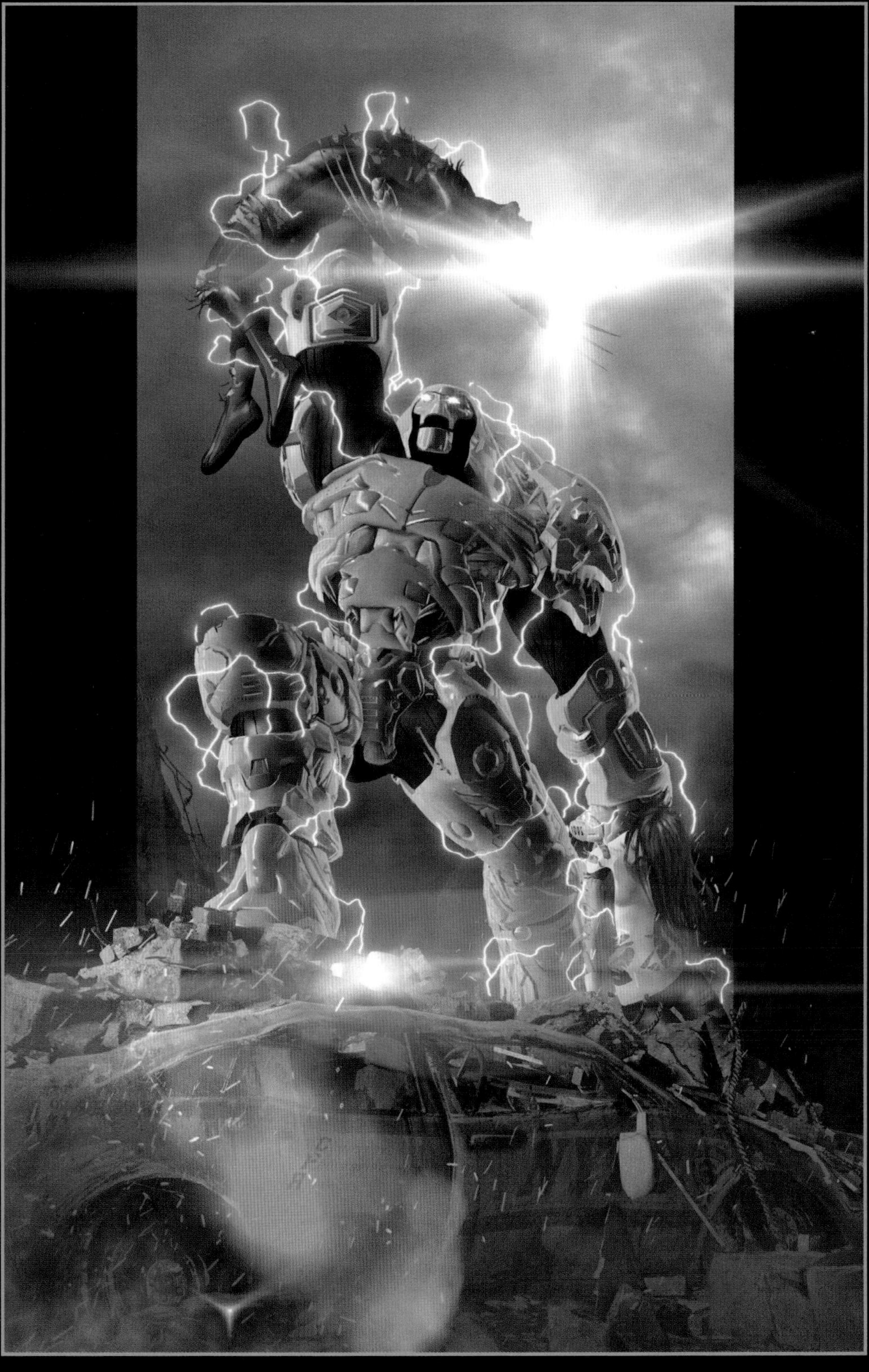

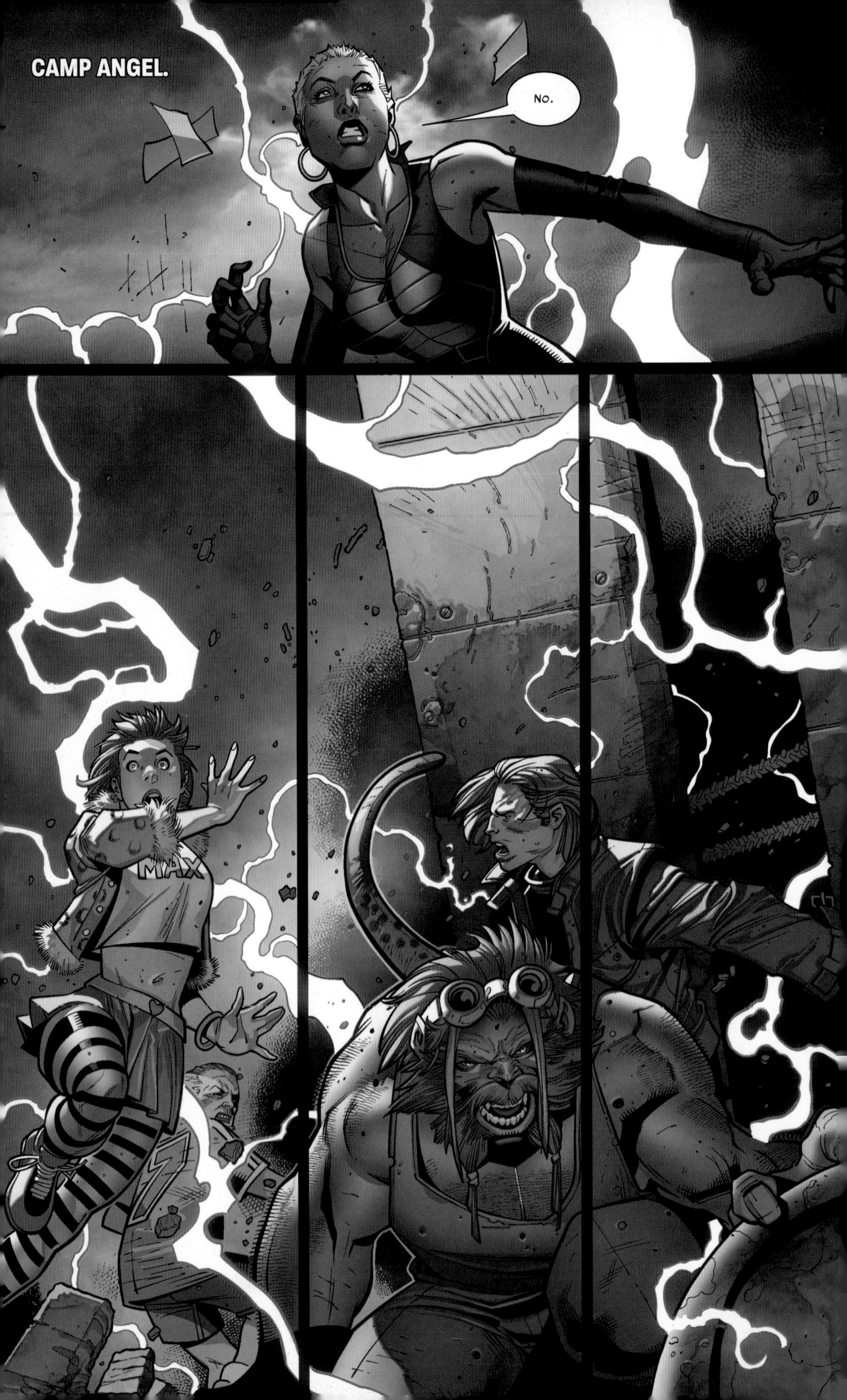
CAMP ANGEL.
NO.
MAX

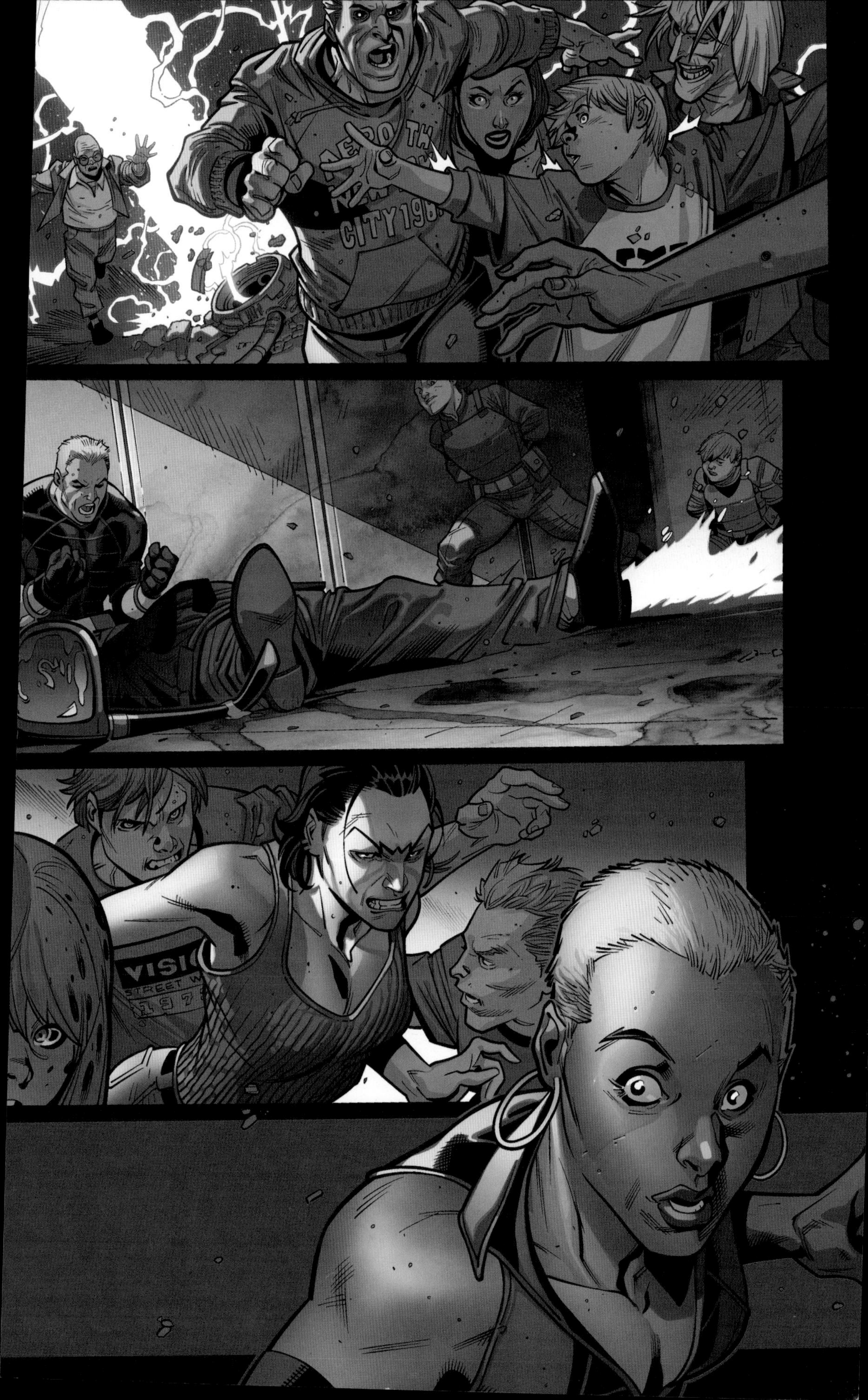
CITY 198

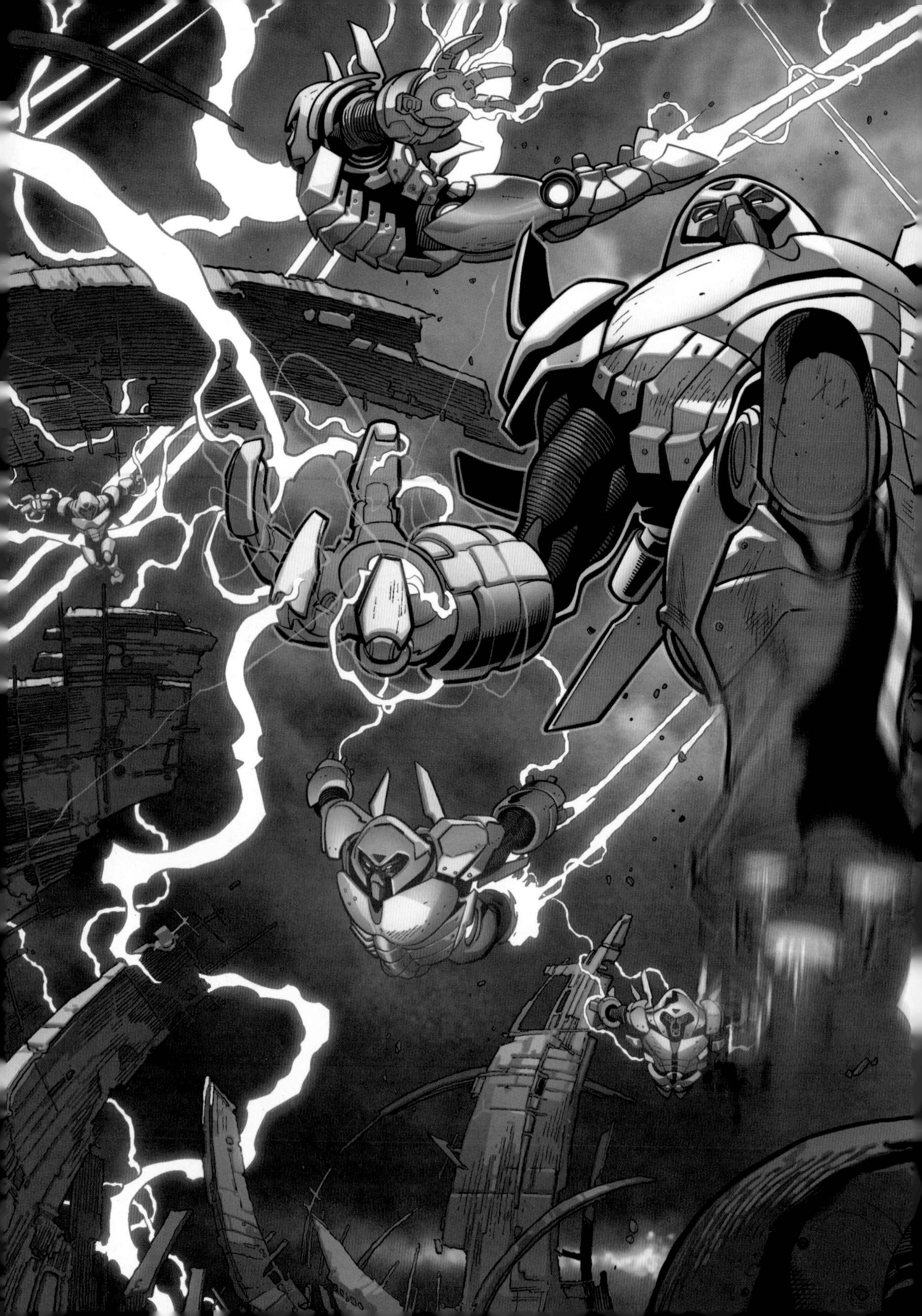

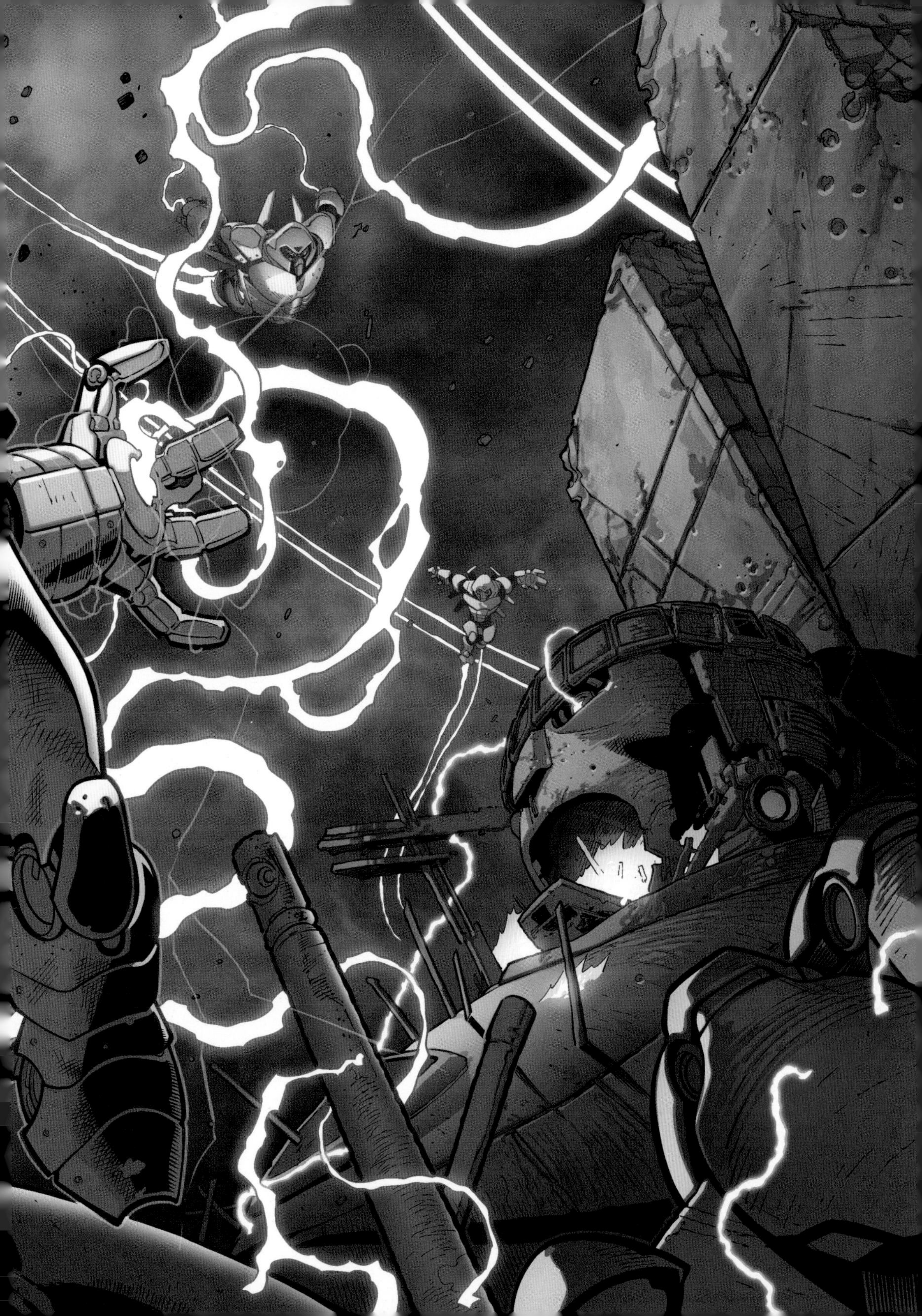

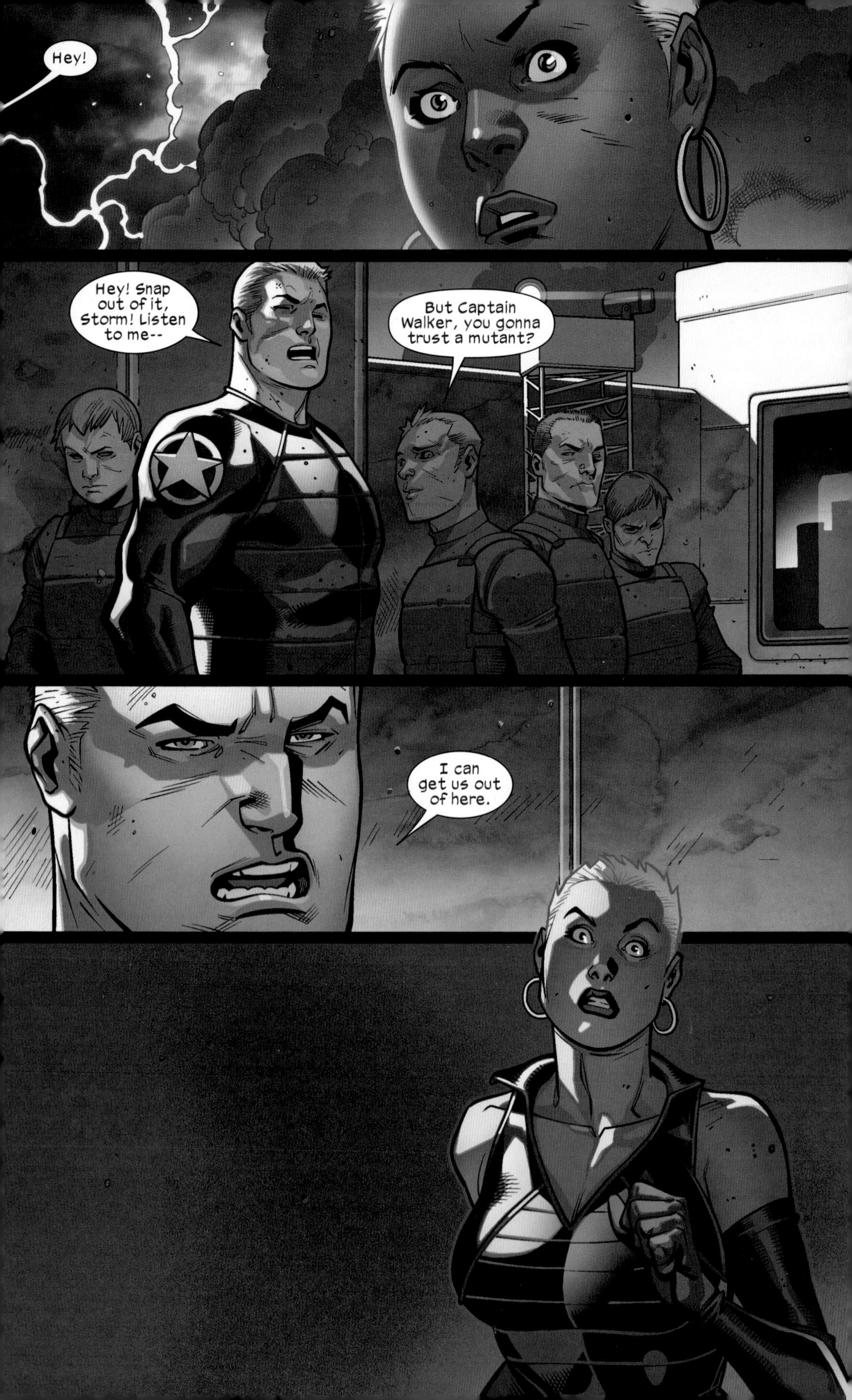
Hey!
Hey! Snap out of it, Storm! Listen to me--
But Captain Walker, you gonna trust a mutant?
I can get us out of here.

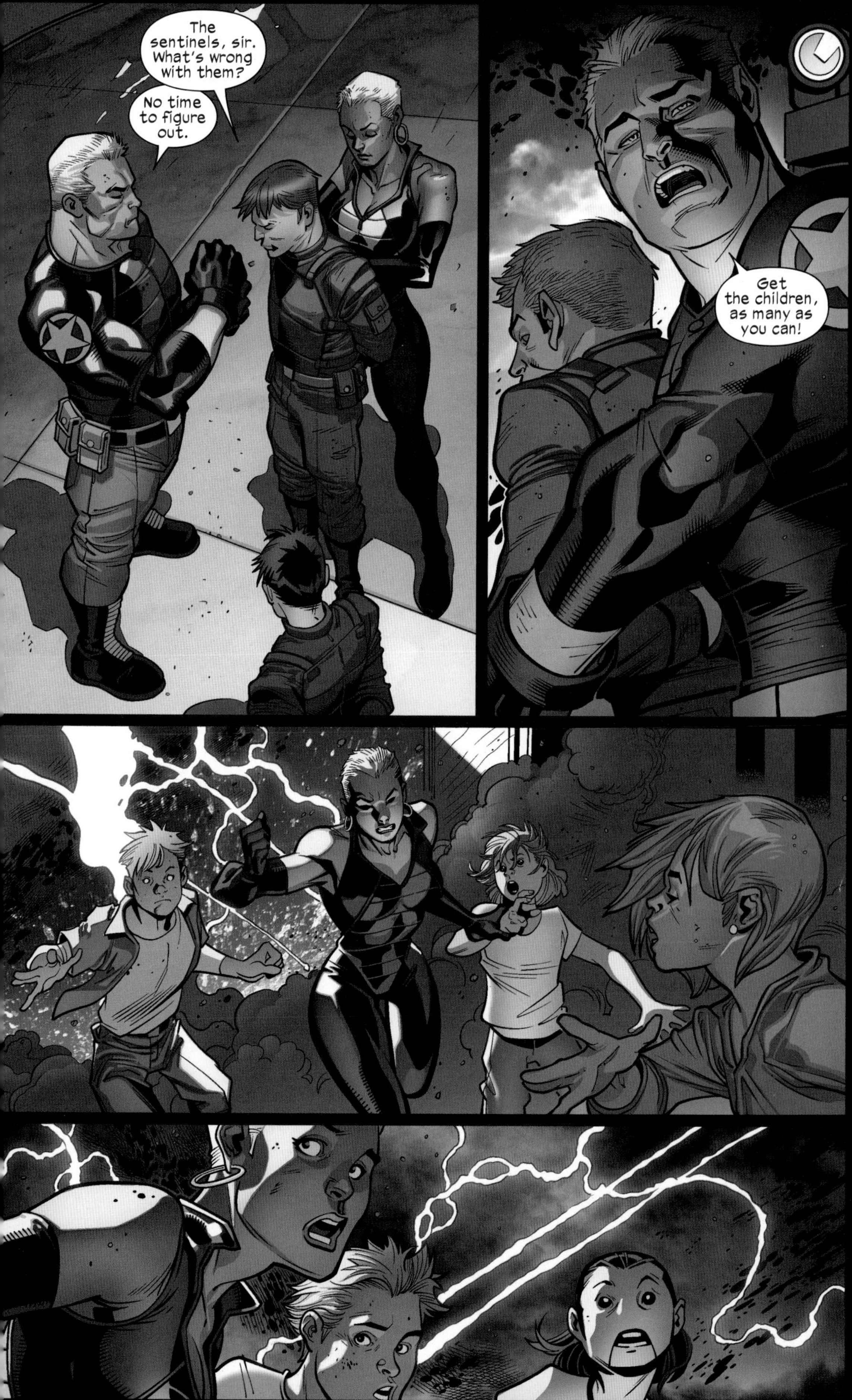
The sentinels, sir. What's wrong with them?
No time to figure out.
Get the children, as many as you can!

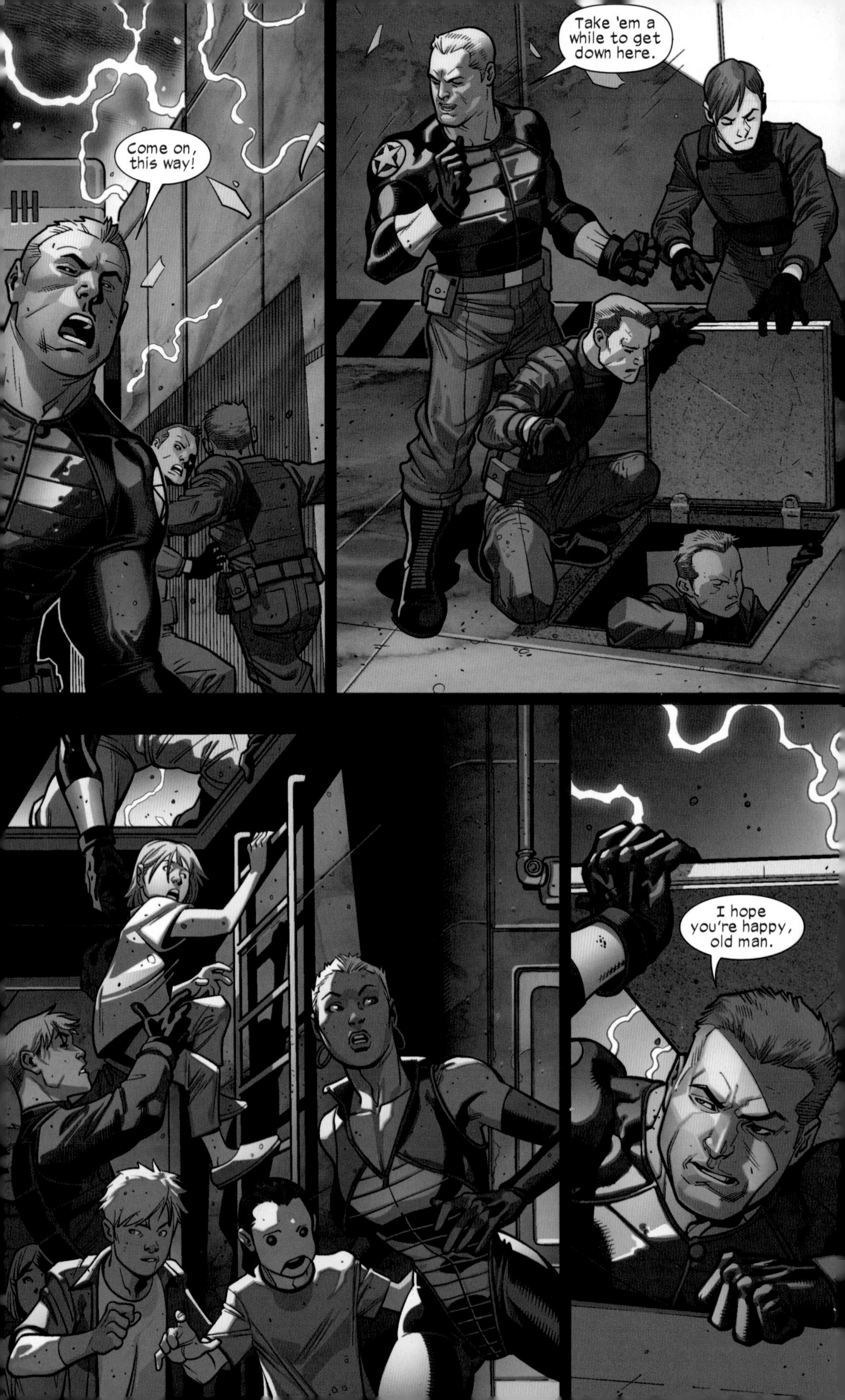
Come on, this way!
Take 'em a while to get down here.
I hope you're happy, old man.

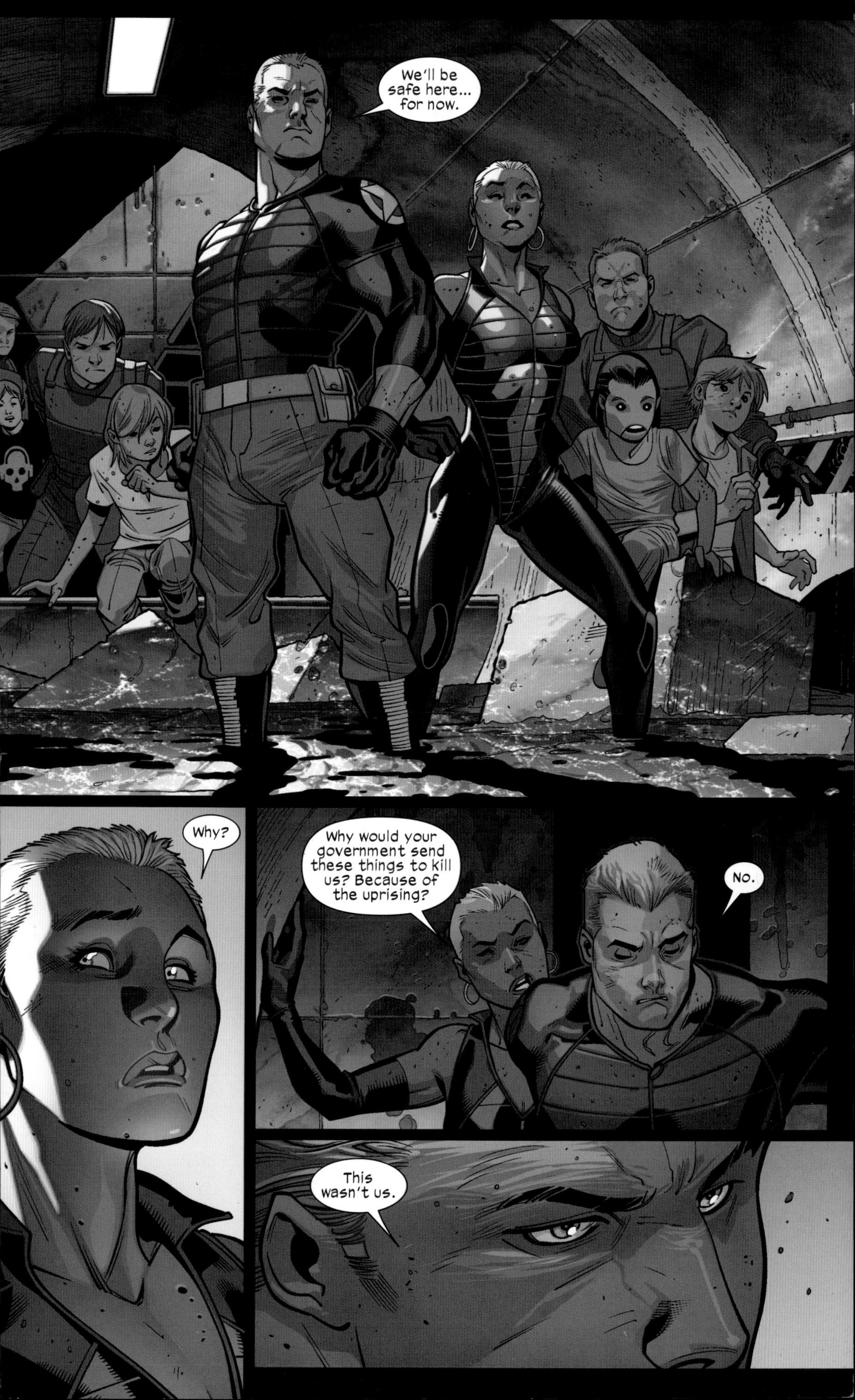

We'll be safe here... for now.
Why?
Why would your government send these things to kill us? Because of the uprising?
No.
This wasn't us.

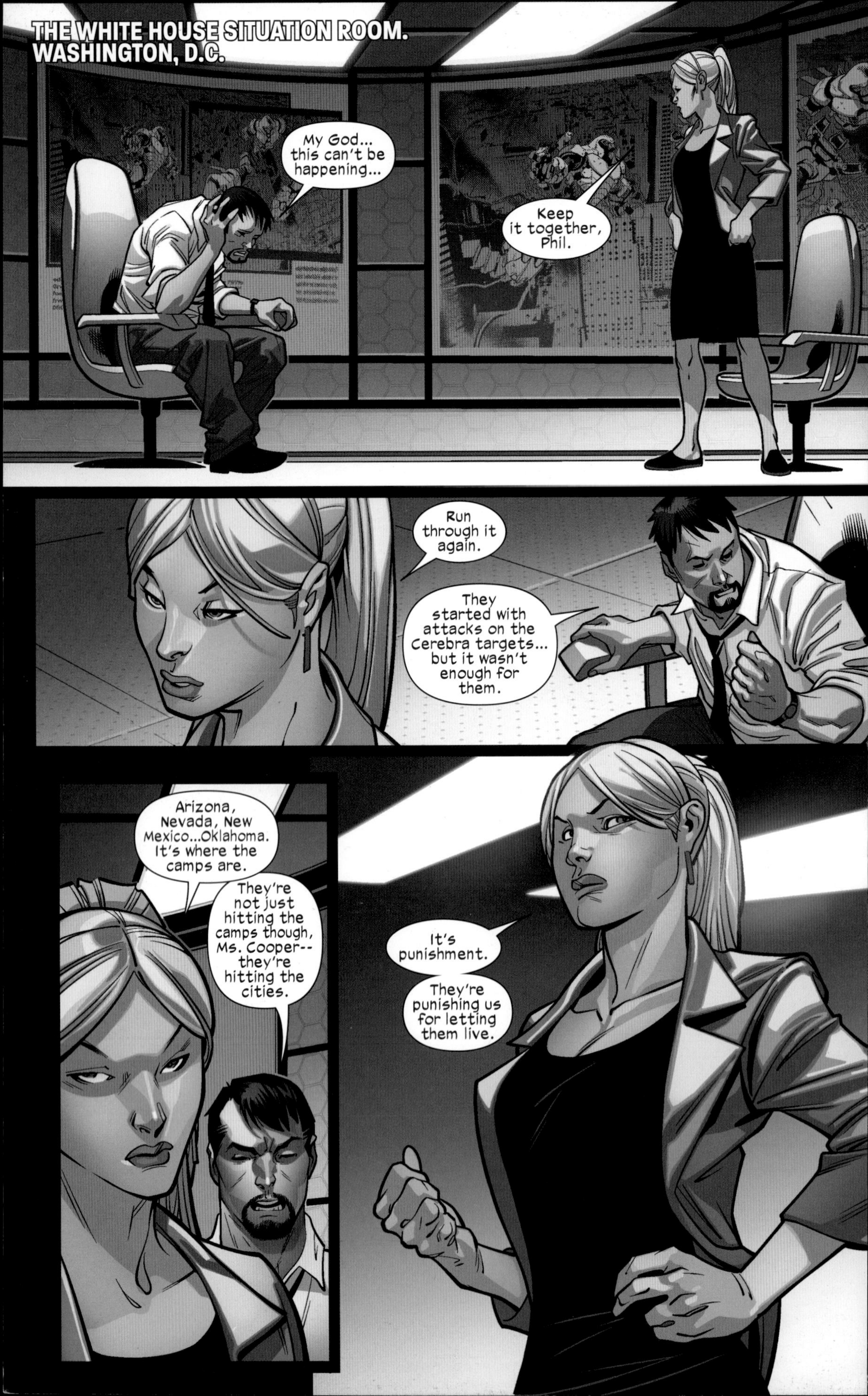
THE WHITE HOUSE SITUATION ROOM.
WASHINGTON, D.C.
My God... this can't be happening...
Keep it together, Phil.
Run through it again.
They started with attacks on the Cerebra targets... but it wasn't enough for them.
Arizona, Nevada, New Mexico...Oklahoma. It's where the camps are.
They're not just hitting the camps though, Ms. Cooper--they're hitting the cities.
It's punishment.
They're punishing us for letting them live.

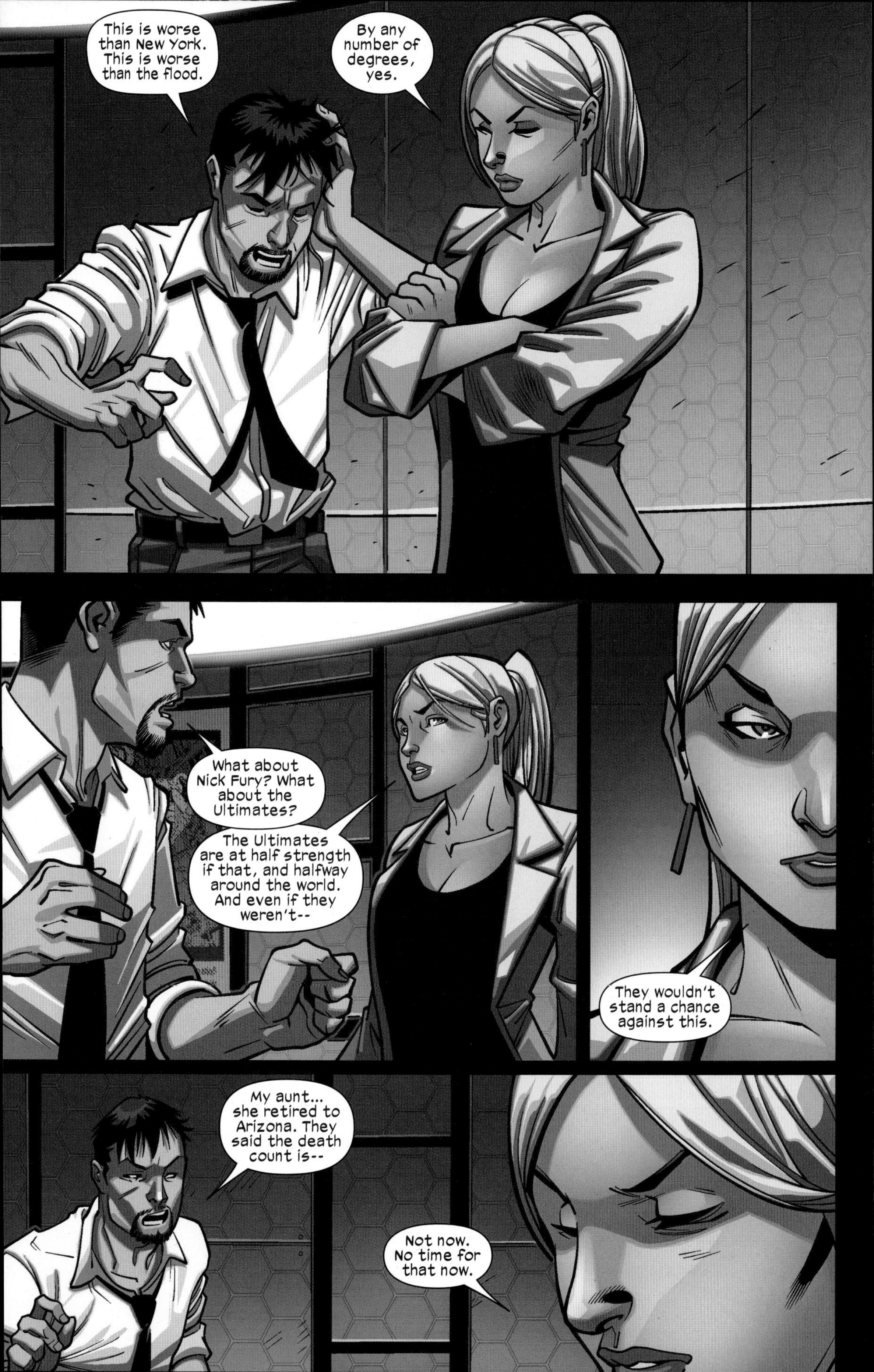
This is worse than New York. This is worse than the flood.
By any number of degrees, yes.
What about Nick Fury? What about the Ultimates?
The Ultimates are at half strength if that, and halfway around the world. And even if they weren't--
They wouldn't stand a chance against this.
My aunt... she retired to Arizona. They said the death count is--
Not now. No time for that now.

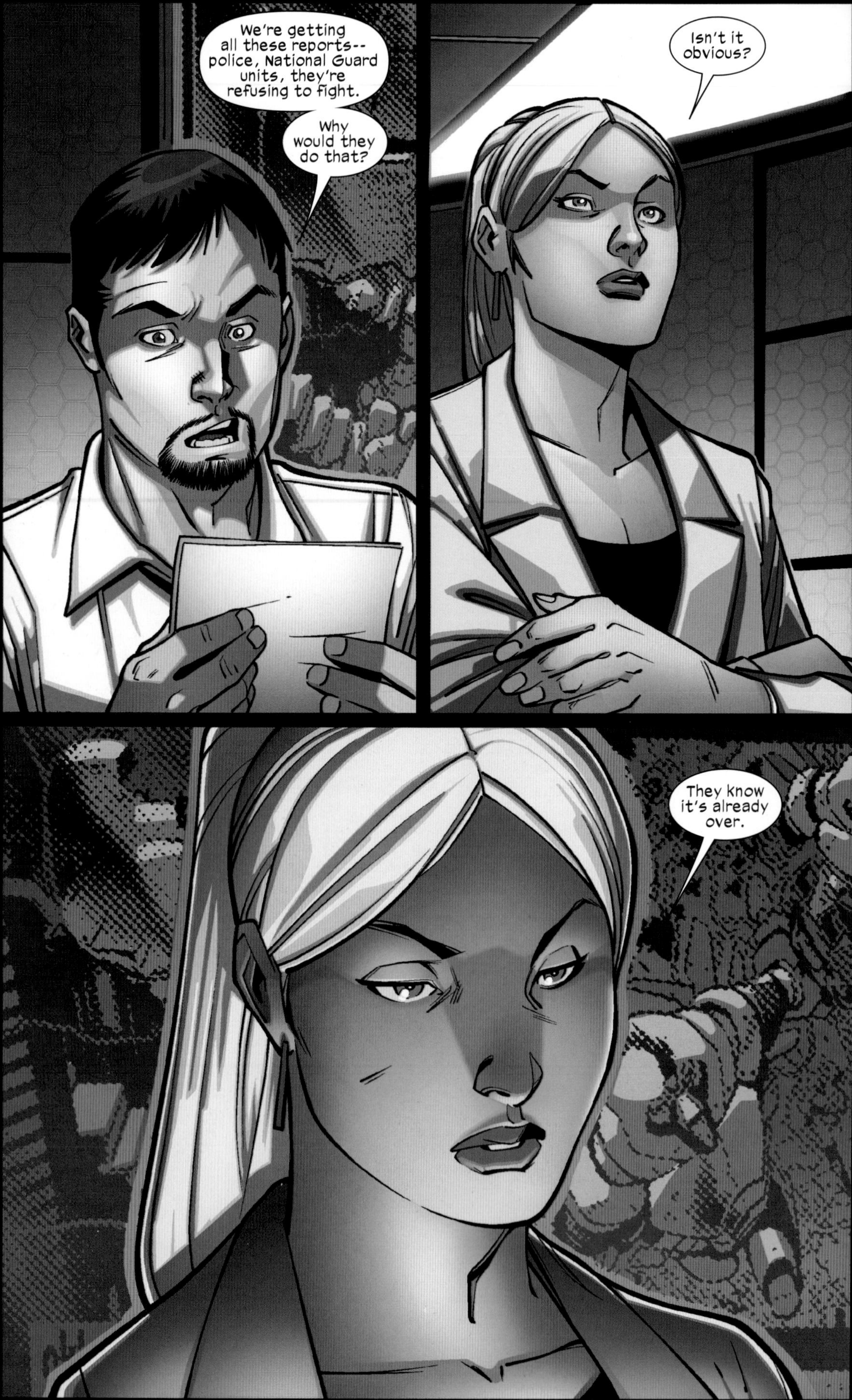
We're getting all these reports-- police, National Guard units, they're refusing to fight.
Why would they do that?
Isn't it obvious?
They know it's already over.

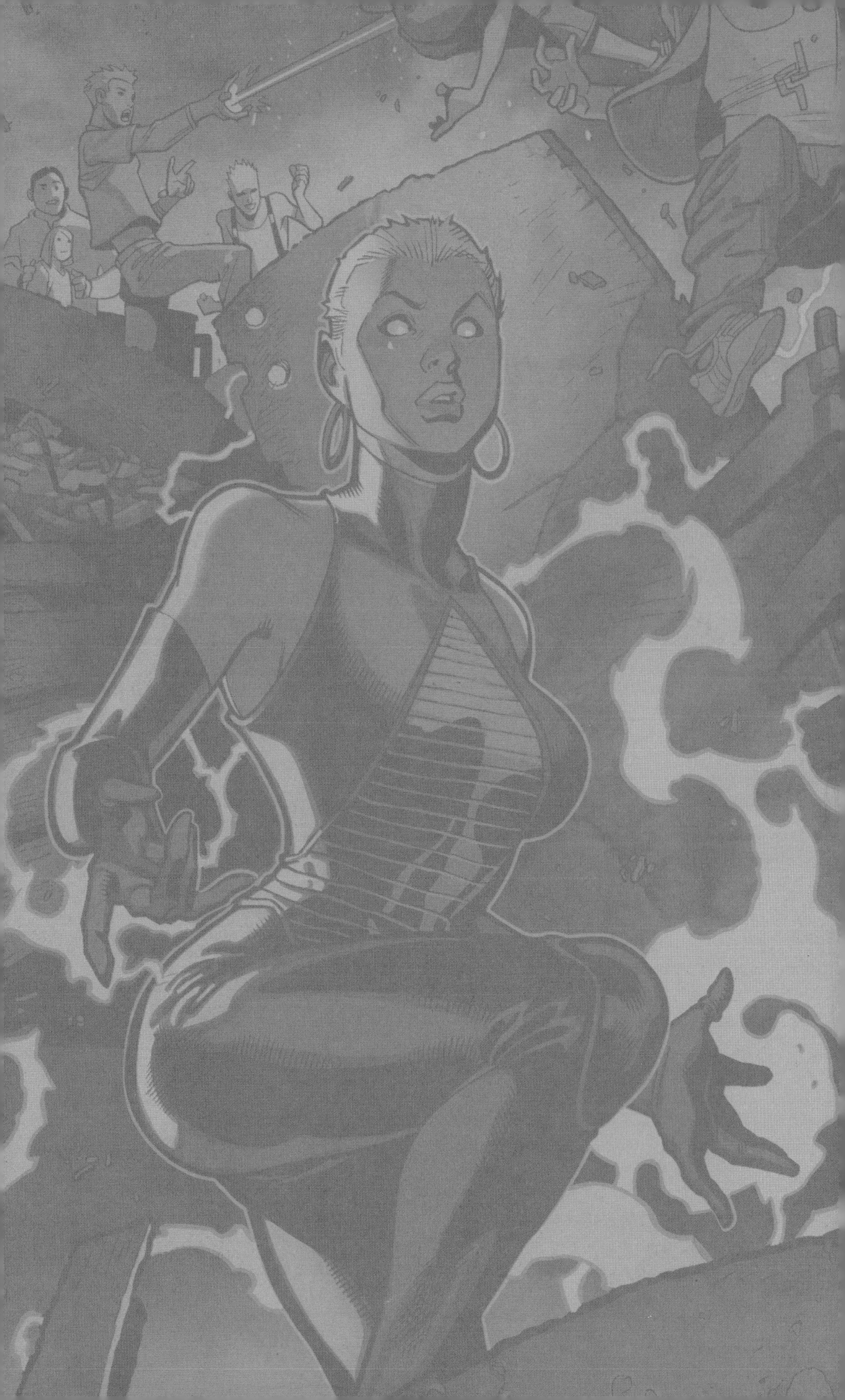

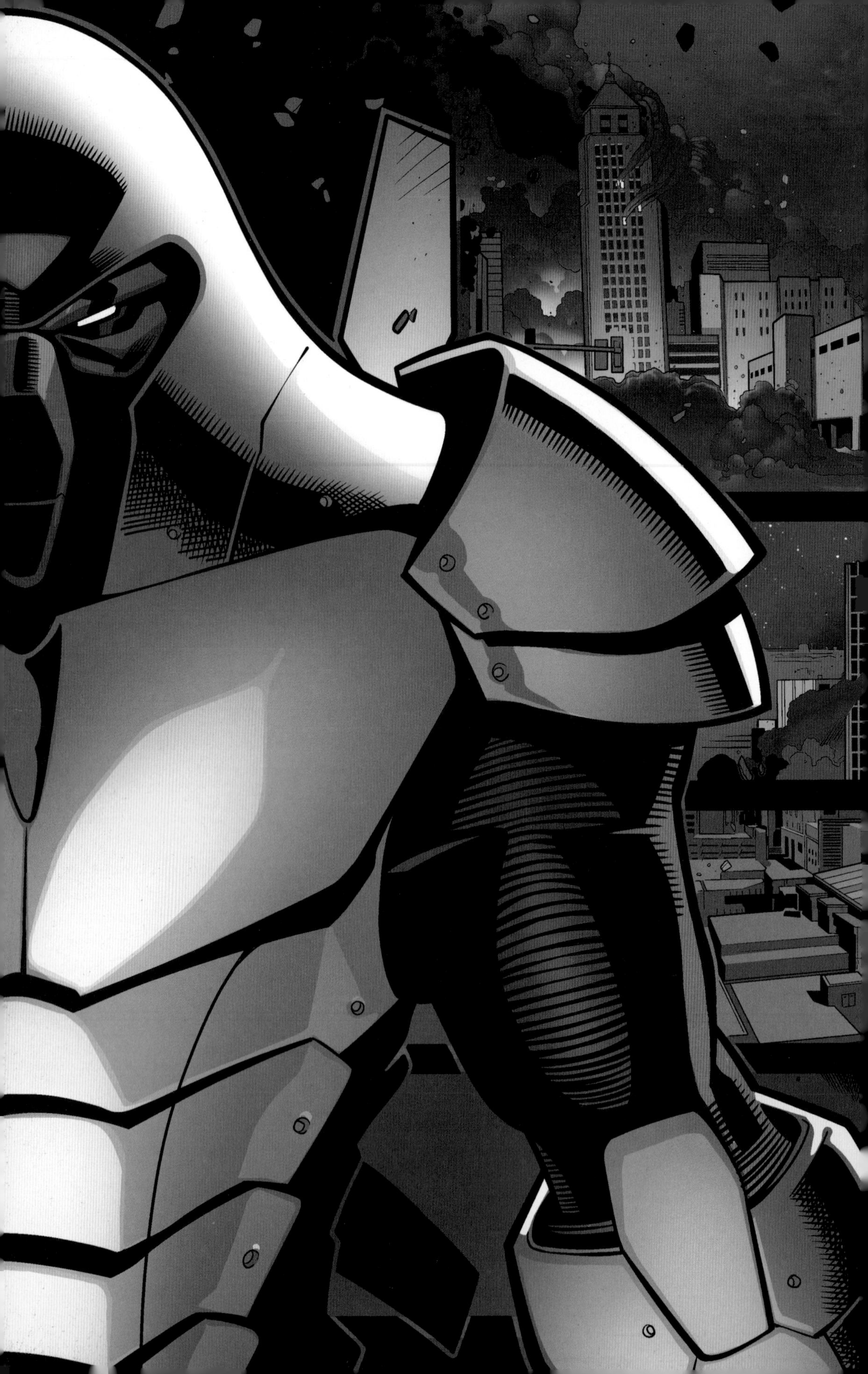

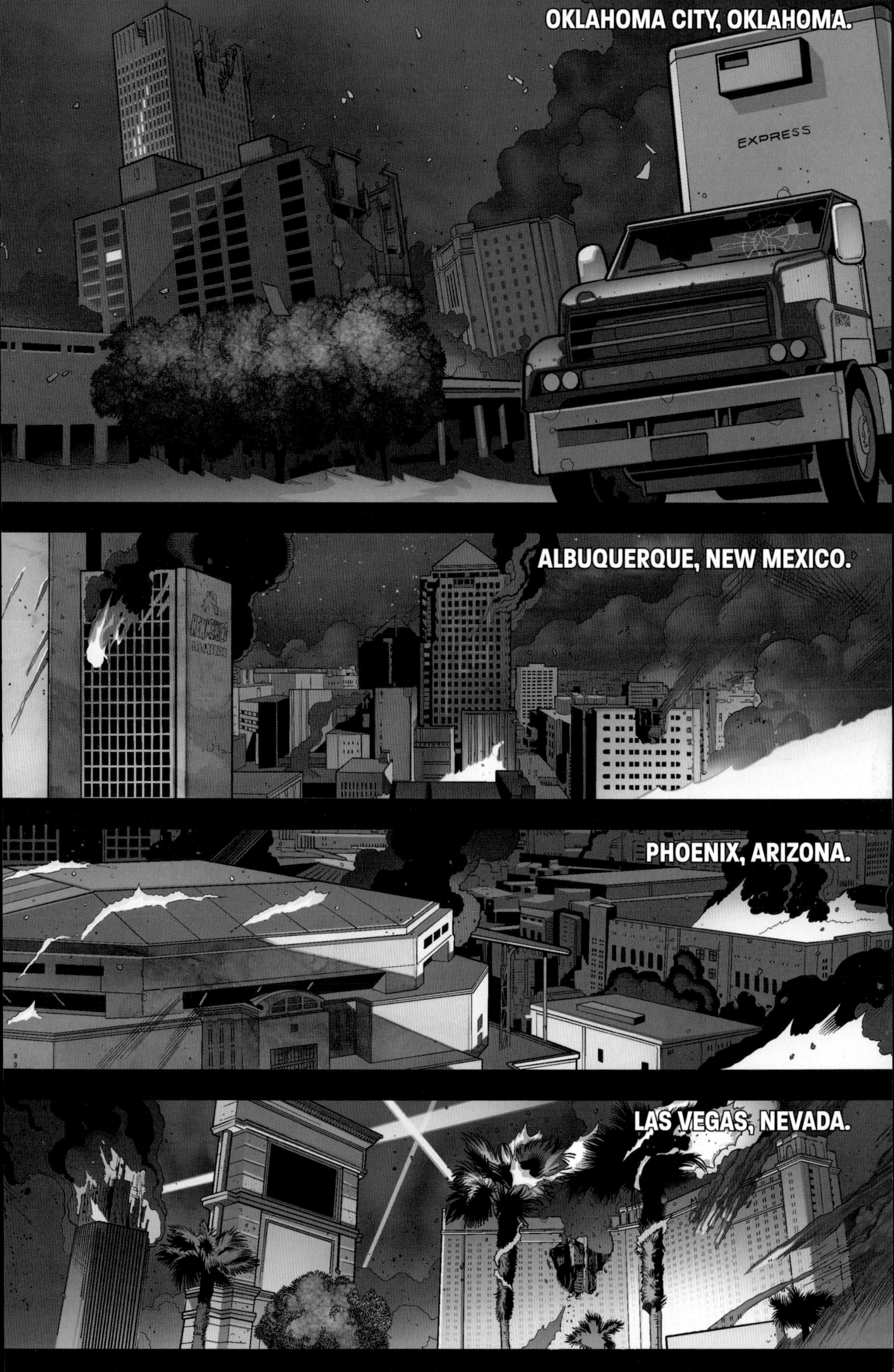
OKLAHOMA CITY, OKLAHOMA.
EXPRESS
ALBUQUERQUE, NEW MEXICO.
PHOENIX, ARIZONA.
LAS VEGAS, NEVADA.

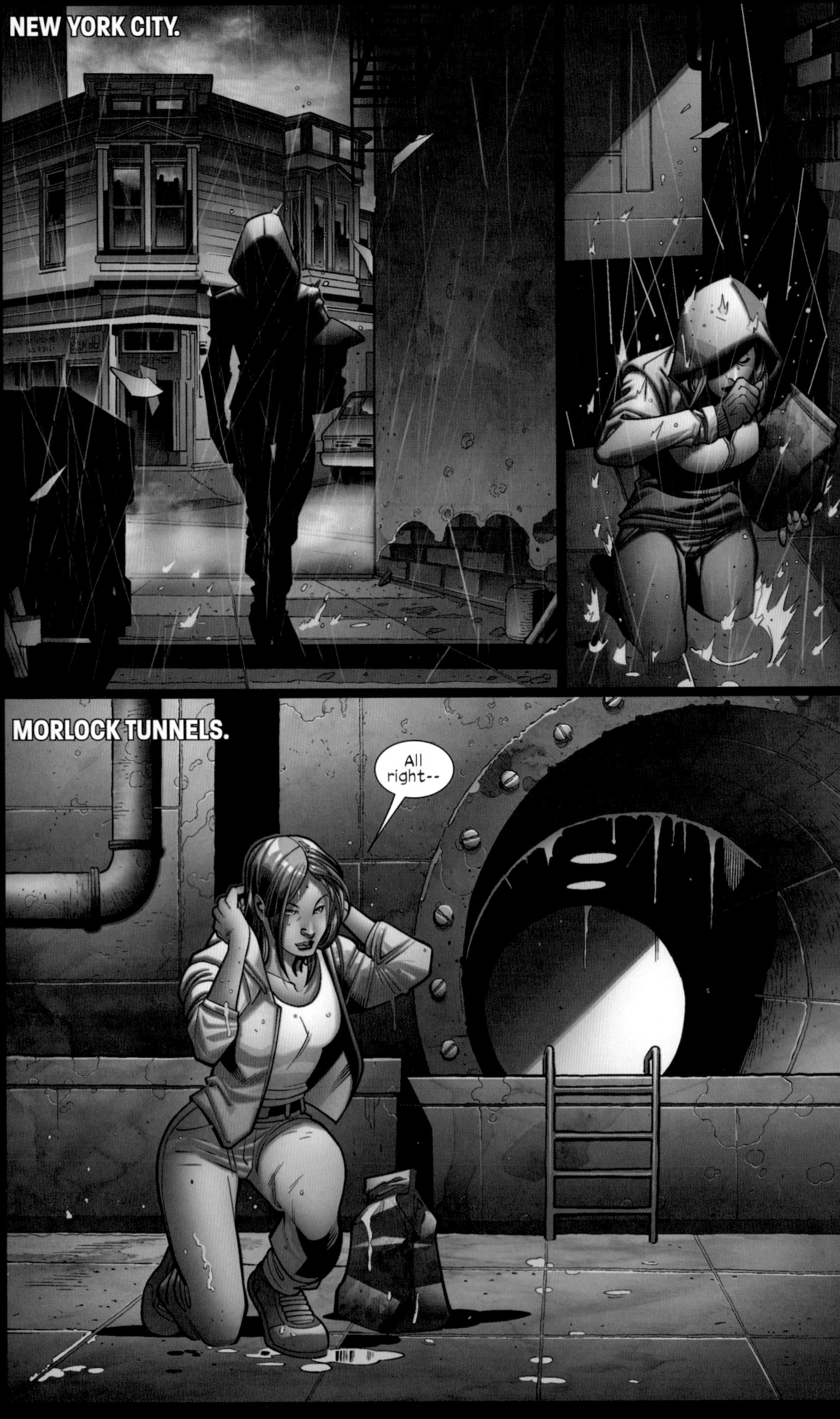
NEW YORK CITY.
MORLOCK TUNNELS.
All right--

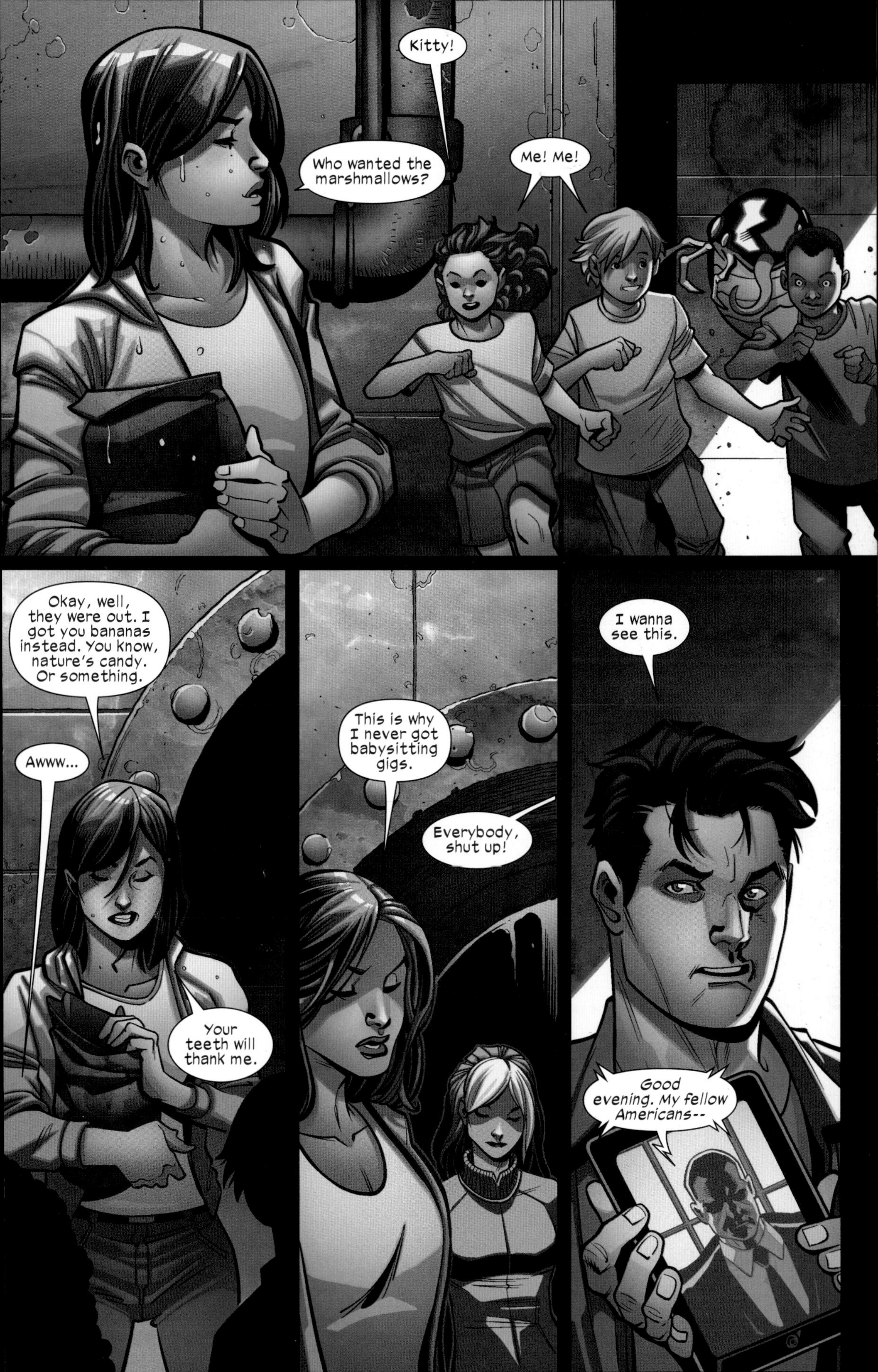
Kitty!
Who wanted the marshmallows?
Me! Me!
Okay, well, they were out. I got you bananas instead. You know, nature's candy. Or something.
Awww...
Your teeth will thank me.
This is why I never got babysitting gigs.
Everybody, shut up!
I wanna see this.
Good evening. My fellow Americans--

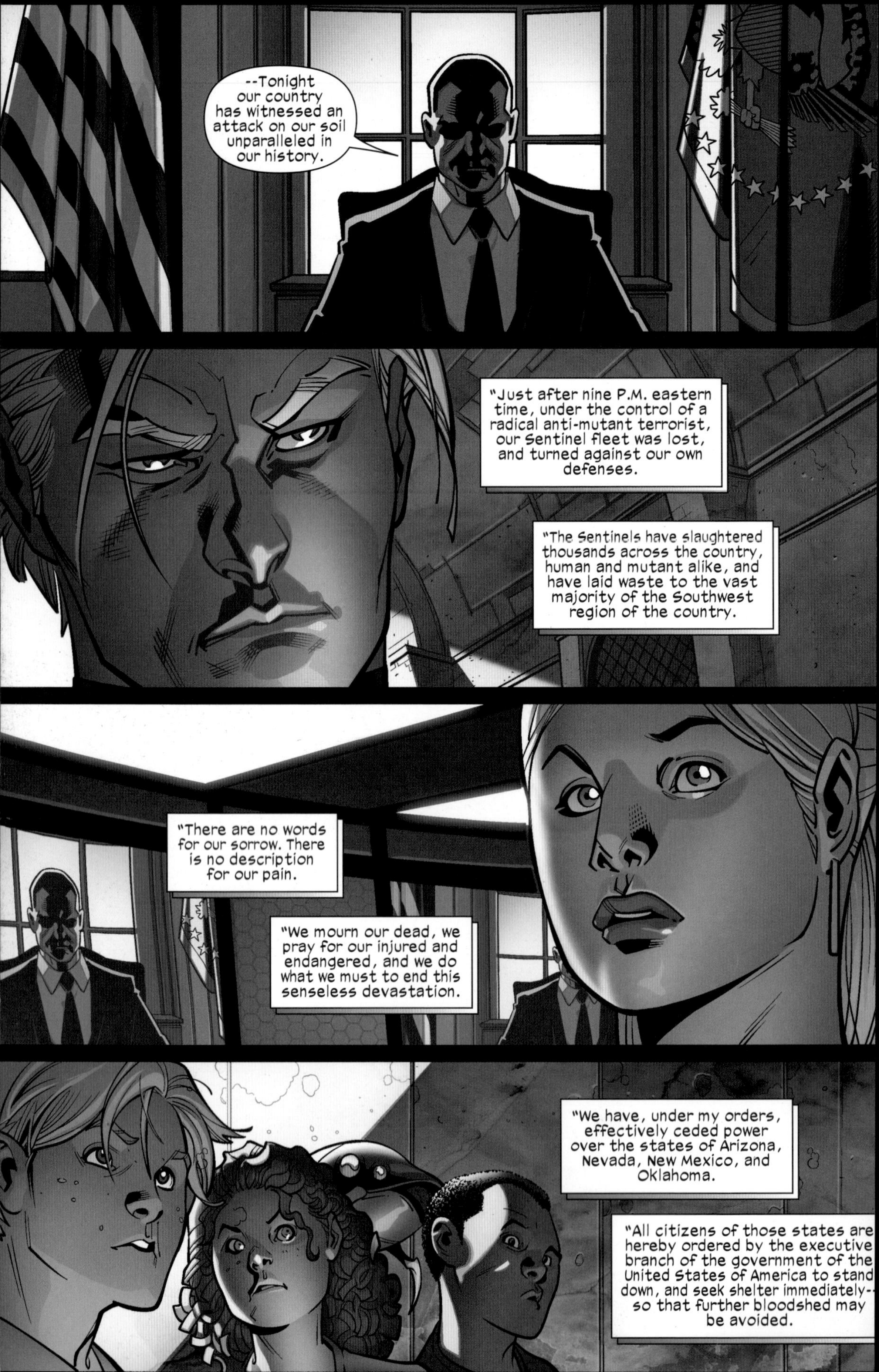

--Tonight our country has witnessed an attack on our soil unparalleled in our history.
"Just after nine P.M. eastern time, under the control of a radical anti-mutant terrorist, our Sentinel fleet was lost, and turned against our own defenses.
"The Sentinels have slaughtered thousands across the country, human and mutant alike, and have laid waste to the vast majority of the Southwest region of the country.
"There are no words for our sorrow. There is no description for our pain.
"We mourn our dead, we pray for our injured and endangered, and we do what we must to end this senseless devastation.
"We have, under my orders, effectively ceded power over the states of Arizona, Nevada, New Mexico, and Oklahoma.
"All citizens of those states are hereby ordered by the executive branch of the government of the United States of America to stand down, and seek shelter immediately--so that further bloodshed may be avoided.

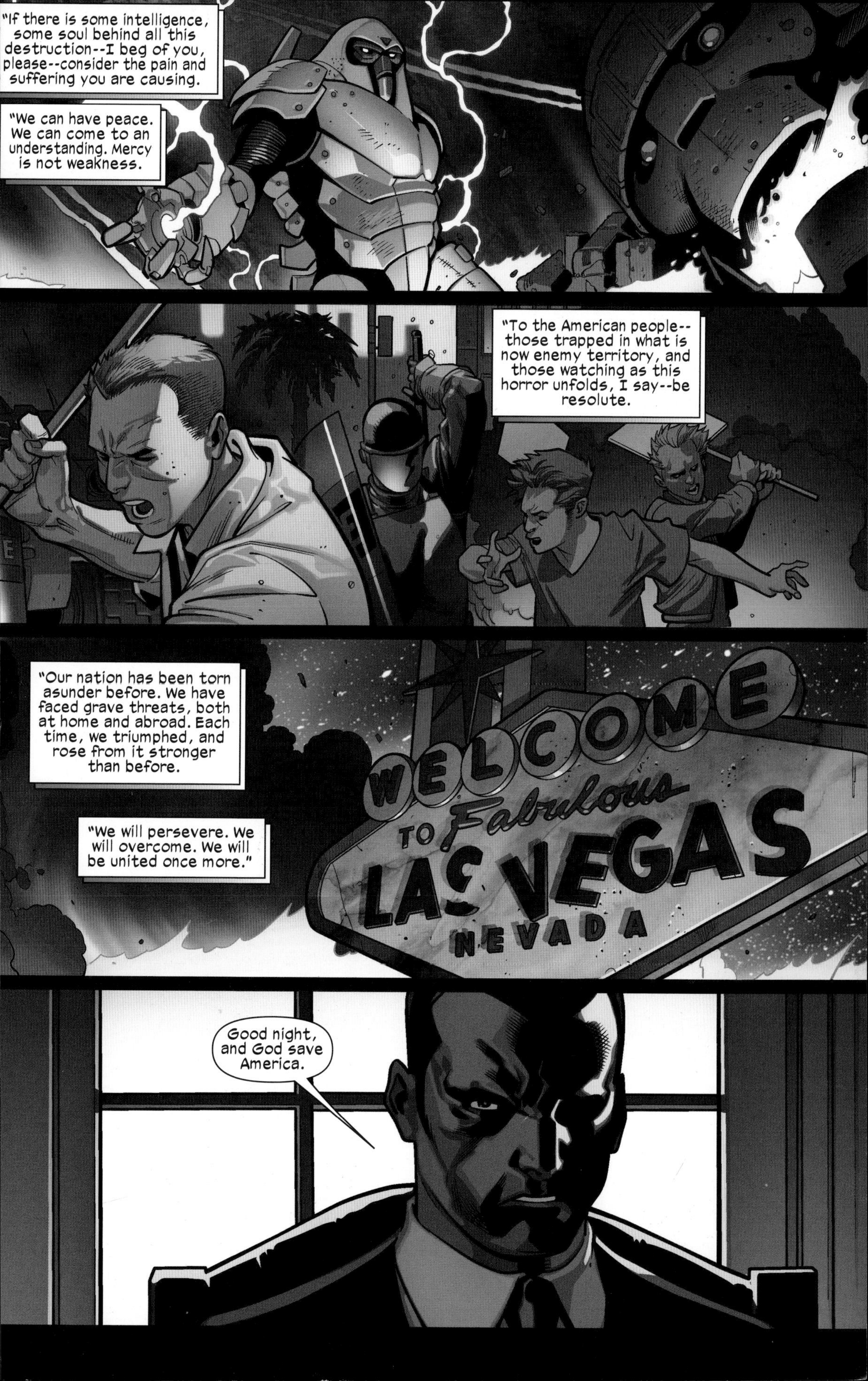
"If there is some intelligence, some soul behind all this destruction--I beg of you, please--consider the pain and suffering you are causing.
"We can have peace. We can come to an understanding. Mercy is not weakness.
"To the American people--those trapped in what is now enemy territory, and those watching as this horror unfolds, I say--be resolute.
"Our nation has been torn asunder before. We have faced grave threats, both at home and abroad. Each time, we triumphed, and rose from it stronger than before.
WELCOME TO Fabulous LAS VEGAS NEVADA
"We will persevere. We will overcome. We will be united once more."
Good night, and God save America.

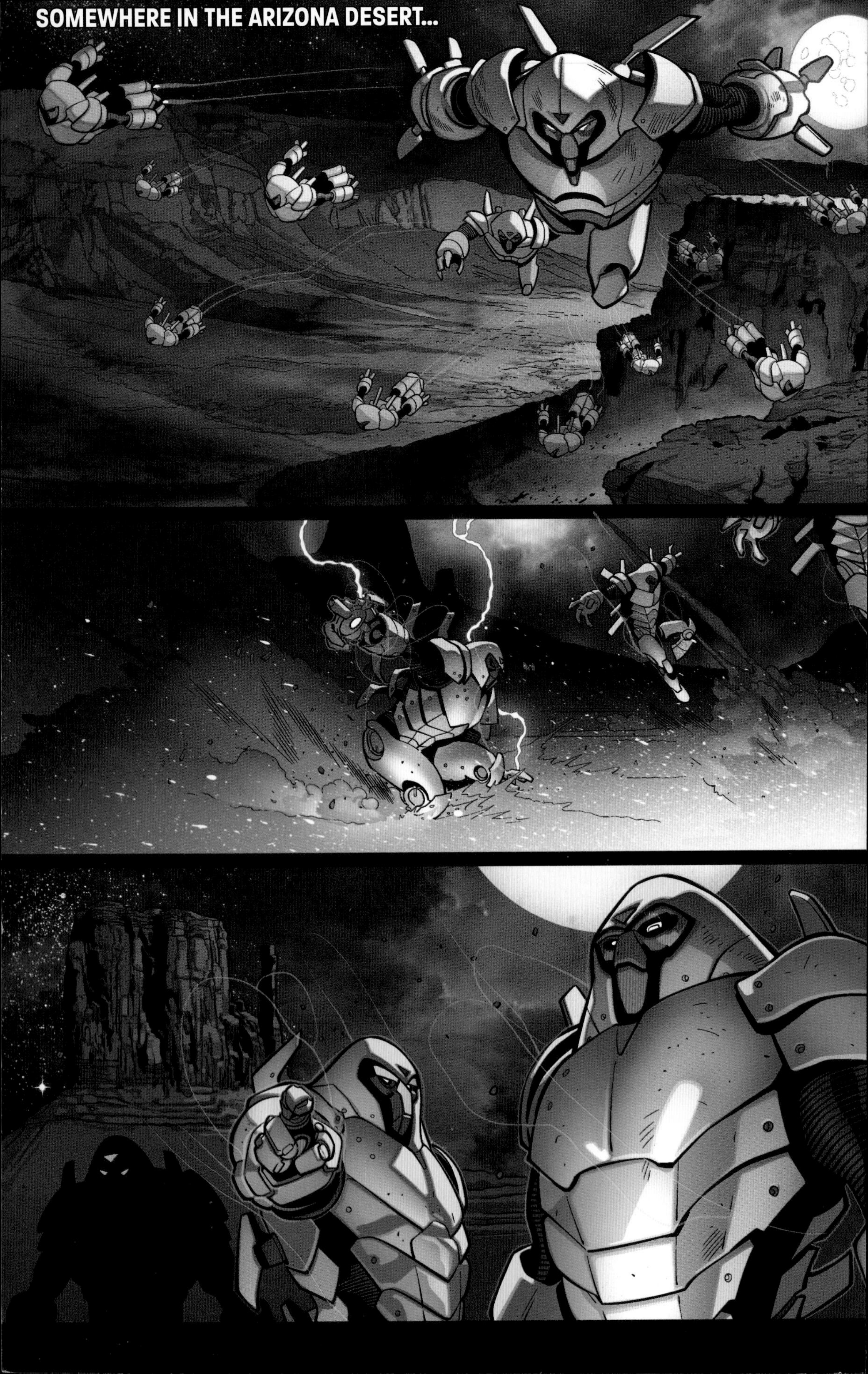
SOMEWHERE IN THE ARIZONA DESERT...

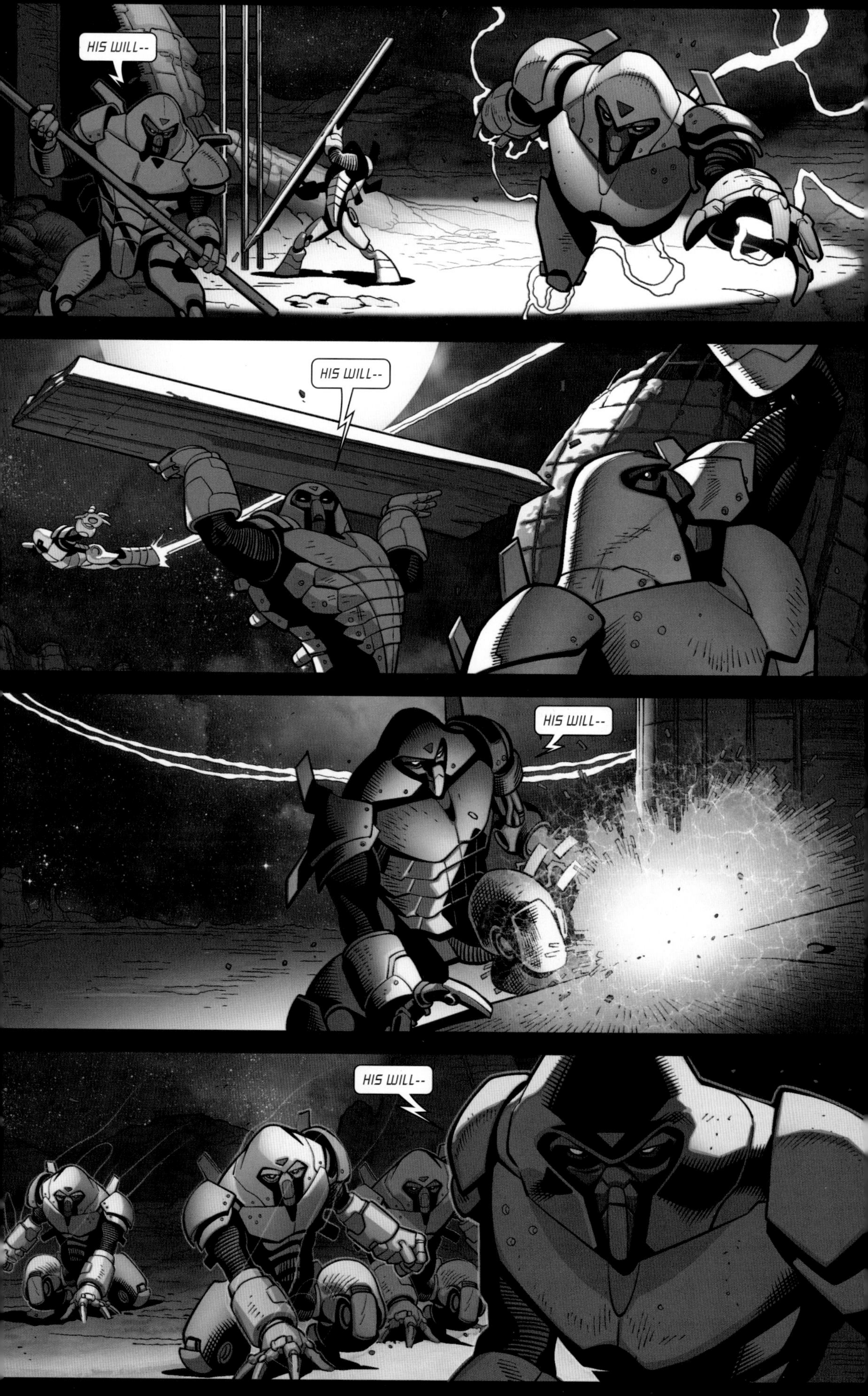
HIS WILL--
HIS WILL--
HIS WILL--
HIS WILL--

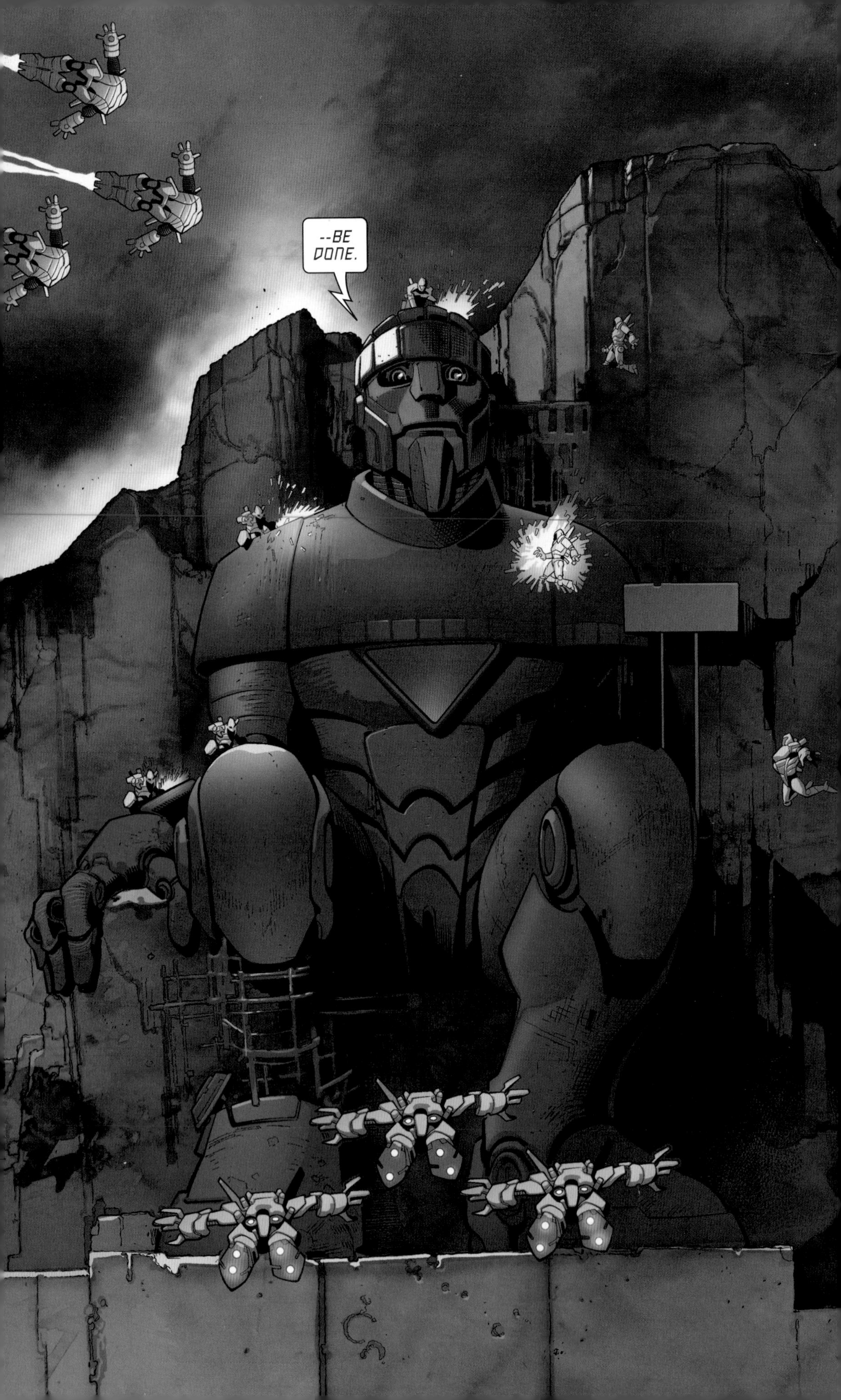
--BE DONE.

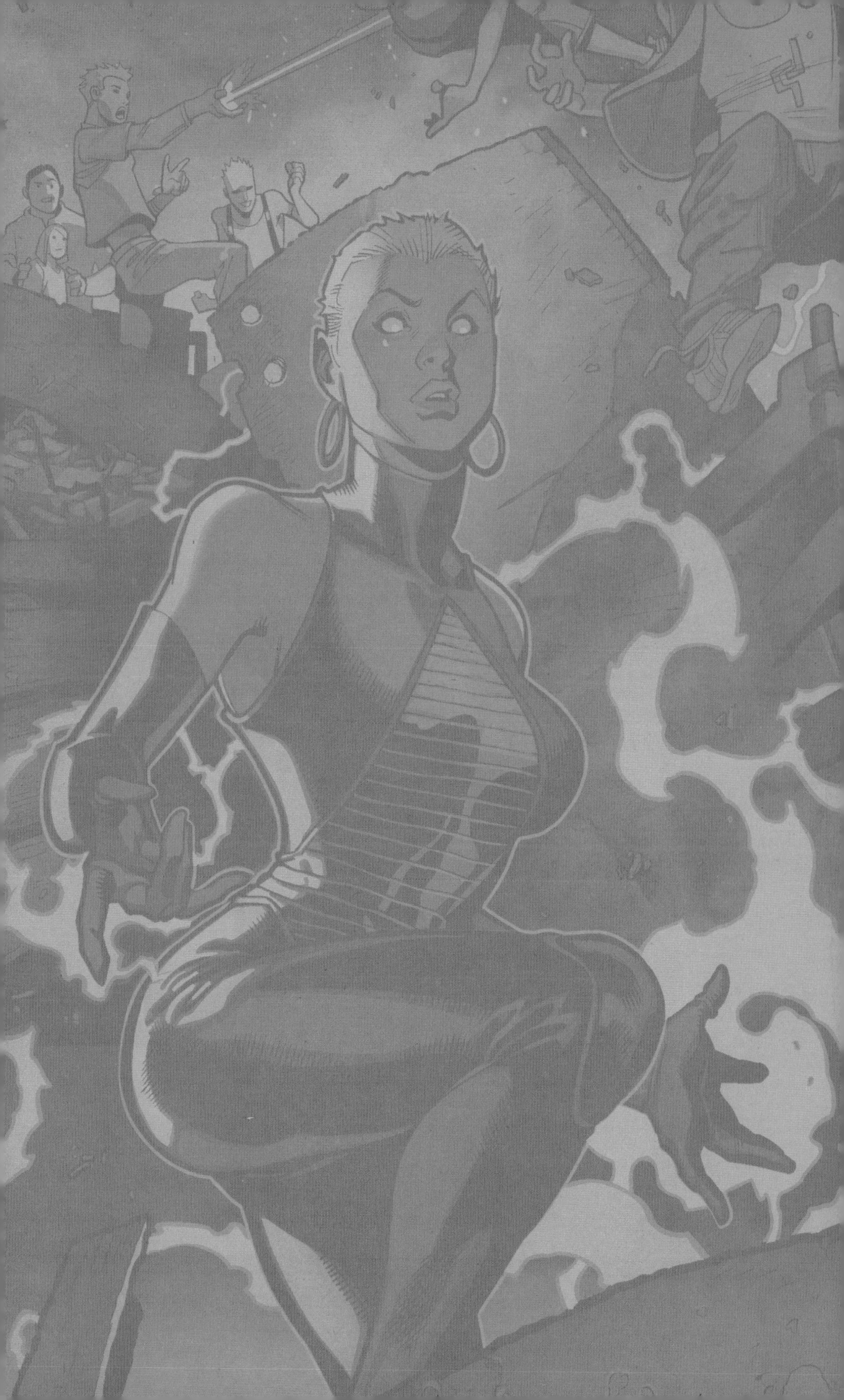

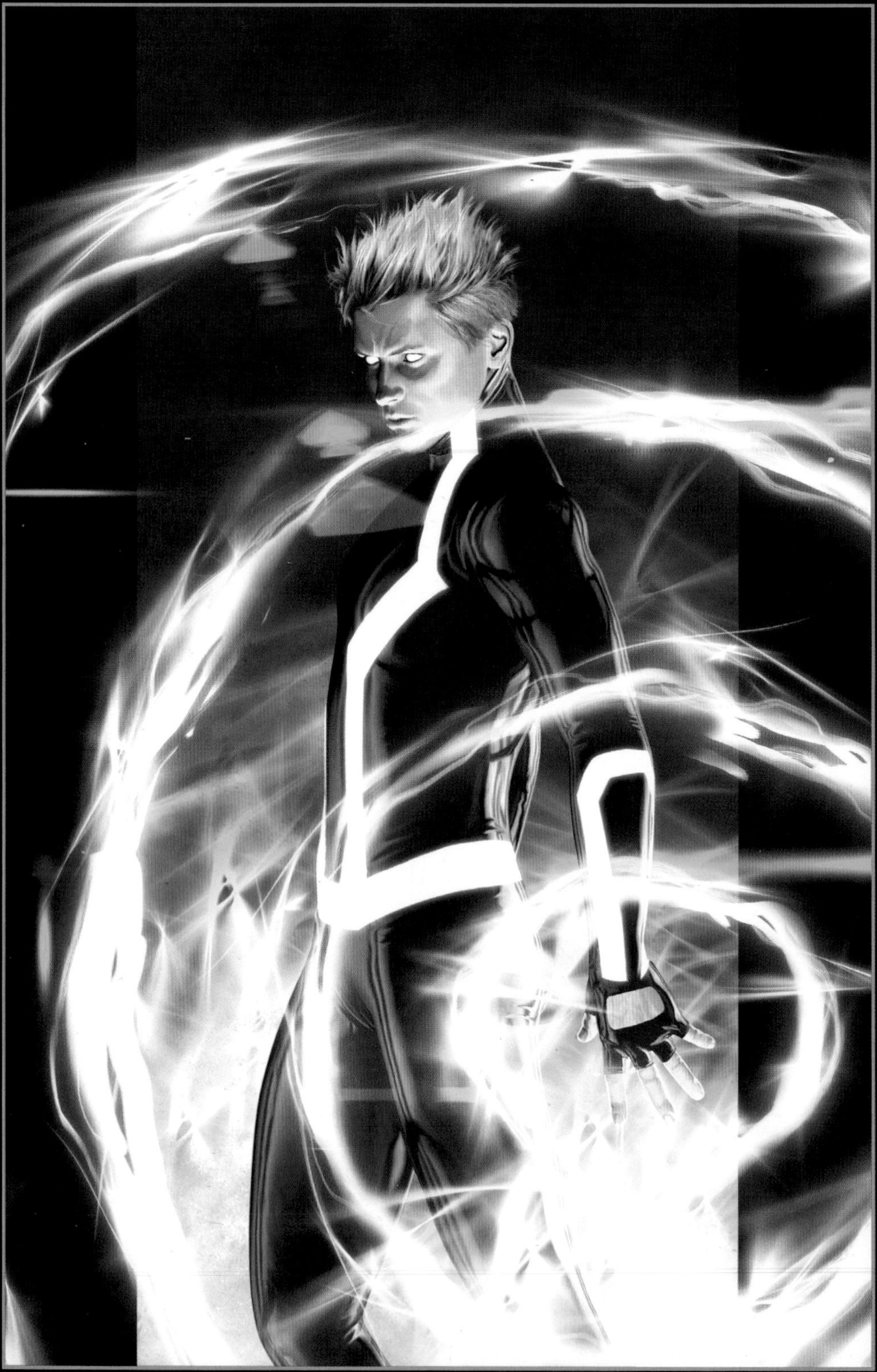

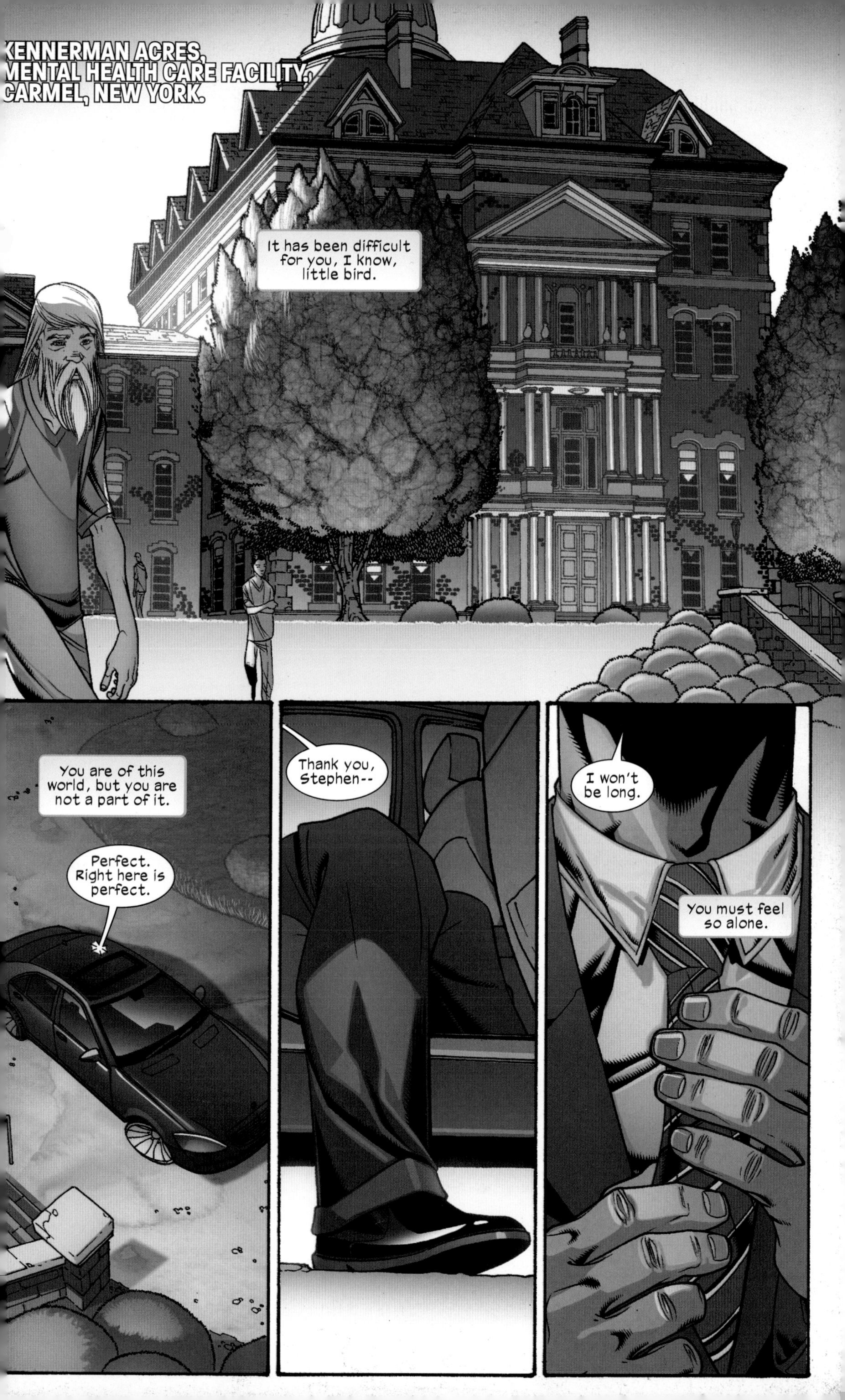
KENNERMAN ACRES,
MENTAL HEALTH CARE FACILITY.
CARMEL, NEW YORK.
It has been difficult for you, I know, little bird.
You are of this world, but you are not a part of it.
Perfect. Right here is perfect.
Thank you, Stephen--
I won't be long.
You must feel so alone.

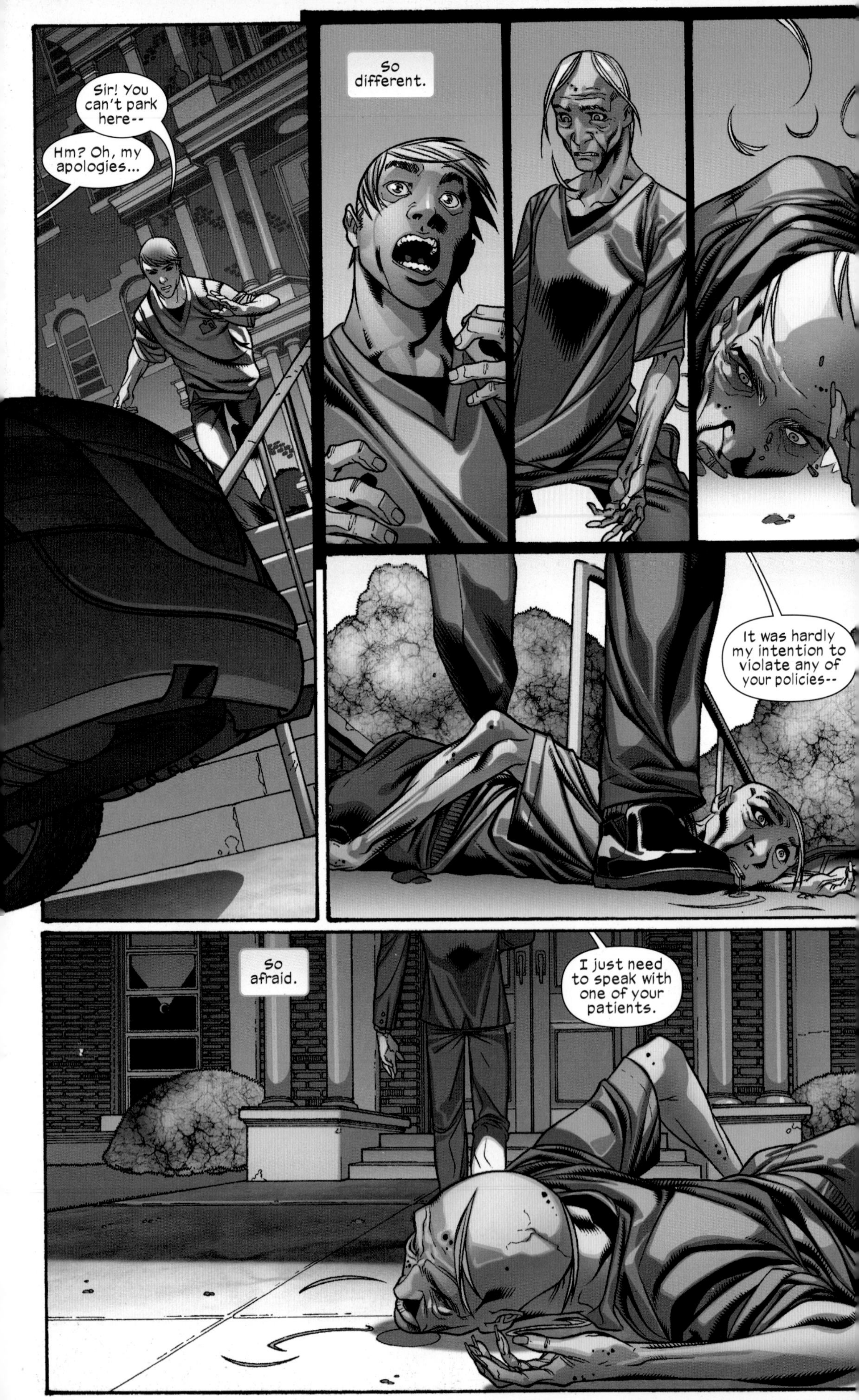
Sir! You can't park here--
Hm? Oh, my apologies...
So different.
It was hardly my intention to violate any of your policies--
So afraid.
I just need to speak with one of your patients.

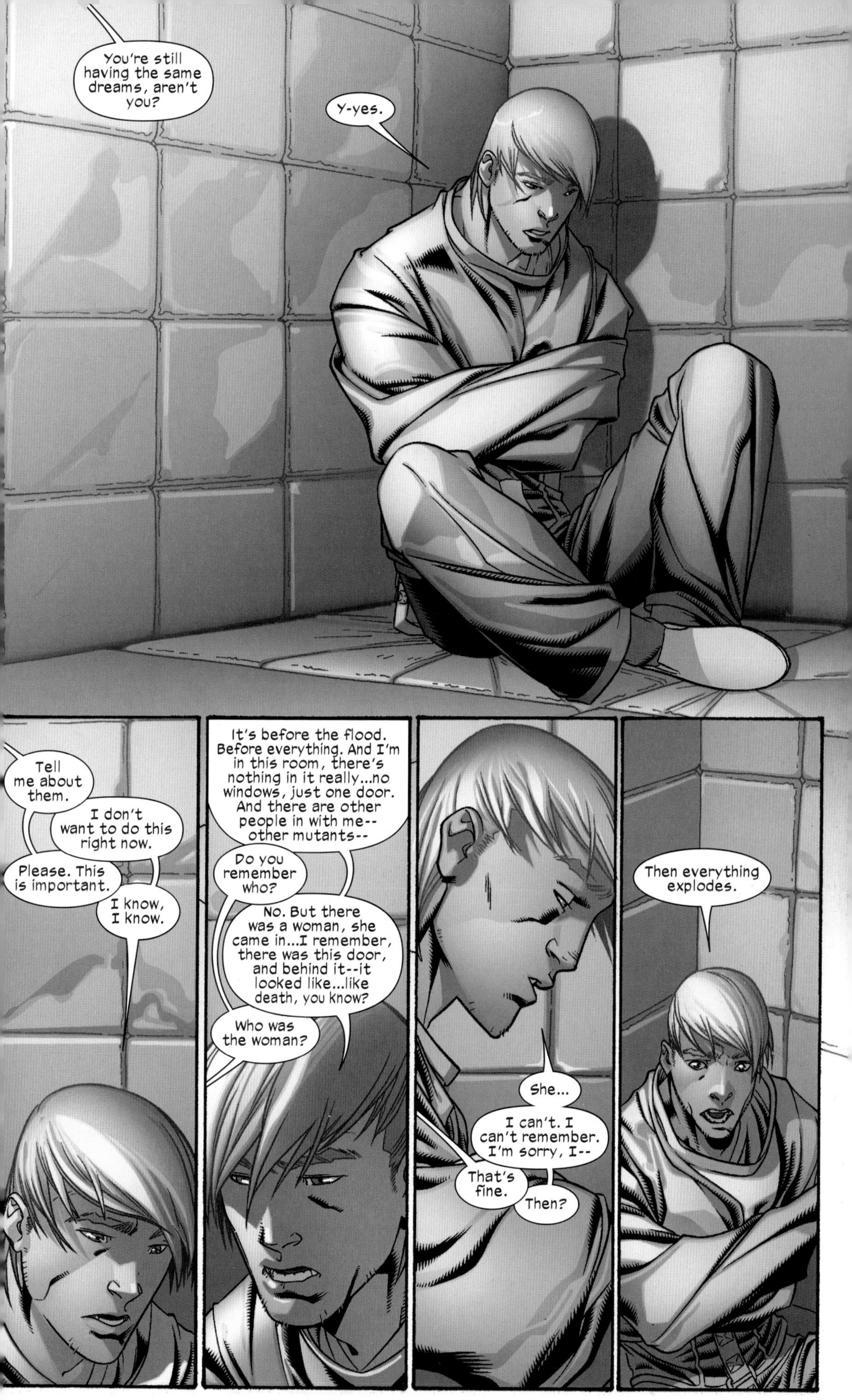
You're still having the same dreams, aren't you?
Y-yes.
Tell me about them.
I don't want to do this right now.
Please. This is important.
I know, I know.
It's before the flood. Before everything. And I'm in this room, there's nothing in it really...no windows, just one door. And there are other people in with me--other mutants--
Do you remember who?
No. But there was a woman, she came in...I remember, there was this door, and behind it--it looked like...like death, you know?
Who was the woman?
She...
I can't. I can't remember. I'm sorry, I--
That's fine.
Then?
Then everything explodes.

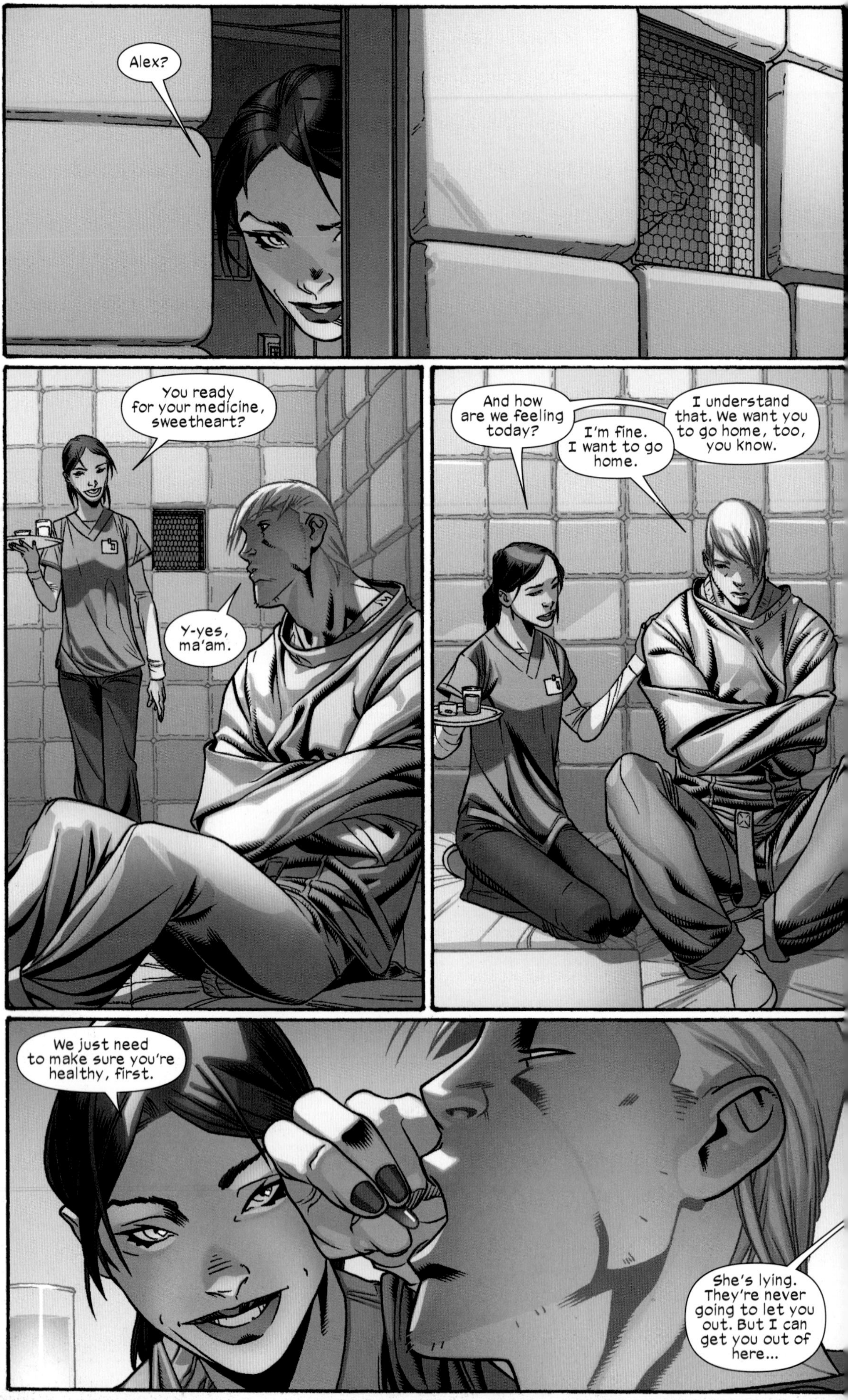
Alex?
You ready for your medicine, sweetheart?
Y-yes, ma'am.
And how are we feeling today?
I'm fine. I want to go home.
I understand that. We want you to go home, too, you know.
We just need to make sure you're healthy, first.
She's lying. They're never going to let you out. But I can get you out of here...

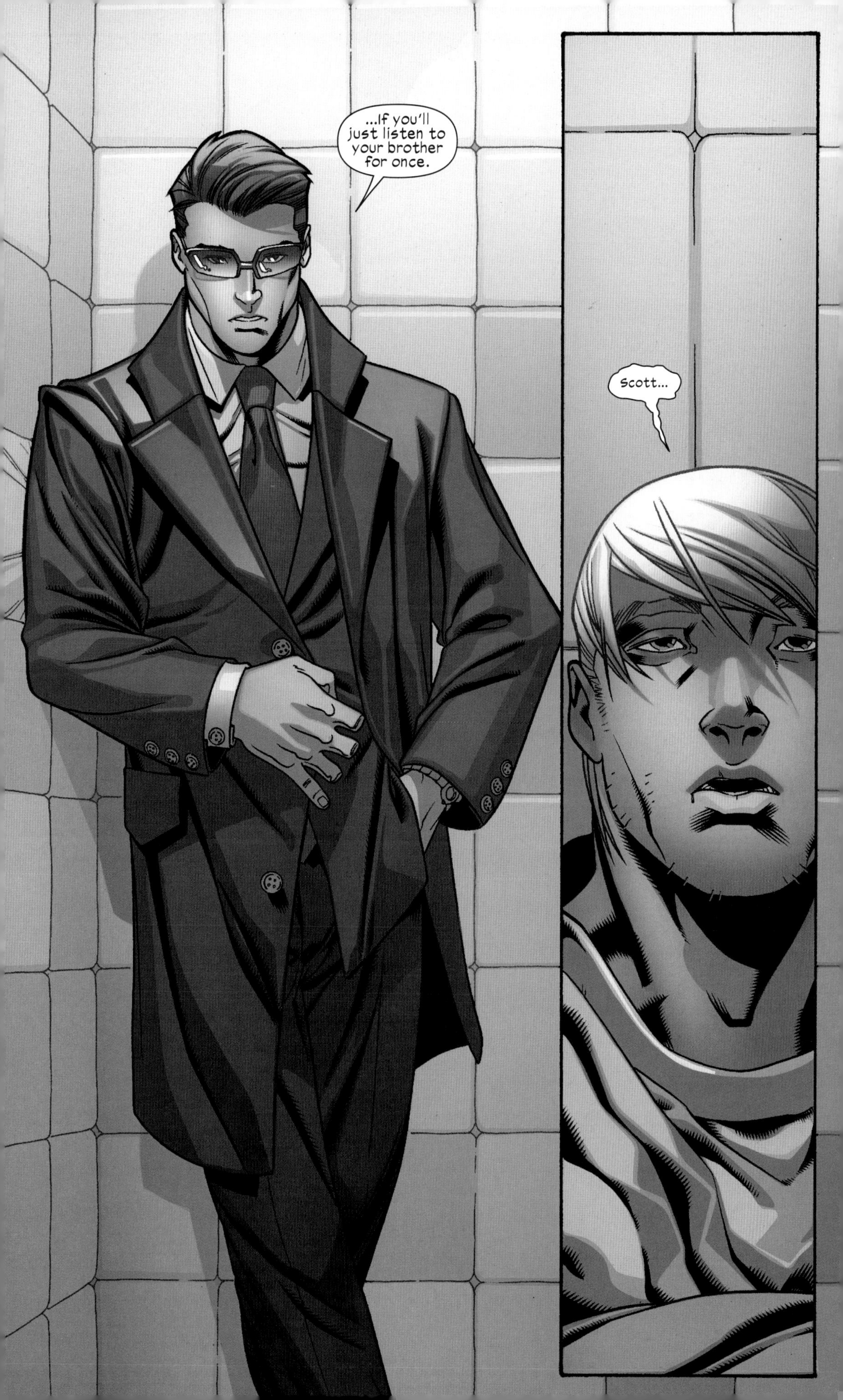
...If you'll just listen to your brother for once.
Scott...

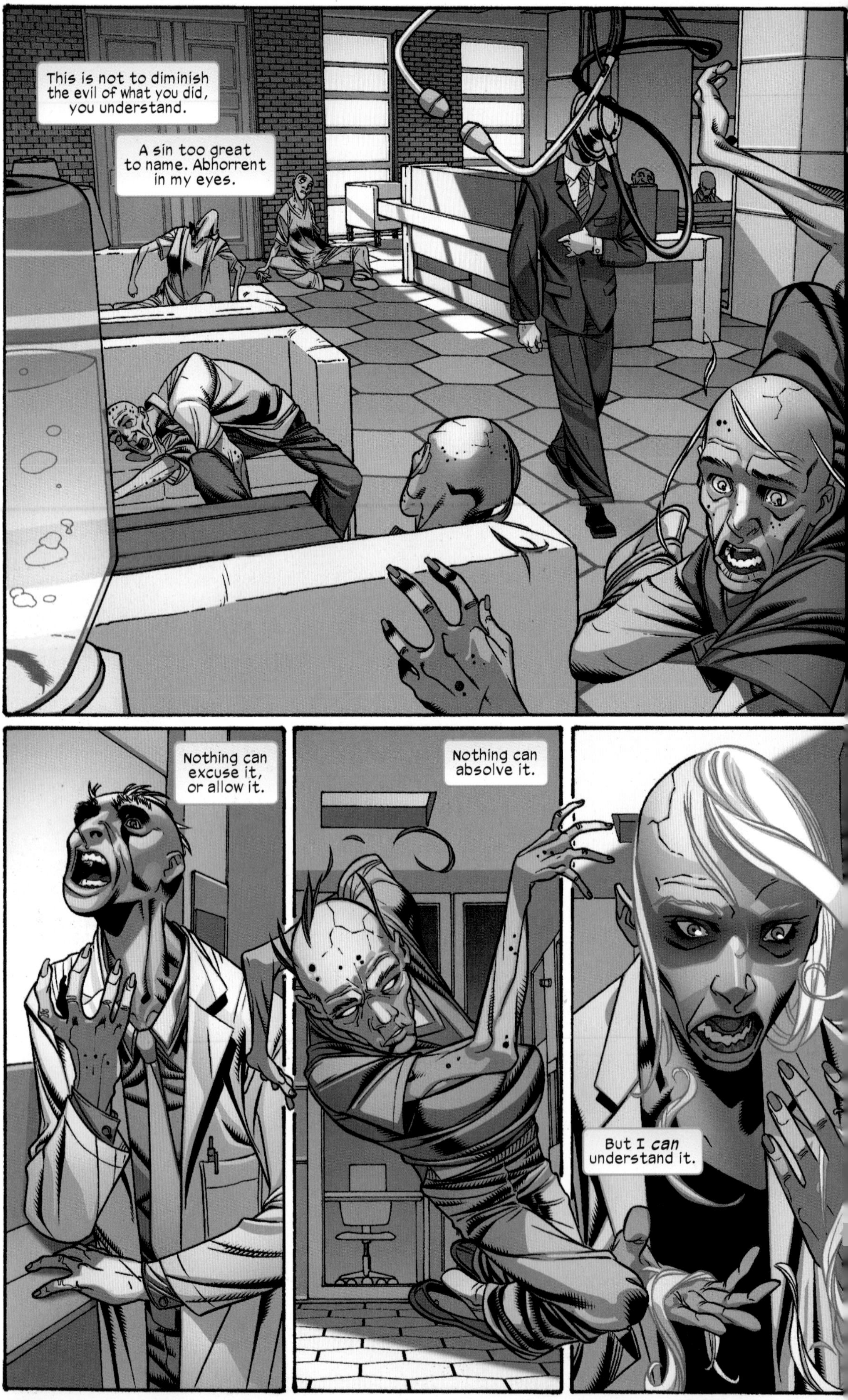
This is not to diminish the evil of what you did, you understand.
A sin too great to name. Abhorrent in my eyes.
Nothing can excuse it, or allow it.
Nothing can absolve it.
But I *can* understand it.

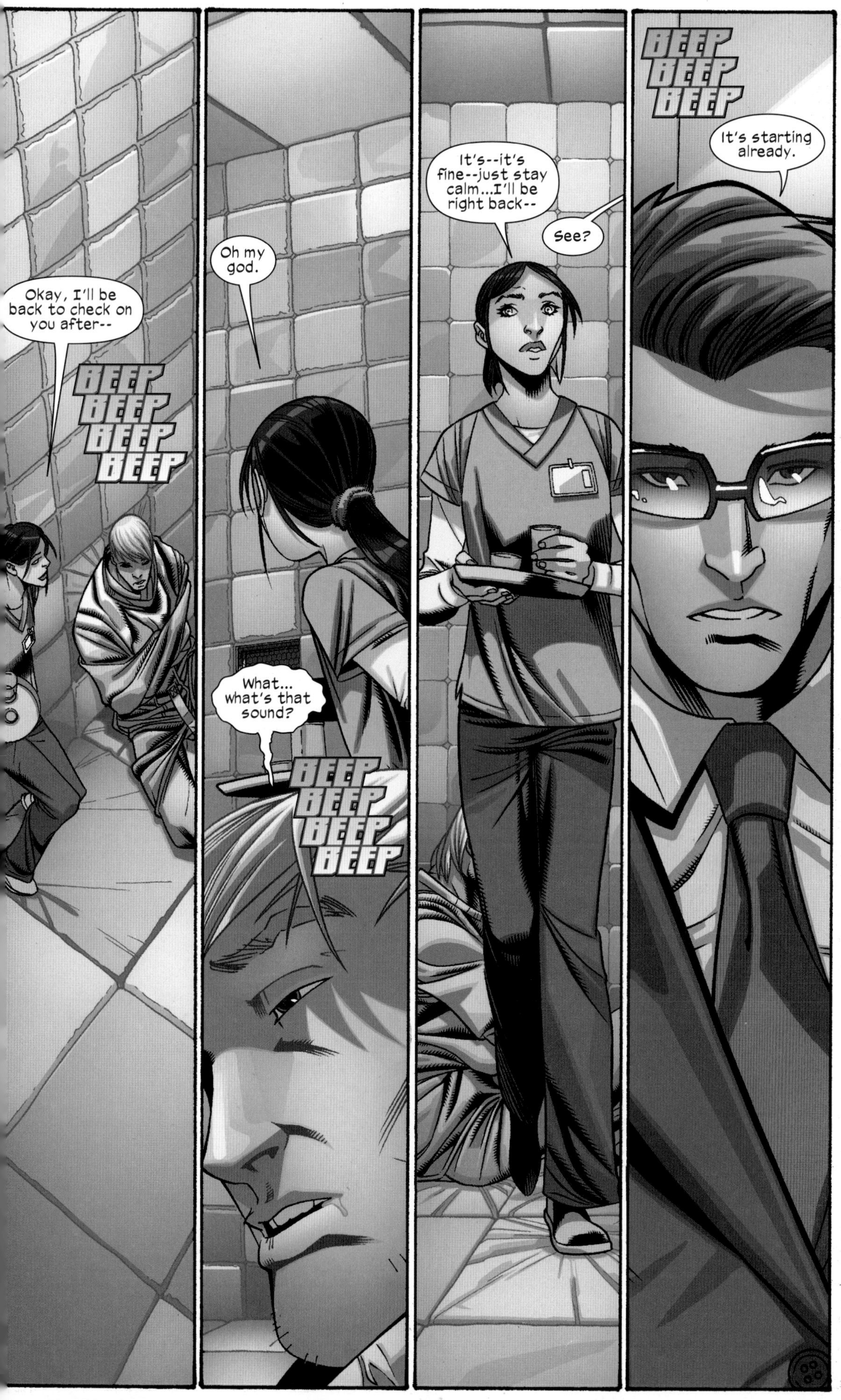
Okay, I'll be back to check on you after--
BEEP BEEP BEEP BEEP
Oh my god.
What... what's that sound?
BEEP BEEP BEEP BEEP
It's--it's fine--just stay calm...I'll be right back--
See?
BEEP BEEP BEEP
It's starting already.

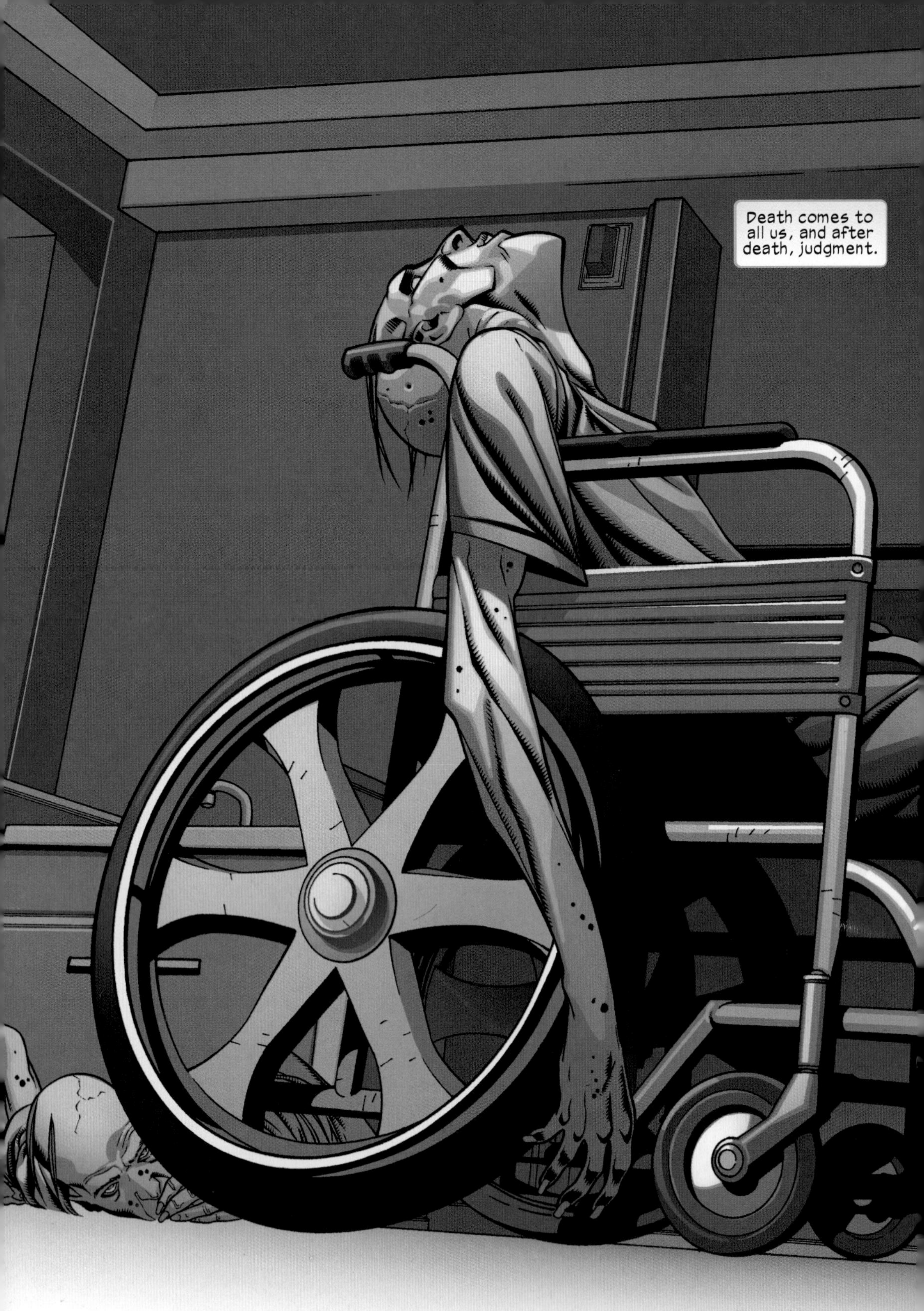
Death comes to all us, and after death, judgment.

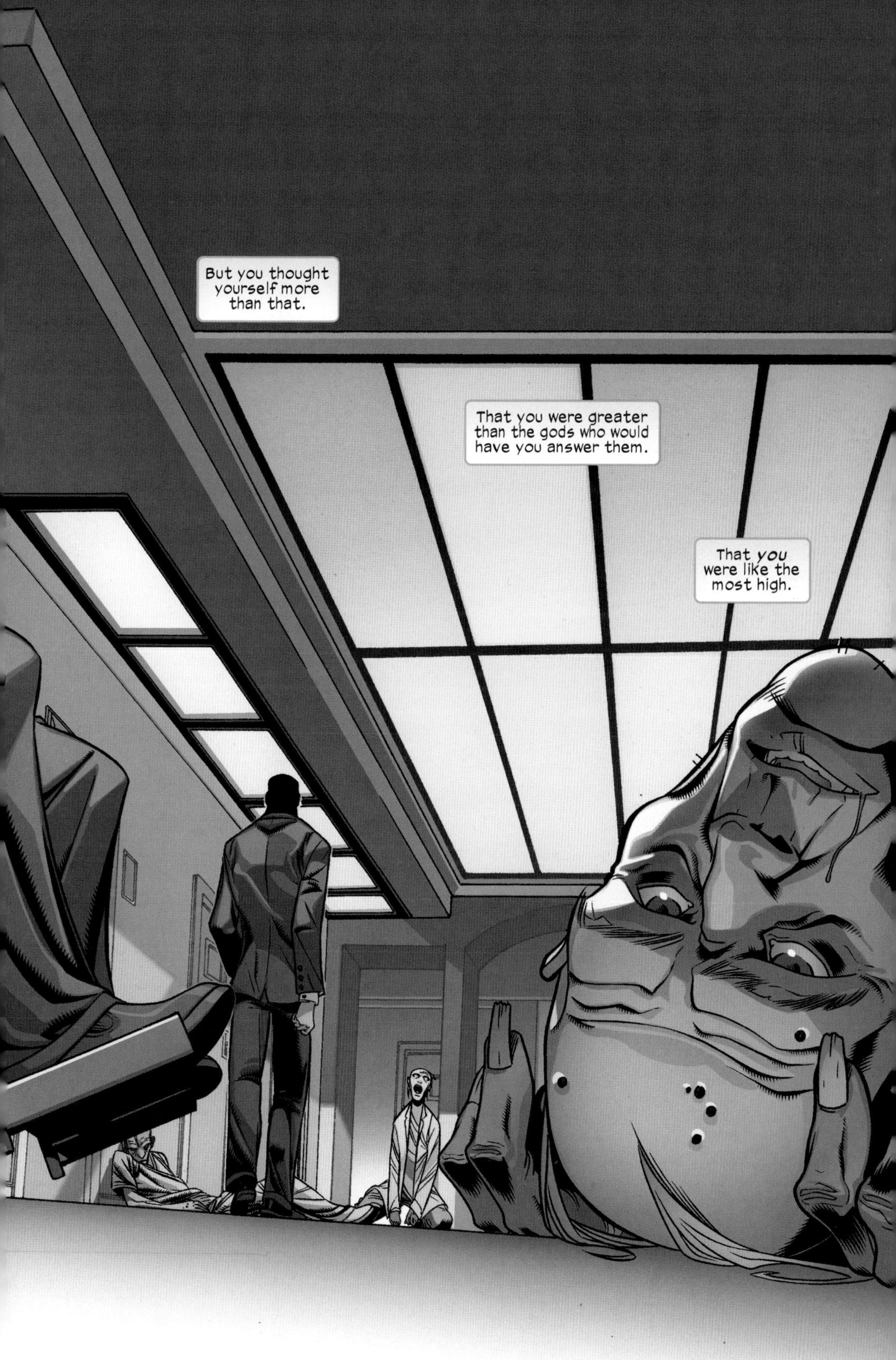
But you thought yourself more than that.
That you were greater than the gods who would have you answer them.
That *you* were like the most high.

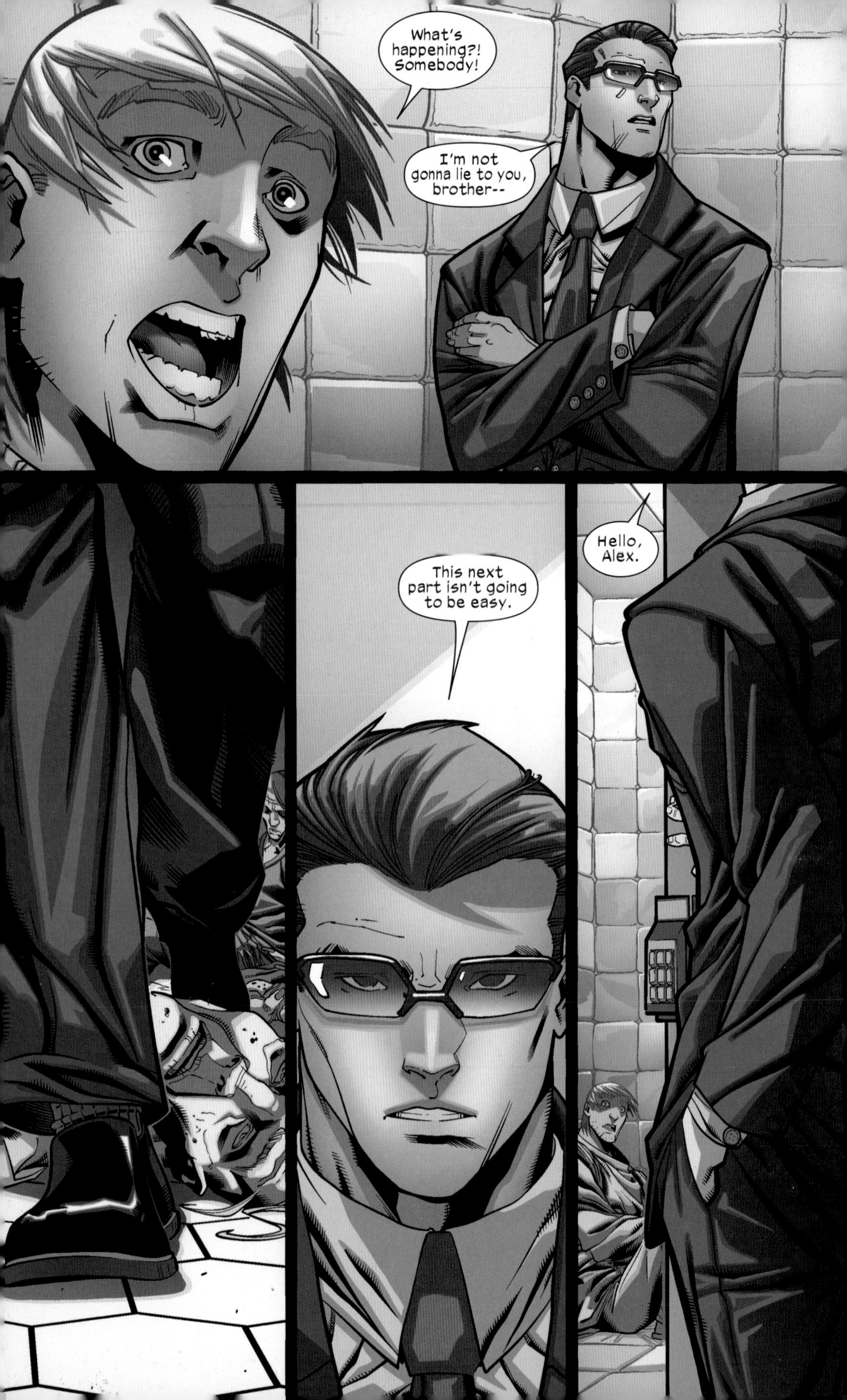
What's happening?! Somebody!
I'm not gonna lie to you, brother--
This next part isn't going to be easy.
Hello, Alex.

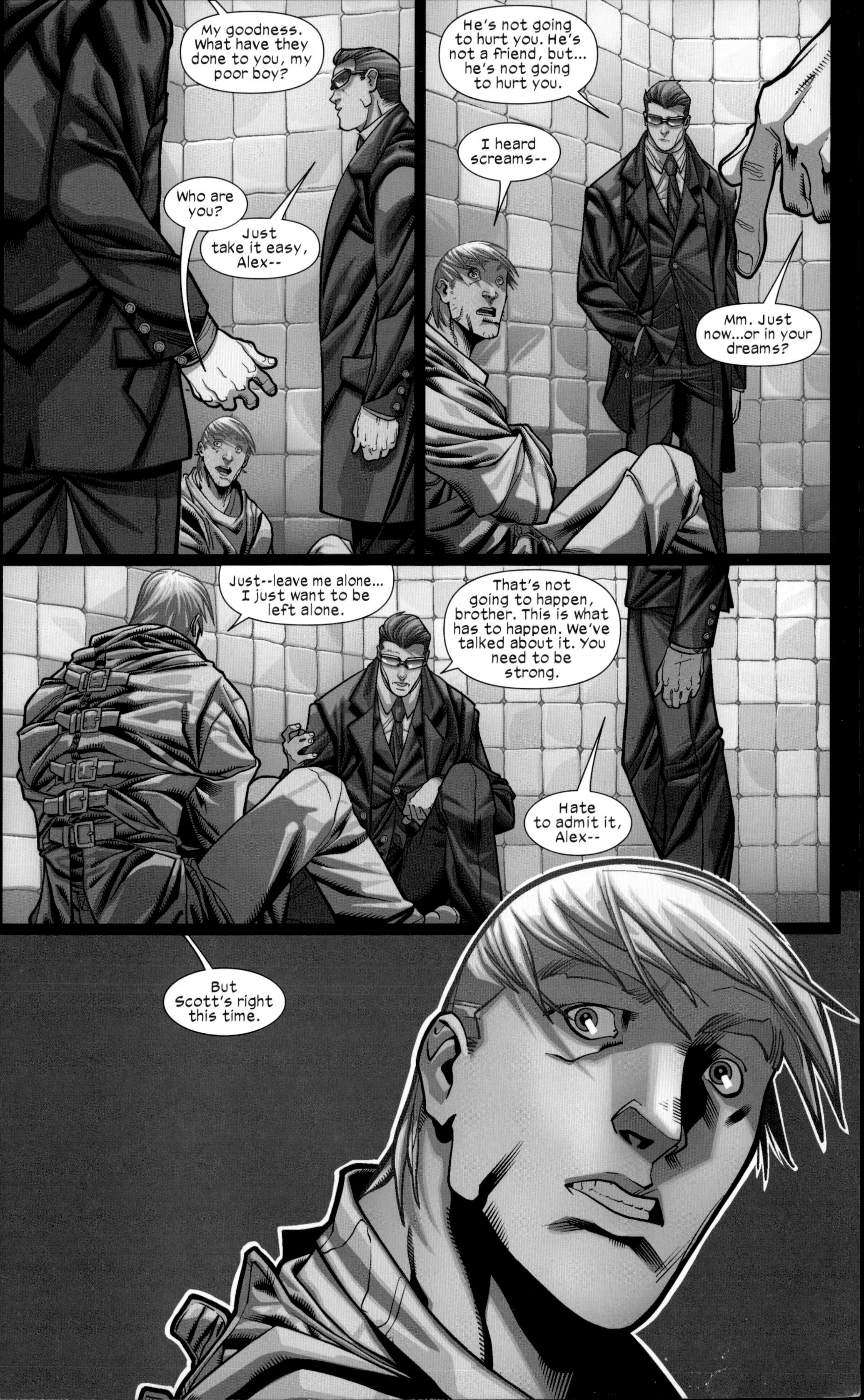
My goodness. What have they done to you, my poor boy?
Who are you?
Just take it easy, Alex--
He's not going to hurt you. He's not a friend, but... he's not going to hurt you.
I heard screams--
Mm. Just now...or in your dreams?
Just--leave me alone... I just want to be left alone.
That's not going to happen, brother. This is what has to happen. We've talked about it. You need to be strong.
Hate to admit it, Alex--
But Scott's right this time.

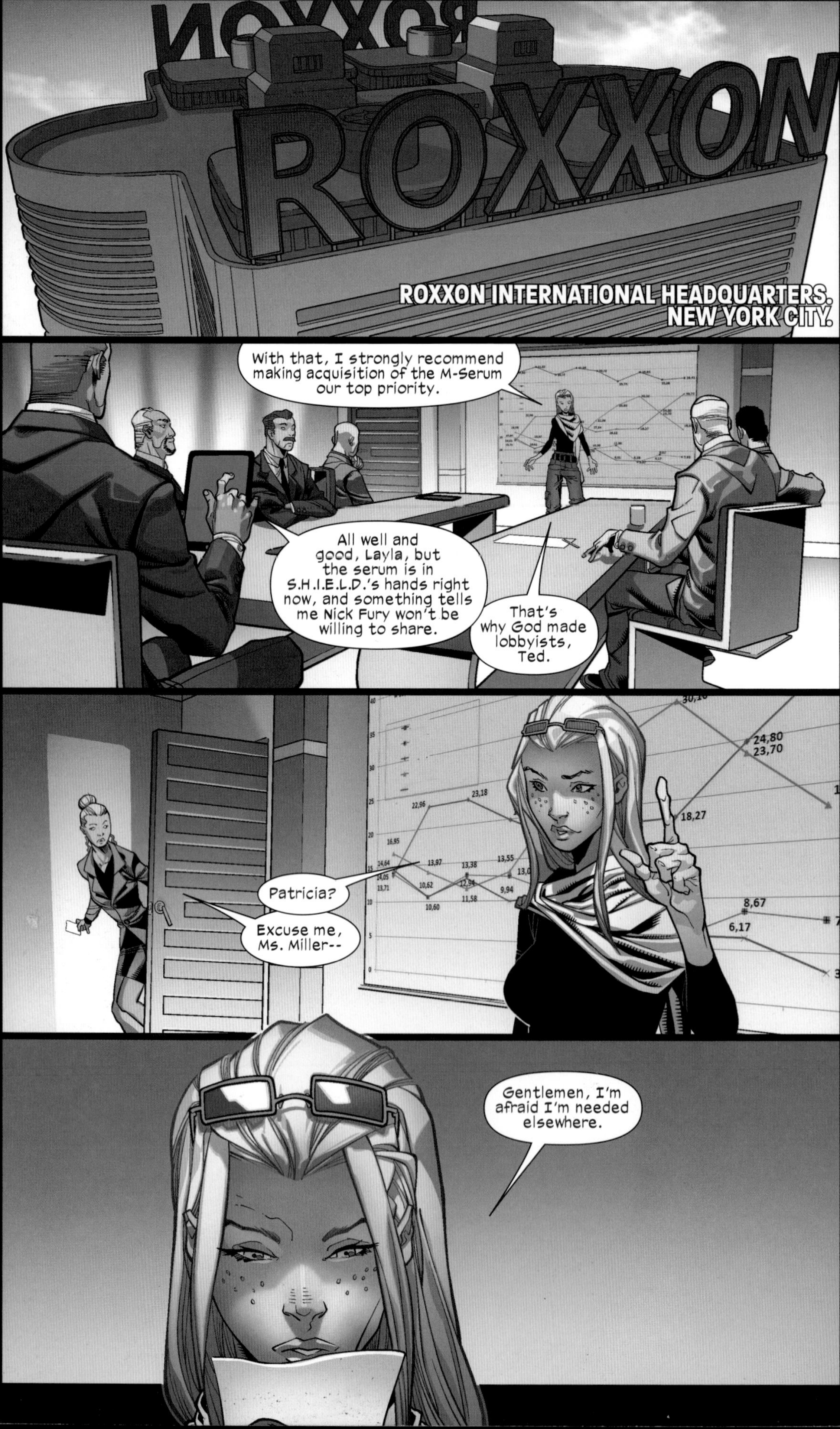
ROXXON
ROXXON INTERNATIONAL HEADQUARTERS. NEW YORK CITY.
With that, I strongly recommend making acquisition of the M-Serum our top priority.
All well and good, Layla, but the serum is in S.H.I.E.L.D.'s hands right now, and something tells me Nick Fury won't be willing to share.
That's why God made lobbyists, Ted.
Excuse me, Ms. Miller--
Patricia?
Gentlemen, I'm afraid I'm needed elsewhere.

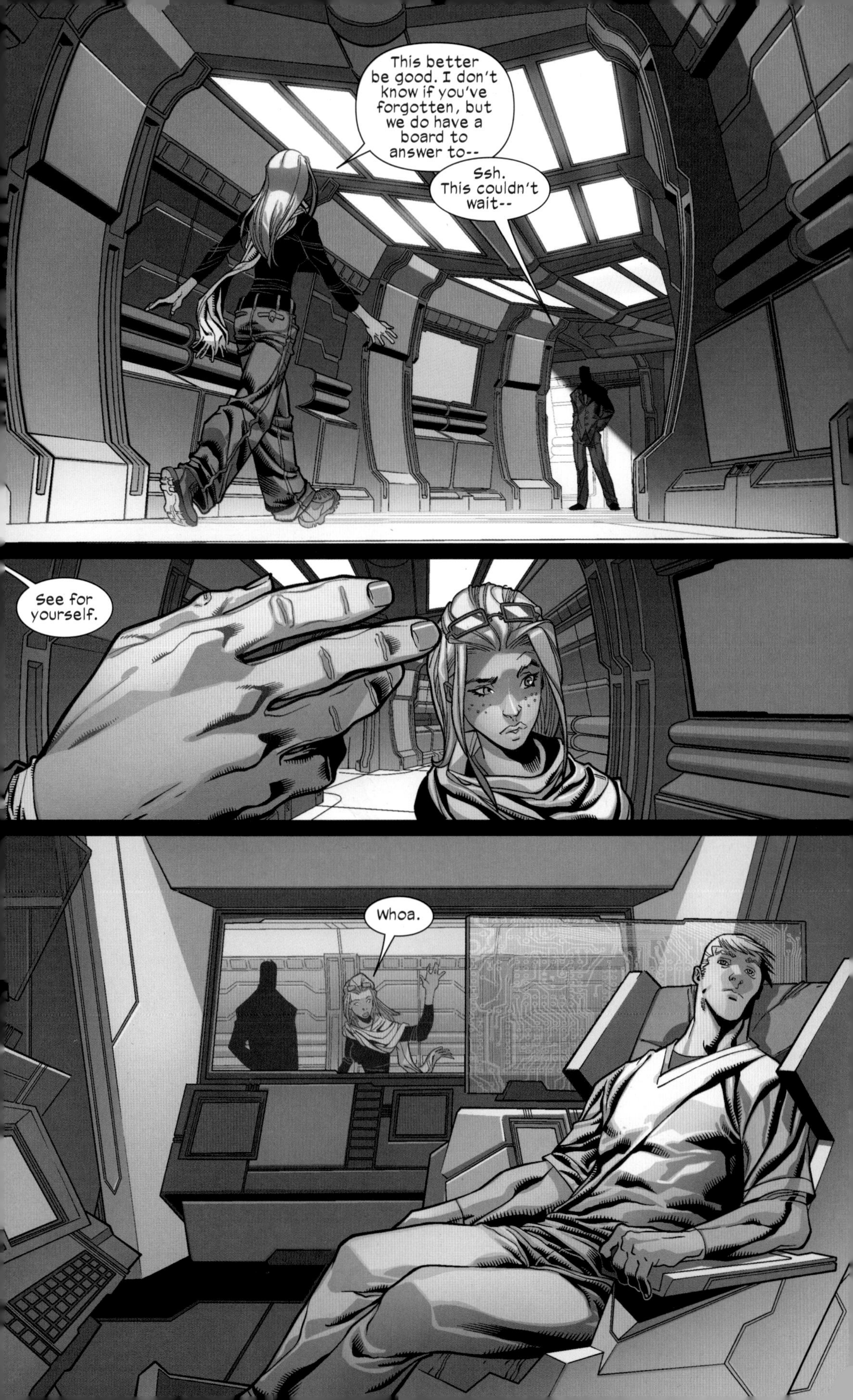
This better be good. I don't know if you've forgotten, but we do have a board to answer to--
Ssh. This couldn't wait--
See for yourself.
Whoa.

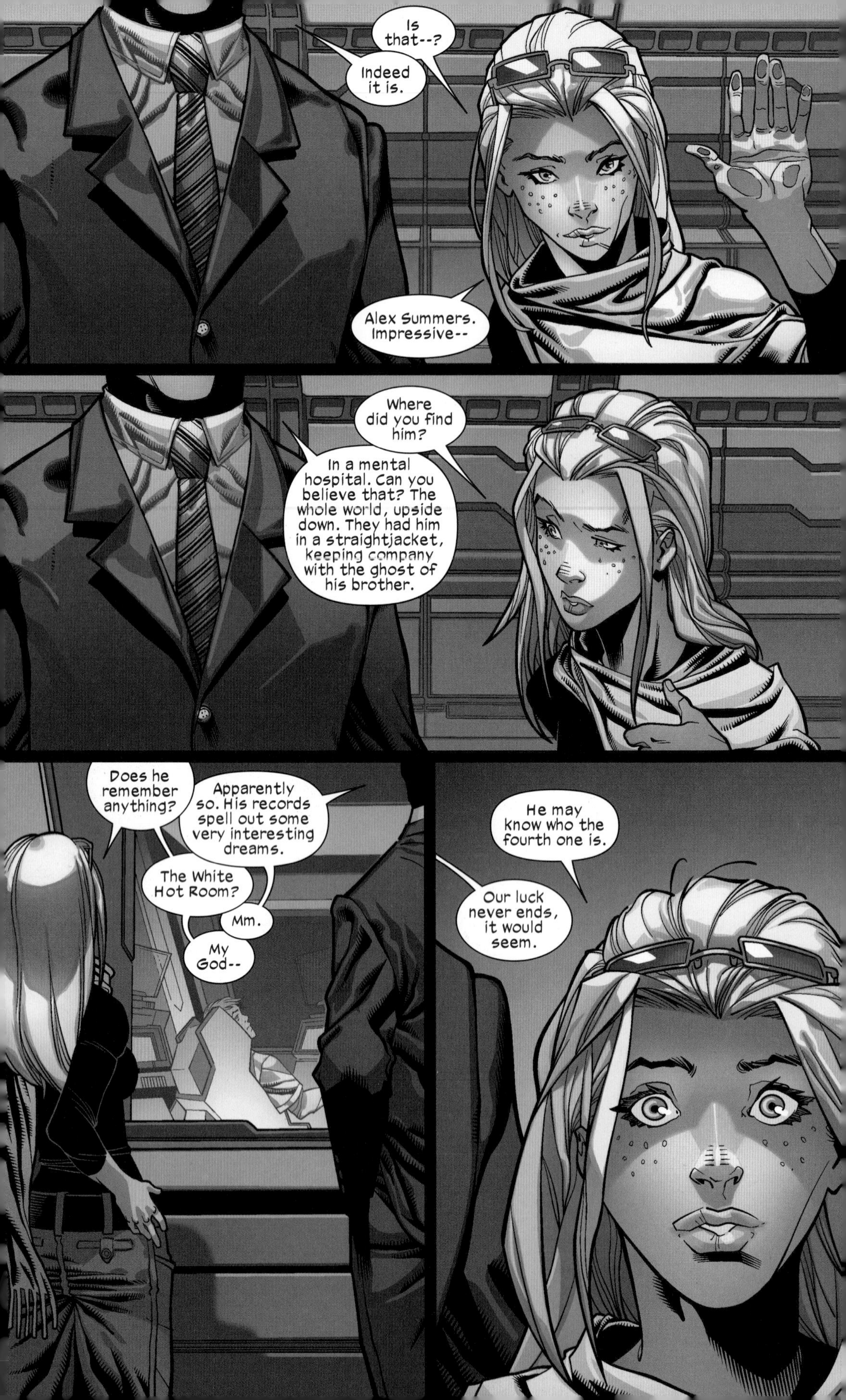

Is that--?
Indeed it is.
Alex Summers. Impressive--
Where did you find him?
In a mental hospital. Can you believe that? The whole world, upside down. They had him in a straightjacket, keeping company with the ghost of his brother.
Does he remember anything?
Apparently so. His records spell out some very interesting dreams.
The White Hot Room?
Mm.
My God--
He may know who the fourth one is.
Our luck never ends, it would seem.

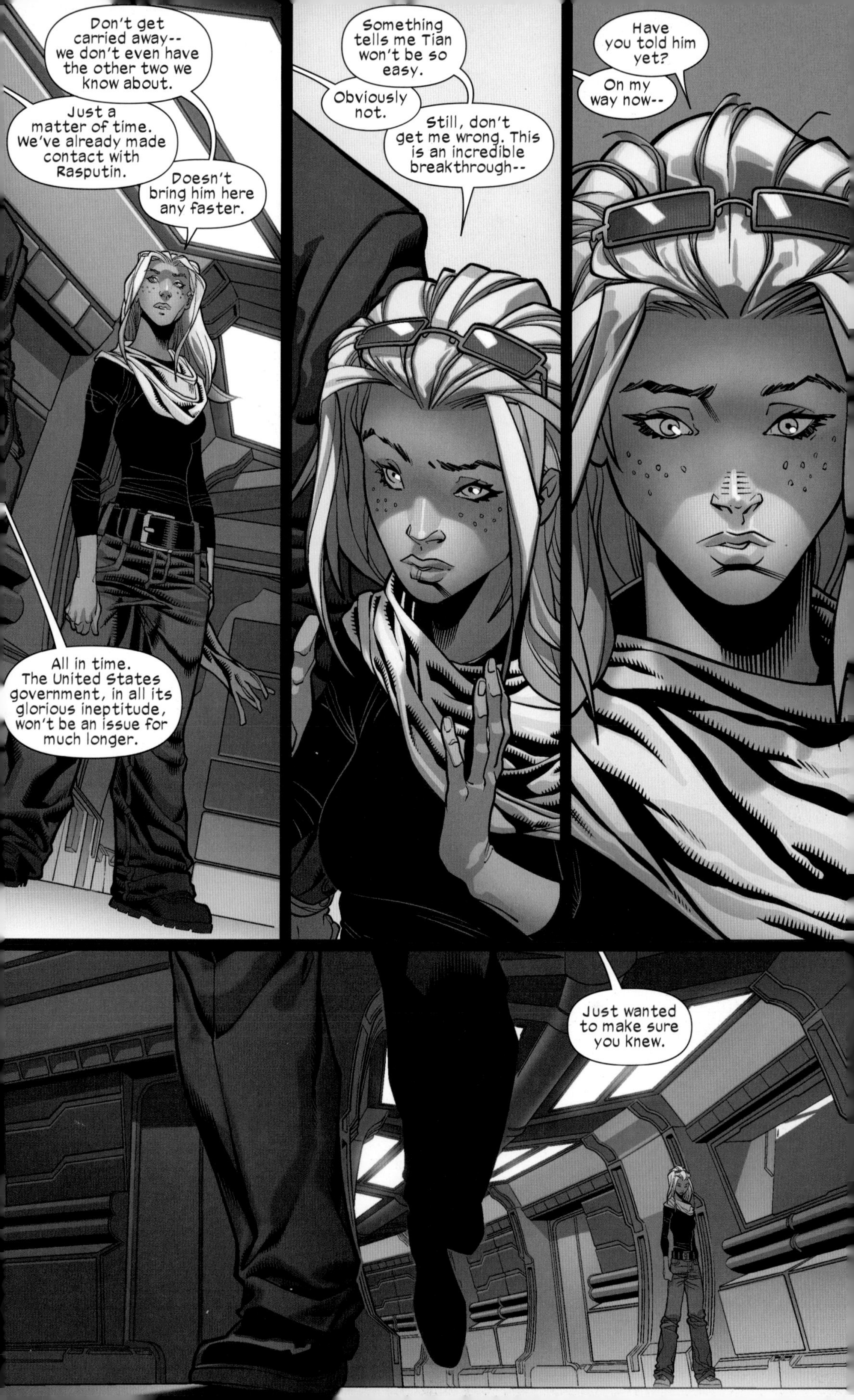
Don't get carried away-- we don't even have the other two we know about.
Just a matter of time. We've already made contact with Rasputin.
Doesn't bring him here any faster.
All in time. The United States government, in all its glorious ineptitude, won't be an issue for much longer.
Something tells me Tian won't be so easy.
Obviously not.
Still, don't get me wrong. This is an incredible breakthrough--
Have you told him yet?
On my way now--
Just wanted to make sure you knew.

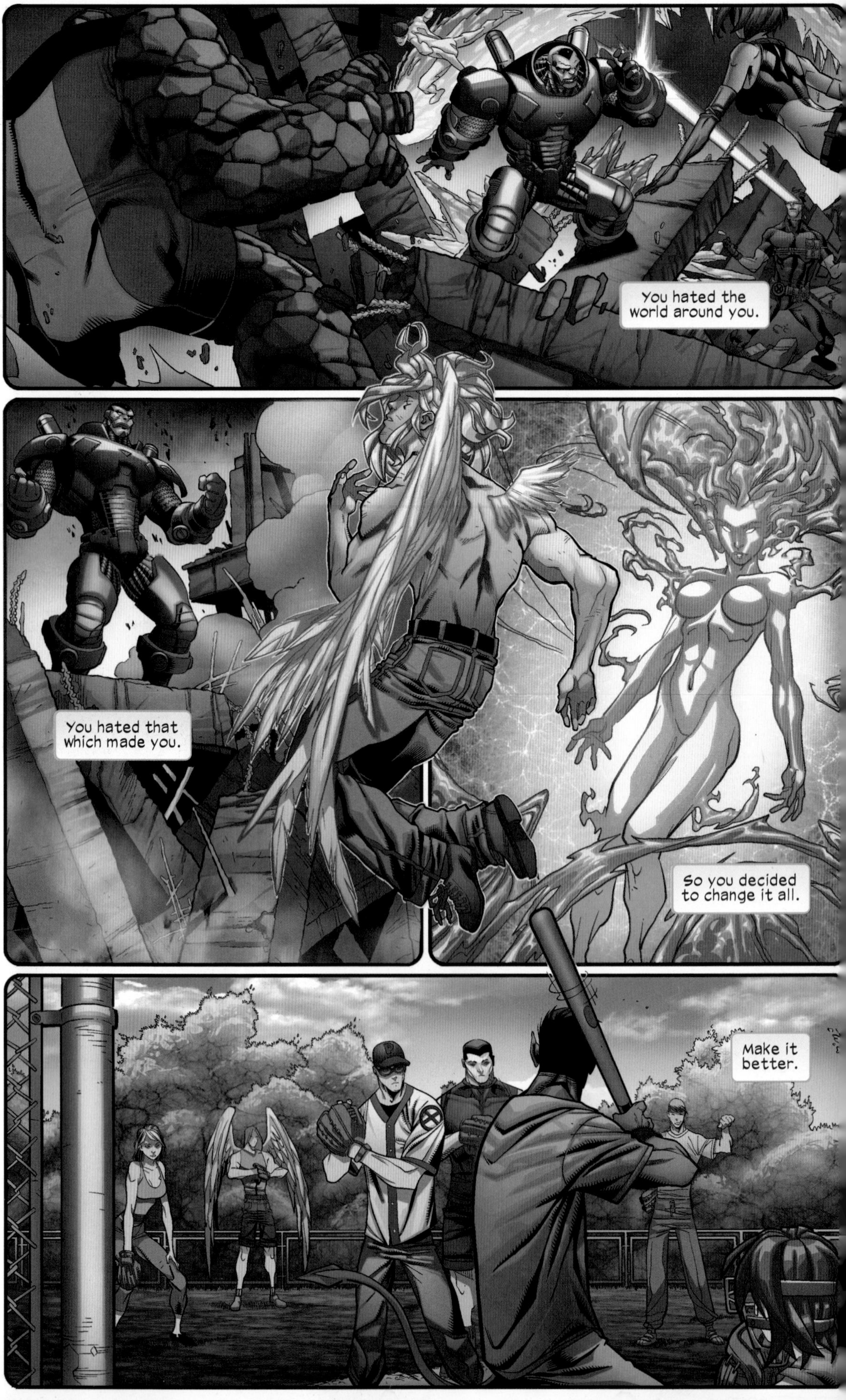
You hated the world around you.
You hated that which made you.
So you decided to change it all.
Make it better.

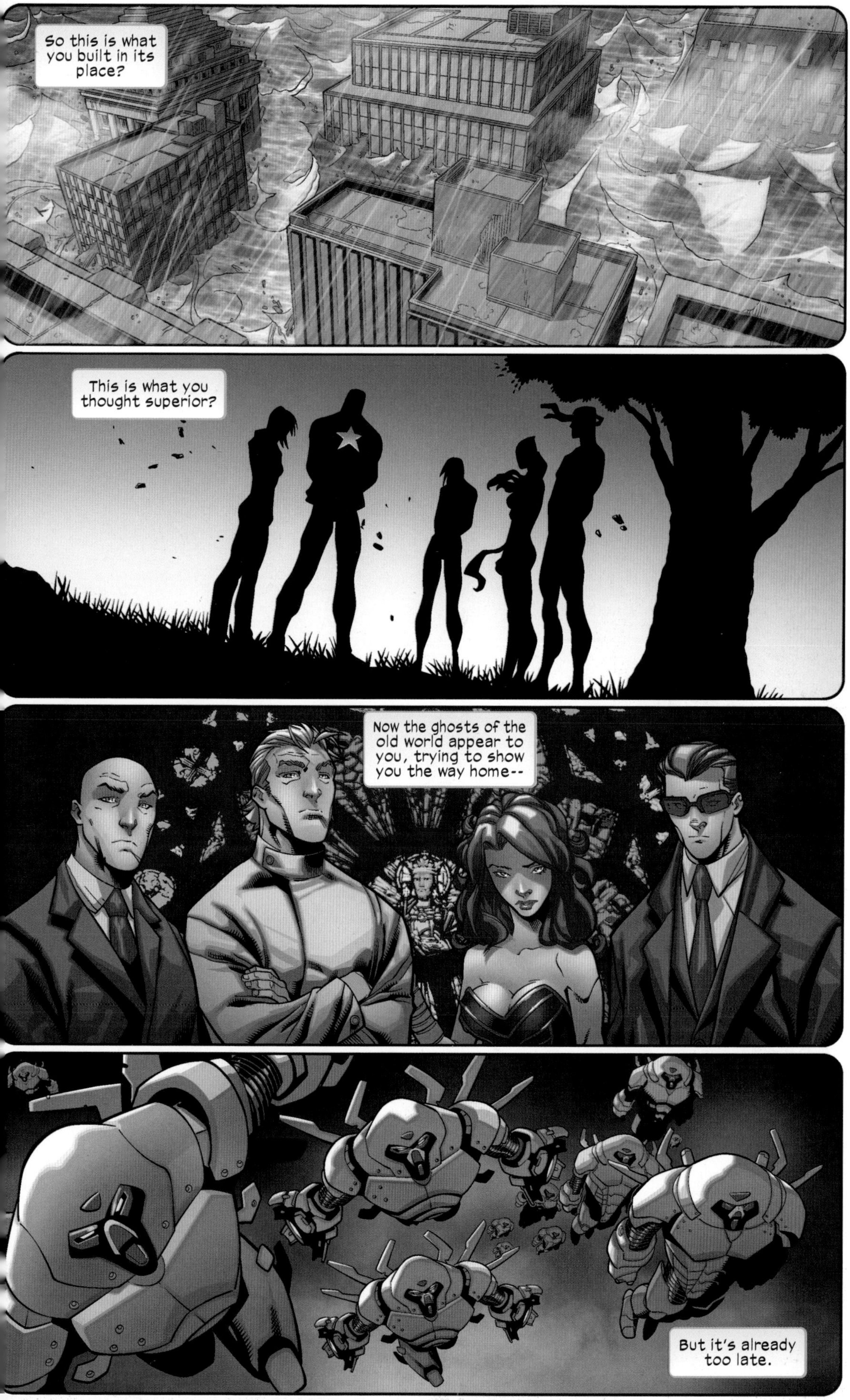
So this is what you built in its place?
This is what you thought superior?
Now the ghosts of the old world appear to you, trying to show you the way home--
But it's already too late.

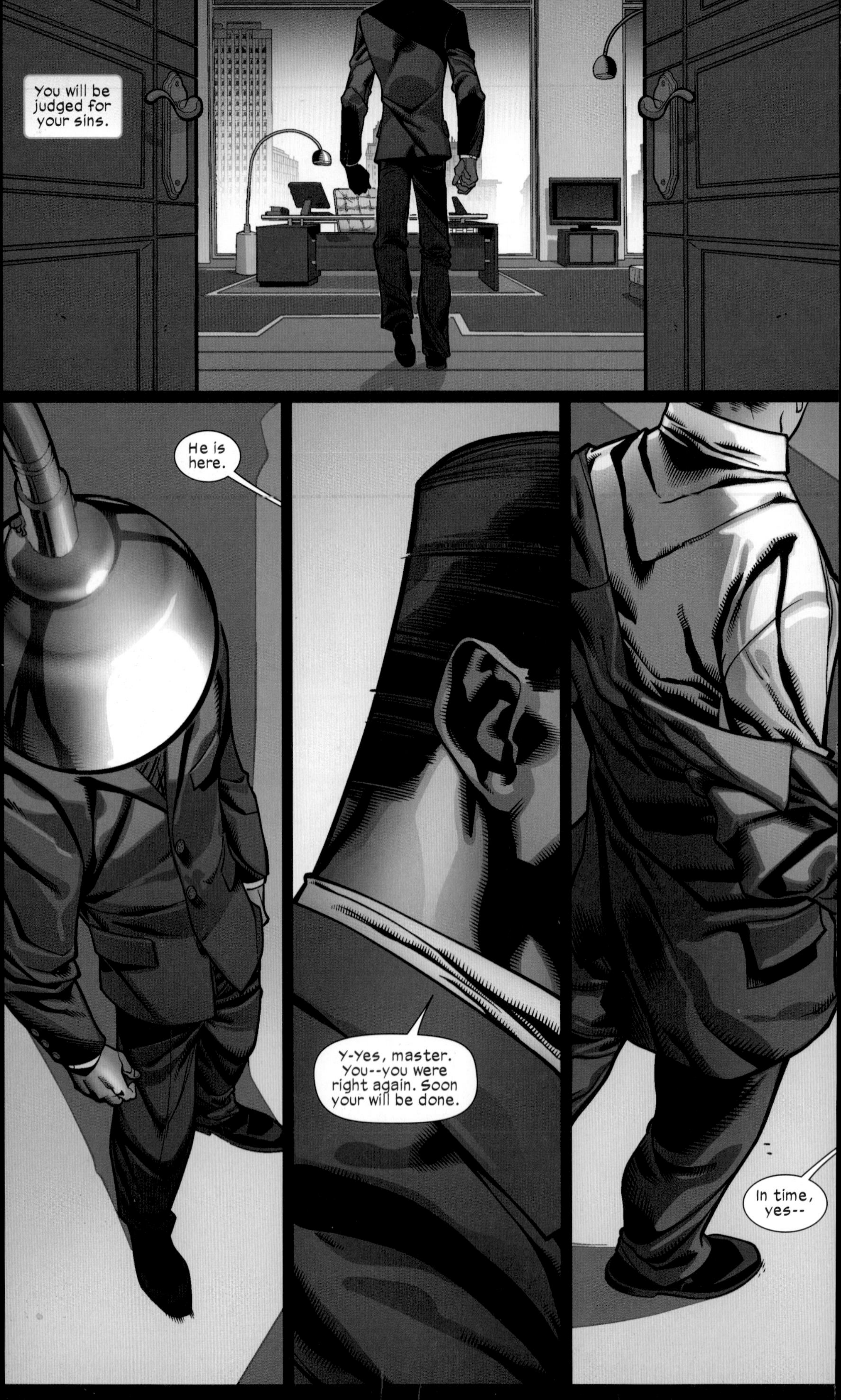
You will be judged for your sins.
He is here.
Y-Yes, master. You--you were right again. Soon your will be done.
In time, yes--

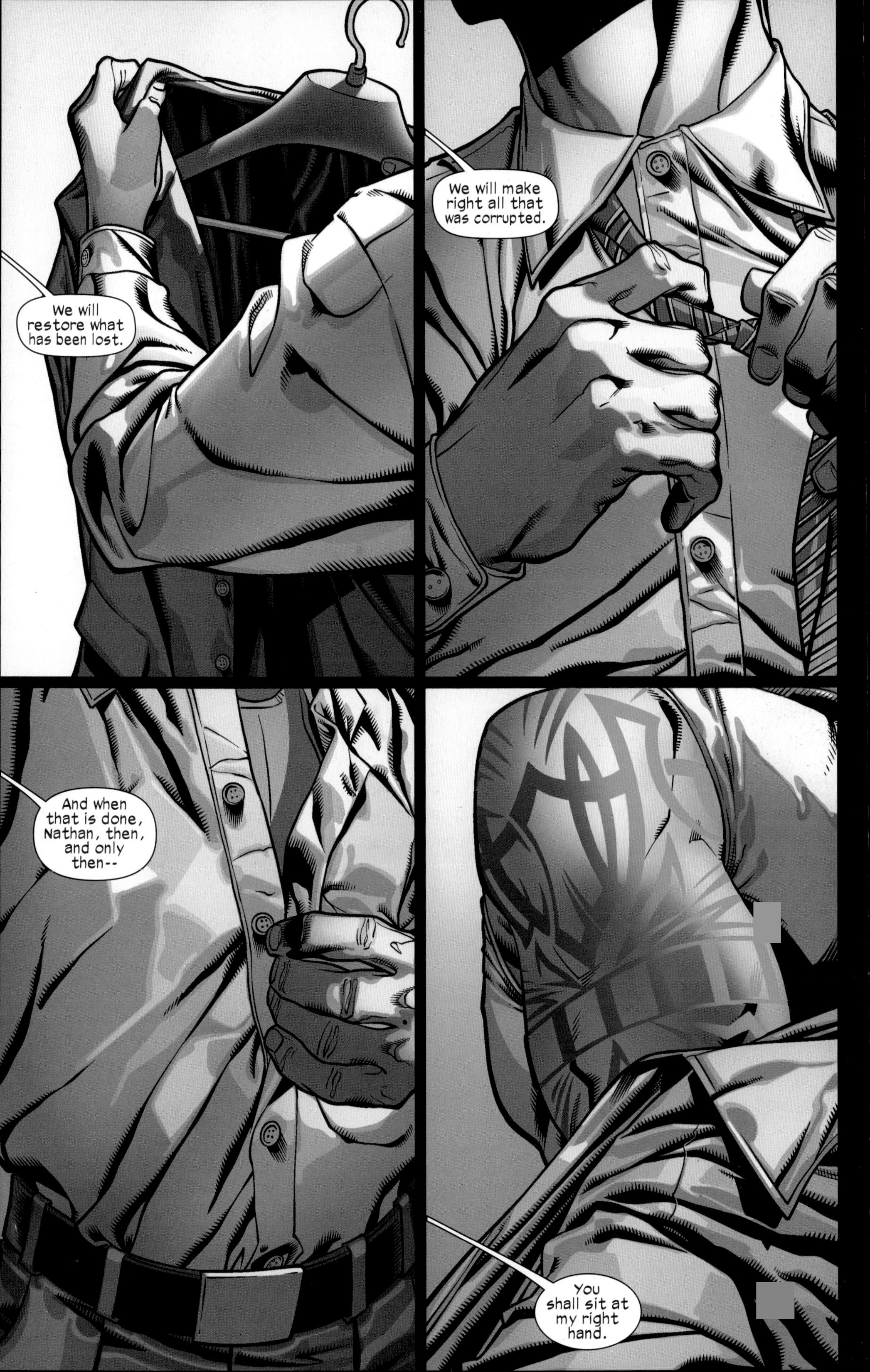
We will restore what has been lost.
We will make right all that was corrupted.
And when that is done, Nathan, then, and only then--
You shall sit at my right hand.

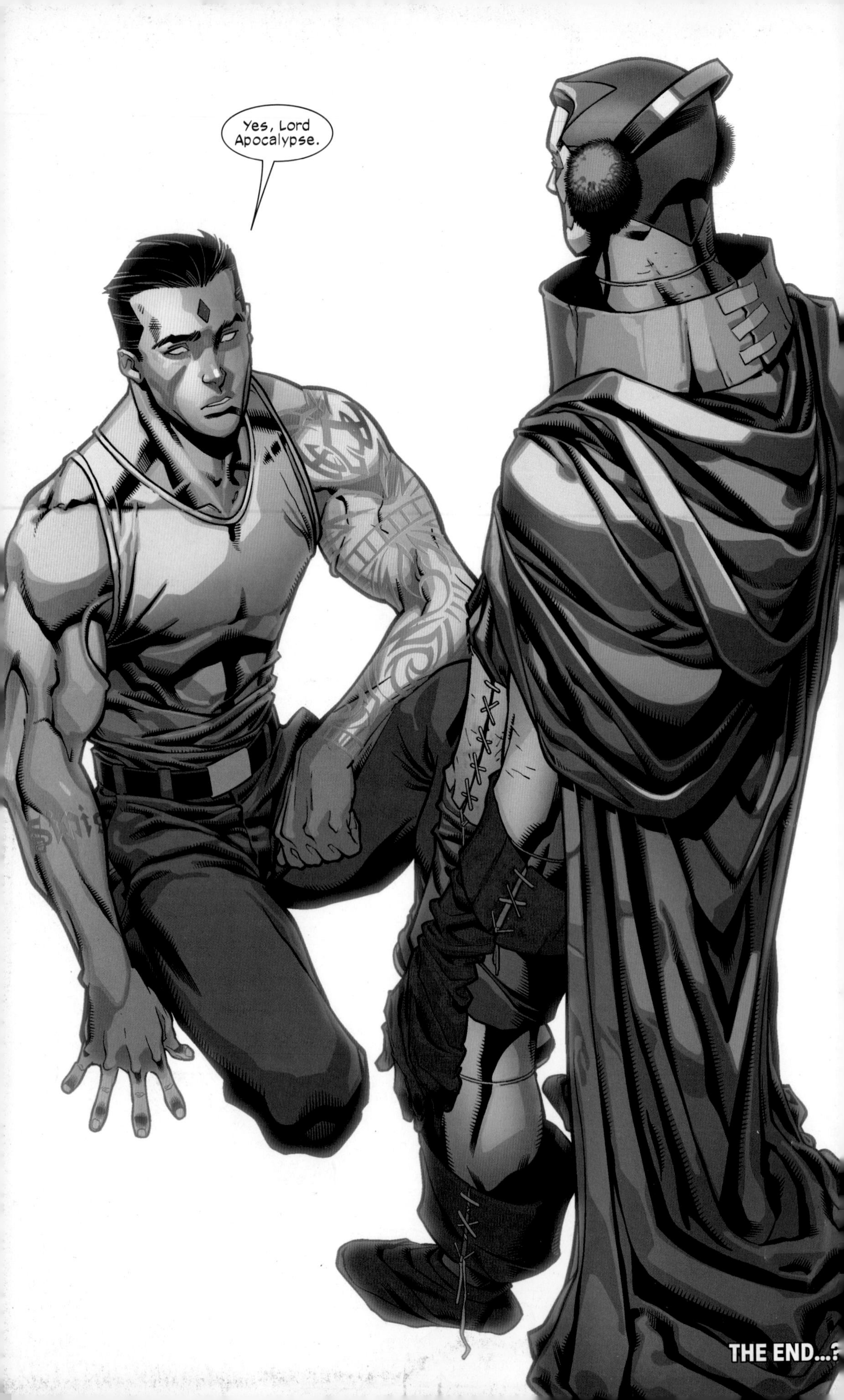
Yes, Lord Apocalypse.
THE END...?